W9-BCW-921

LEAN SIX SIGMA FOR LEADERS

LEAN SIX SIGMA FOR LEADERS

A practical guide for leaders to transform the way they run their organisation

MARTIN BRENIG-JONES
JO DOWDALL

WILEY

Library of Congress Cataloging-in-Publication Data

Names: Brenig-Jones, Martin, author. | Dowdall, Jo, 1975- author.
Title: Lean six sigma for leaders : a practical guide for leaders to
  transform the way they run their organisation / Martin Brenig-Jones, Jo
  Dowdall.
Description: Hoboken : Wiley, 2018. | Includes bibliographical references and
  index. |
Identifiers: LCCN 2017058782 (print) | LCCN 2018006783 (ebook) | ISBN
  9781119463368 (epub) | ISBN 9781119463375 (pdf) | ISBN 9781119374749
  (hardback) | ISBN 9781119463375 (ePDF)
Subjects: LCSH: Leadership. | Six sigma (Quality control standard) |
  Strategic planning. | BISAC: BUSINESS & ECONOMICS / Leadership.
Classification: LCC HD57.7 (ebook) | LCC HD57.7 .B744 2018 (print) | DDC
  658.4/013—dc23
LC record available at https://lccn.loc.gov/2017058782

Cover Design: Wiley
Cover Image: © Rova N/Shutterstock

Set in 11.5/14pt GoudyStd by SPi Global, Chennai, India

Printed in Great Britain by CPI Group (UK) Ltd, Croydon CR0 4YY

10 9 8 7 6 5 4 3 2 1

Contents

Foreword

Ian Swain, CEO, BQF

This is a different sort of Lean Six Sigma book, that not only guides leaders through the principles and the approaches, but provides case studies and stories from leaders who have used it. It goes beyond the theory and talks about practice, addressing real life challenges and considering Lean Six Sigma from a range of perspectives.

There is a lot more to Lean Six Sigma than problem solving and process improvement! The principles set out by Martin and Jo can underpin all aspects of leadership. These are in line with the fundamental concepts of excellence set out in the EFQM Excellence Model: adding value for customers; creating a sustainable future; developing organisational capability; harnessing creativity and innovation; leading with vision, inspiration and integrity; managing with agility; succeeding through the talent of people; sustaining outstanding results. Also aligned is the concept of applying learning, creativity and innovation to what an organisation does and how it does it, to improve what the organisation achieves.

This book also outlines how Lean Six Sigma can be used by leaders to support 'other' aspects of the leadership role which they may have thought to be separate or mutually exclusive. As the Agile movement grows for example, and its value is increasingly recognised outside of the world of software development, the book shows that it's possible to harness both Agile and Lean Six Sigma, and do so with pragmatism.

Martin and Jo have also considered the fit with strategy deployment, process management, innovation and winning hearts and minds.

Managing change is a theme that runs through every section of this book, in leaders' stories and case studies especially. I would urge you to read this section! It's refreshing in its honesty and you're likely to recognise the circumstances and situations described. The stories are also shared with the benefit of hindsight, which we all know is a wonderful thing.

Years of experience are shared in the book. It doesn't matter what type of leader you are, or where you are, you should read it!

Preface

We've written this book for you, assuming that you are 'anyone in a leadership role in any kind of organisation' and that you are interested or intrigued to learn about the use of Lean Six Sigma. It's based on a heck of a lot of practical experience over many years, meeting and working with leaders in all sorts of positions, in all sorts of organisations, in all sorts of sectors!

Following on from the success of *Lean Six Sigma for Dummies* we were kindly invited to write this book by Wiley Publishing. I (Martin) must admit that I have often joked in executive workshops that given the title *Lean Six Sigma for Dummies* that book was written very much with executives in mind and you have taken this in good heart as you often do see yourselves as 'dummies' when it comes to this kind of thing. Of course, that isn't at all fair but what I have discovered is that you want to be able to pick up a book, read it through quickly, pick up the key points very much focused on your role as a leader, whilst not getting bogged down in the technical detail of different tools. You want to see how you and your organisation can use this 'stuff' – and by the way, you don't even have to call it 'Lean Six Sigma'. In fact, I was rather hoping the title would be 'Lean Six Sigma … or whatever you want to call it … for Leaders'. We will explain why, but most importantly we wanted to write a book that you could relate to, with plenty of real life examples, real case studies, from real leaders' perspectives.

So, Part I covers how Lean Six Sigma can be used (and is most frequently used) as an approach to solve problems – business problems, technical problems, production problems, HR problems, financial problems – any problems!

In Part II we look at how Lean Six Sigma principles can be applied in a variety of different ways including how Lean Six Sigma is increasingly being used to turn strategy into action. To be fair, this approach is more commonly linked to 'Lean' than 'Six Sigma' but we think this is ok, as we see Lean Six Sigma increasingly being an 'umbrella' which, nowadays at least, incorporates both Lean and Six Sigma (plus other useful 'change' tools, as we will see).

We also look at how Lean Six Sigma links to creating a process based system and everyday operations. Why not? It provides great foundations for running effective organisations, is focused on customers, how things get done (those processes), people involvement, and measuring results in a smart, sensible way using some nifty visual tools. We call this 'Everyday Operational Excellence' – you can call it whatever works well for you in your organisation!

We then look at the big and challenging subject of leadership and change, the people and cultural dimension – sorry but you can't ignore it and, after all, isn't this what it's all about? Making improvements, making changes to the way work gets done in organisations – and that is all about CHANGE! This is critically important and not just in theory as you will see when you read the case studies at the end of the book, all written by leaders who have done it for real.

In between all this we have squeezed in chapters about how leaders can use Lean Six Sigma to create a system for innovation and design, integrate it with agile thinking, and apply it to make digital transformation more likely to deliver effective results.

In Part III, we look at how it is important to involve everyone and how leaders can work with different parts of the organisation – HR, employees, managers as well as practitioners. Admittedly we could continue … But we wanted to make this book relatively 'light' and easy to read, taking a leaf out of our Dummies experience.

Finally, the case studies – and stories – and personal perspectives which we have gathered from a deliberately wide selection of leaders and organisations. You will see that these really come from the heart as well as the mind and it is interesting to see what these have in common, even across different organisations.

There aren't any rules about reading this book, if you are like me, you won't read it like a novel, for example, *Far from the Madding Crowd* – there is no big surprise at the end – so dip in and out, you might want to read the case studies first, or you might not.

Whichever way you read it, whoever you are, we hope you find it helpful.

Acknowledgements

I'd like to thank Martin Brenig-Jones for inviting me to co-author this book about Lean Six Sigma, and the team at Catalyst who constantly inspire me and the clients lucky enough to work with them. Thanks also to the clients I work with, who always teach me something new. They do say that if you choose a job you love you'll never have to work a day in your life … I get that! And the biggest thanks to my friends and my brilliant family for their patience, amazing love and support. I'd like to dedicate this book (my parts of it!) to Buckley.

Jo

So many people have been fabulous in their support for us in writing this book.

First of all, a special mention has to go to Jo Dowdall who came in during the writing phase and has been an absolute godsend. I had seen Jo's great writing style from reading her famous quirky blogs. She has been absolutely brilliant, taking on so many ideas and writing so well and so fast with such good humour. We have worked really well together to the extent that we edit each other's work back and forth and it's now hard to tell who wrote what.

Second, I would like to thank all the other contributors: my other colleagues in Catalyst, particularly Vince Grant, Chris Merriman and James Dwan but also Barbara Bird, Rita Green, Moore Allison, Mark Jones, Jim Stephenson, Rob Row, Helen Smith, Linda Nicholas and Marie Helene Vander Elst for their deep expertise and wisdom. I must also thank my past and present clients for their time in helping to write the case studies which I feel really bring the book to life. Huge thanks to Kevin Barrett and of course to Wayne Fisher, Rachel Angell, Beau Ormrod, Lorraine Daly, Mark Canning, and a particular thanks to Alec Gilbert, Mike Baddeley, and the amazing 'post it note' Derek Kennedy. Also to several others from organisations where I have shaped my thinking – Michelle Egan, Katie McConochie, Katie Brown, Rushmi Laidlaw, Klas Fischer, Sandra Nixon, Caroline Holyhead, Karen Leftley, Estelle Clarke, Guy Butler, Nick Mathias, Sue Smallwood-Brown. There are many others and I apologise if I have not mentioned you by name. Thank you all for your insights, your time and your wonderful words. I would also like to thank those colleagues in Catalyst who have listened to me and my ideas on phone calls, on train and car journeys, in particular Jenny Levers who acted as a sounding board for the initial ideas and structure for the book but also the great support from Elizabeth Wilkinson, Rosie Stone, and Charmaine Willetts.

Thank you also to Ian Swain, at the BQF, for his encouragement and for kindly agreeing to write the Foreword which is much appreciated.

I would also like to say how I have thought of the late John Morgan (my co-author on the Dummies book). He continues to be a great influence on my thinking, he may have gone but his ideas live on.

Finally, of course, I would like to thank my family, especially my wife, Di, who has had to put up with me being very bad at doing household chores over many months, with the continuing excuse that I have been writing this book. You have been a rock, a star and a great support. I promise to get out and get to work on the hedges.

I am not quite sure how many cups of tea have been consumed in the writing of this book, but I know it is a heck of a lot. I think you all deserve a glass of something bubbly!

Thank you.

Martin

PART

I

Using Lean Six Sigma to Solve Business Problems

1

Introduction

Why this Book?

Another book about Lean Six Sigma?

Ah but this is different, it's about leadership and it is definitely not a technical book about the dark arts of black belts or advanced statistics. We hope you'll find it helpful no matter what kind of role you are in. We hope it will make you think that maybe there is more to this than you had thought. We hope you can put some of the ideas into practice. Come and join the party!

Let's start by trying out one of our favourite Lean Six Sigma tools, 'negative brainstorming' on that very subject – leadership.

If you haven't discovered it yet, this 'tool' (as Lean Six Sigma practitioners like to call techniques which can be employed to help facilitate workshops and the like) is really good fun – and it works.

So how do you use negative brainstorming?

In our experience there are two main steps. Firstly, grab a flipchart and pen, and say to the group 'Okay, so describe what good leadership looks like.'

This is a tough question and is likely to stall quickly, so before they get bogged down, say 'Let's turn the question around, what are the characteristics of really **bad** leadership?'

This inevitably creates a few chuckles around the room and immediately engages everyone including the negative diehards. Everyone seems to know what BAD leadership is like and they will have no trouble describing examples of it.

Here are a few examples from workshops we have run with senior executives:

Being a poor communicator

Dictating everything from above

Not involving people in decision making

Saying one thing and doing another

Rubbishing a company programme

Not living the company values

Pushing blame down

Jumping to solutions without any real facts.

You can add more to this list as there are sure to be plenty of ideas.

You will have real difficulty writing down their ideas fast enough and keeping up with them, so the second approach is to use Post-it notes and ask them to write down each idea on a separate note. Then you put them all onto a wall or flip chart. Personally, we both like getting them to shout out ideas as it creates a real buzz and it's clear who is participating.

Once they have filled up at least one flip chart sheet, you say 'Okay well we seem to be pretty good at this! However, what we really want is "excellent leadership" so let's look at our collected notes and see if they can give us ideas by turning the negatives into positives.'

So, work down the list and literally change the negatives into positives.

Looking at the list above, this might become ...

Being an excellent communicator

Not being a dictator

Involving people in decision making

Doing what you say you will do

Supporting company programmes

Living the company values

Not pushing the blame down!

Not jumping to solutions without getting the facts.

You can continue with your list of negative ideas, turning each one around.

The discussion as a team is helpful, engaging and we have found this one simple 'tool' can really make a difference in getting teams involved and opening up thinking. We probably all know somewhere deep in our minds what the characteristics of good leadership look like but simply reversing the question seems to help dig out that thinking and gets a serious discussion going in a way which is more enjoyable. Maybe it is because we're Brit and we are pretty expert at being negative about just about everything given half a chance; but underneath it we genuinely do want to be good leaders ourselves and we want to work with good leaders too.

Okay so negative brainstorming, it's a great tool, try it in your next team meeting on 'How can we run the worst team meeting ever!?'

Our experience with teams is that within 15 minutes you can run the negative idea generation and turn these ideas around into positive thoughts, create a 'guidelines for effective team meetings' flip chart which you can then use in future at YOUR team meetings. The team will buy into it too. After all, they were involved in its development.

I (Martin) wanted to start by illustrating that when you get under the somewhat weird and off-putting name, 'Lean Six Sigma', it may surprise you. If you can get beyond the odd name and any residual stigma or preconceived ideas you might have about Six Sigma being just about super high levels of quality, then there is a lot 'under the bonnet' of Lean Six Sigma which any manager or leader will find more than just useful.

With so many books written on the subject it may seem rather crazy to write another. However, from my experience working with many executive teams, what managers or leaders want to know is a little different from the rather technical descriptions that are covered in the traditional books on the subject.

I am often Asked the Question 'What Exactly is Lean Six Sigma?'

Over the last few years it's come to mean a number of things but, in reality, most organisations use it as a tried and tested approach to implement continuous improvement. In Catalyst, we use the name to encompass a wide range of methods, tools and techniques which have their origins in different histories and backgrounds. This range is developing and changing over time as more and more organisations build ever increasing experiences of using the approach in very different situations.

The latest most successful implementations of Lean Six Sigma – or whatever you want to call it (more on this later) – bring together thinking, principles, approaches, tools and techniques from the following:

- Lean thinking
- Six Sigma
- Change Management
- Agile and, most recently,
- 'Digital Transformation'.

Lean Thinking

Let's take a look at some of the background, starting with Lean. If you'd like a serious grounding in Lean and Six Sigma then pick up a copy of *Lean Six Sigma for Dummies*. When we wrote that book we wanted to 'demystify' the approach and make it accessible to everyone. We are going to paraphrase some of the basics here with the emphasis on the leadership aspects behind the approach.

When people talk about the roots of Lean thinking, the word 'Toyota' is often quoted. In fact, Toyota call their system 'The Toyota Production System'. The concept of the word 'Lean' goes back to 1987, when John Krafcik who is now the CEO of Waymo (including the Google driverless car project) worked as a researcher in his earlier career at MIT. He was looking for a label for the Toyota Production System (TPS) phenomenon that described what the system did. On a whiteboard, he wrote the performance attributes of the Toyota system compared with traditional mass production.

TPS:

- Needed less human effort to design products and services.
- Required less investment for a given amount of production capacity.
- Created products with fewer delivered defects.
- Used fewer suppliers.
- Went from concept to launch, order to delivery and problem to repair in less time and with less human effort.
- Needed less inventory at every process step.
- Caused fewer employee injuries.

Krafcik commented:

It needs less of everything to create a given amount of value, so let's call it 'Lean'.

The Lean thinking world grew rapidly with the focus on reducing non-value-adding activities or waste. The Japanese word is *Muda*.

But, to sustain success, organisations need a lot more than knowledge about the tools and techniques. It all boils down to leadership. After all, it would not have taken root in Toyota if it hadn't had strong leadership commitment to create the environment needed to embed the principles and thinking into the **organisation as a system**. As Toyota chairperson Fujio Cho says:

The key to the Toyota way is not any of the individual elements but all the elements together as a system. It must be practised every day in a very consistent manner – not in spurts. We place the highest value on taking action and implementation. By improvement based on action, one can rise to the higher level of practice and knowledge.

As we said in *Lean Six Sigma for Dummies*: the system focuses on training to develop exceptional people and teams that follow the company's philosophy to gain exceptional results. Consider the following:

- Toyota creates a strong and stable culture wherein values and beliefs are widely shared and lived out over many years.
- Toyota works constantly to reinforce that culture.

- Toyota involves cross-functional teams to solve problems.
- Toyota keeps teaching individuals how to work together.

Being Lean means involving people in the process, equipping them to be able, and feel able, to challenge and improve their processes and the way they work. Never waste the creative potential of people!

All of the above has implications for leadership. It won't just happen without commitment and 'commitment' alone isn't enough either – you will need to stir it into action.

There is a lot more to Lean thinking but these five principles underpin the approach:

1. Understand the customer and their perception of value.
2. Identify and understand the value stream for each process and the waste within it.
3. Enable the value to flow.
4. Let the customer pull the value through the processes, according to their needs.
5. Continuously pursue perfection (continuous improvement – or Kaizen in Japanese).

Introducing Six Sigma

Lean has its origins in Japan, while Six Sigma has its roots in the US from the 1980s, when we can trace the origins back to Motorola. The then CEO Bob Galvin was struggling to compete with foreign manufacturers and Motorola set a goal of tenfold improvement in five years, with a plan focused on global competitiveness, participative management, quality improvement and training. Quality engineer Bill Smith coined the name of the improvement measurements: Six Sigma. All Motorola employees underwent training, and Six Sigma became the standard for all Motorola business processes.

The word soon spread around US major businesses into Allied Signal, and in the 1990s it reached the ears of Jack Welch, the dynamic CEO of General Electric (GE). Jack Welch was initially sceptical as he viewed Six Sigma as a 'Quality' programme but he agreed to pilot test the approach insisting that all Six Sigma projects should have a clear measure of success. The expression Return On Six Sigma or ROSS was born. Within a few months it was clear that Six Sigma projects could return attractive financial (and other) benefits and Welch dictated the use of Six Sigma across the entire group of GE businesses.

So once again, it was strong leadership, albeit a very different style of leadership compared with Toyota (Jack Welch was known in GE as 'Neutron Jack'), that drove the initial success; and through the experience in GE the world learned that Six Sigma was far from 'just a quality programme' and also that the approach was proven to work in all kinds of businesses not 'just manufacturing'.

When Jack Welch introduced Six Sigma, he said:

> We are going to shift the paradigm from fixing products to fixing and developing processes, so they produce nothing but perfection or close to it.

The recognition that it is the *process* that needs to be changed is central to both Lean and Six Sigma. We will come back to this!

Six Sigma enhances the Lean approach considerably.

For example, Six Sigma has strong roots – with measurement and data analysis extending an already great Lean toolkit by bringing a range of additional tools focused on how to measure, how much to measure and statistical tools, many of which are relevant for everyone in business or indeed leaders responsible for running any kind of organisation in whatever sector.

Six Sigma also brings a powerful problem-solving method which can easily be integrated with Lean tools. This method has now become the standard problem-solving approach for many organisations and has stood the test of time and application in all kinds of different sectors. The original thinkers in Motorola who devised the Six Sigma method must be astonished at how this approach has spread throughout the world and is still growing in popularity more than 30 years since it was first conceived.

We have occasionally heard leaders say that 'we are not ready for Six Sigma' and this is almost always down to confusion about the name.

When those statisticians in Motorola influenced the creation of the name 'Six Sigma' they had absolutely the right intentions with the aim of inventing a great aspirational goal for everyone to aim for – a very high level of quality. However, to understand exactly what they meant by Six Sigma requires a rather complicated, overly mathematical explanation which is likely to turn off many leaders before they reach a real understanding. To be honest it isn't technically that relevant to a lot of applications of continuous improvement which can benefit so much from the principles behind Six Sigma and the tools underpinning it. The name stuck though and has entered the business vocabulary whether we like it or not.

It has put a lot of leaders off the whole approach though! This is a real shame as there is so much which is relevant to leading and running organisations today, especially as we enter a new digital transformation era.

Don't get too worried about the name 'Six Sigma'! It is an issue, we agree. Some of our clients feel strongly enough to use a different 'brand' instead of Lean Six Sigma – here is a selection which we have seen over the years:

- Operational Excellence
- Business Excellence
- Think Process
- Continuous Improvement
- Continuous Innovation
- Relentless Simplification
- For a Better Life

There are also 'coded' expressions that mean something specific for a particular organisation – like 'e3'.

In all these cases when you look 'under the bonnet' you will find the same approaches, principles and tools which all come from the latest Lean Six Sigma stable. Make it work for you, adapt it for your organisation, make it fit so that people feel curious and want to join in.

One of the most powerful and common applications for Lean Six Sigma is to tackle business problems. We will look at this from a leadership perspective in the following chapters.

Lean Six Sigma Principles

Lean Six Sigma is based on a set of principles which are based on the roots mentioned above:

1. Focus on the customer
2. Identify and understand how the work gets done
3. Manage, improve and smooth the process flow
4. Remove non-value-add steps and waste
5. Manage by fact and reduce variation
6. Involve and equip people in the process
7. Undertake improvement activity in a systematic way

We will draw on these principles throughout this book.

2

Business Problem Solving

LET'S HAVE A look at the Lean Six Sigma problem-solving method with a particular focus on leadership.

First, as with all problem solving, we start with a problem – and in the world of Lean Six Sigma, 'problem' is not a bad word. We know that our processes are not perfect and problems are everywhere. A continuous improvement mindset will always be looking for opportunities to improve things. In a later chapter, we will look at how leaders can set up systems to select the 'right' problems to work on but for this chapter let's assume we have selected a problem and we are starting a Lean Six Sigma 'project' to tackle this problem.

The five phases of the Lean Six Sigma problem-solving method are:

Define – Measure – Analyse – Improve – Control (DMAIC).

These are shown in Figure 2.1.

The aim is to take a problem, which may well be ill-defined to start with, and work through the phases to understand the current situation (Measure); then to work down to discover the root causes of the problem (Analyse); with this knowledge we can move into the Improve phase where we initially consider different options to

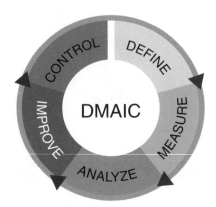

Figure 2.1   The DMAIC phases

solve the problem, select the most appropriate option, plan and test it before finally implementing the chosen solution; and ensure ongoing controls are in place so that the improved process can carry on being operated without the risk of things failing again (Control).

There is of course a lot more to it, but in essence that is how DMAIC works.

Looking at this in a bit more detail: here is a summary of the DMAIC problem-solving approach. The medical analogy works well. I (Martin) was working with a team of doctors in one organisation and one of them mentioned the similarities between the stages in treating a patient and the DMAIC phases in business problem solving.

DEFINE – what do you think needs improving? *So, what seems to be the problem? Listening and organising our thinking.*

MEASURE – use facts and data to understand how your processes work and perform. *Fact Finding/Symptoms. Let's do a few tests and measures and find out what is really going on here.*

ANALYSE – use facts and data to determine the root cause(s) inhibiting your performance to the customer. *Diagnosing/Causes. Analysing the situation using a variety of root cause problem-solving skills, using data and process analysis to narrow down the possibilities until we can identify the most likely root causes.*

IMPROVE – identify, select, and test the most appropriate solution(s), validating your approach with data. *Prescribing/Solutions. Let's consider a number of treatment options before selecting the best one for this situation, testing it out and reviewing how well it works.*

CONTROL – implement the solution and use data to help you hold the gains, and prompt new opportunities. *Implementing, Sustaining, Learning/Benefits. Continue the treatment programme and minimise the chance of any recurrence. Monitor the situation on an ongoing basis looking for any signs of new problems. Continue to look for further opportunities for improvement.*

Starting with Define

This is the phase where we set up our project, we've selected the problem and we need to allocate a small team to work on cracking it. This will be led by a trained Lean Six Sigma practitioner. The Define phase is important. Get the groundwork right and the project will progress well through the subsequent phases; so it is worth investing the time needed at this stage and not rushing off too quickly into 'instant solutions'. If there really is an obvious 'instant solution' then you shouldn't be going through a problem-solving method anyway – just go and do it!

Although all the phases are important, the Define phase is a particularly important one for leaders to be actively involved with. It sets the initial direction.

All too often, though, leaders 'think' they know the solution to problems but their suspicions can be proved incorrect when using this problem-solving approach as it reveals the 'root cause' of the problem rather than just the symptoms. *We can't emphasise this enough.* There is a tendency in some organisational cultures to be seen to be taking 'action' and action is perceived as changing things. Deming (the great guru of quality from the last century) would shudder in his grave at the thought. He'd call that 'tampering with the process', i.e. not thinking it through, not basing decisions on data or facts, and going for a knee-jerk quick fix. The intention is good but the effect can cost a lot of money and create more waste – for example, extra 'checking' is added into a process, it doesn't solve the problem but causes time delays and extra cost, not to mention frustration and hassle.

So, yes, this is all about leadership but it's likely to be a different style of leadership from that seen in many organisations. To be truly successful at this 'stuff' might well require a 'change of thinking' and that is not easy to achieve.

During the Define phase, we carry out a number of key tasks.

One of these is to write up an **improvement project charter** – this is a simple one-page document which has a number of elements – such as the example in Figure 2.2.

Improvement Charter Template

Project title:	Date commenced:

Why *High level business case describing why this project is important and how it links to our business plans*

What *The problem and goal statements, the scope, and the CTQ and defect definitions for the relevant customers and processes*

Problem statement	Goal statement
In frame	Out of frame
CTQs	Defect definition

Who *The process owner, Champion, team leader, and team members. Who are they and what are their roles, responsibilities, and time commitments? What involvement is expected of the champion? How often should they meet?*

Name	Roles & responsibilities	Time commitment

When *High level timeframes for the phases. This could be mapped to the eight steps.*

	Date	Date	Date	Date	Date	Date
Define						
Measure						
Analyse						
Improve						
Control						

Figure 2.2   **Example Charter Template**

Problem Statement

The **problem statement** describes what is *not* happening that should be happening; a good problem statement is worth spending time in writing and getting the team involved. It shouldn't mention any possible 'solutions' and it also shouldn't mention any possible 'causes'. So, for example, here is a really bad problem statement ...

> Sales of online products have dropped over the last three months because our Google Advertising is not being updated with new offers, and we need to spend more money on Adwords.

Phew – that contains a cause (a good problem statement is unlikely to contain the word 'because') AND it contains a solution, 'spend more money on Adwords'.

This is definitely not a Lean Six Sigma problem statement.

A better version would look like this, simply stating what is going wrong but without the (tempting to add) 'because' and the 'fix'.

> Sales of online products have dropped over the last three months.

This does look a bit 'bare' but it is ok as a start. It isn't going to stay like this for long as we can update it after the next phase (Measure), when we have got more facts and data about what is really happening.

After we have collected data we can update the problem statement so it might look more like this ...

> Sales of online products have dropped over the last three months, monthly sales have dropped from £275k to £185k and our forecast is down by 25%.

We've deliberated chosen a sales example as that is not an area that you might have thought Lean Six Sigma could be applied to. But it certainly can. After all, the sales process is a process, a system of working, a 'way of working' just like any other process.

Just to give you a flavour, here is a sample of problem statements from a diverse range of projects.

Here is an example from manufacturing.

> Machine set-up times vary between shifts and machines. This causes inconsistent outputs and knock-on planning issues affecting on time in full delivery to customers.

Note that it is ok to have the consequences or impact of the problem in the problem statement. It adds weight to the rationale for tackling it – i.e. *This causes inconsistent outputs*.

Don't be confused by the use of the verb 'to cause' which is ok, as opposed to the noun 'the cause' which is not ok, in a problem statement. Also try to avoid the use of the word 'because'. Ah, don't you love the English language!

Here is another problem statement example, this time from a Housing Association.

> We charged tenants for 2400 repairs last year for which we considered they were liable. 1200 of these were appealed and over 60% of the appeals were upheld in their favour.

This is clearly a pressing problem and it is tempting to jump straight to a reason why we think this is happening (the cause), and then to 'prescribe' a shoot-from-the-hip (or lip) solution. As leaders (and depending on your style of leadership) your pronouncements may be taken rather too seriously by those whom you are leading and they may follow you blindly if you decide to go down a rapid, action-oriented solution path (i.e. your guess) without really knowing if it will work.

If your organisation has a 'gung ho' culture of action, you will know exactly what I mean.

However, we can also imagine some of you might be thinking, 'well surely some action is better than spending too long "defining, measuring and analysing"'. When done well, Lean Six Sigma problem solving doesn't need to take an inordinate amount of time to get to the right solution but it will certainly feel strange at first, and you may have to defend the approach until it has proven itself in practice. Later we will show how Lean Six Sigma is now learning from the rapid paced world of Agile to speed up improvement projects.

The Business Case

Another key element of the improvement charter is the **Business Case**. This isn't what you might be expecting if you are new to the Lean Six Sigma approach. The business case here is a short statement written at the Define phase which states the business reason why solving this problem is important. This is typically going to link the project to a business issue, for example for financial or operational reasons. As a leader you can write this from the perspective of the 'voice of the business'. Consider the question, 'Why is it important to be tackling this problem now from a business perspective?'

For example, say that the problem is the above mentioned sales issue where online sales have dropped. The importance to the business here is easy to identify so the business case would be something like:

> Falling revenue in online sales, which attract a higher margin than sales through other channels, is impacting on overall profitability of the product line 'X'. This product line is key to our business strategy.

Another problem statement example could be a need to speed up a process, by reducing the time it takes to do something, known in the Lean Six Sigma world as reducing cycle time. In this case, there might be a less obvious link between the process issue (which is what the problem statement is focused on) and the business case. However, reducing cycle time could impact on customer satisfaction and also reduce waste in the process. Both are valid business reasons for going ahead with the improvement project but you as the leader will need to be sure that you can see the link.

Ask the question, 'How will solving this problem affect the overall business?'

If you don't have a good business case then you don't have a good project! Lean Six Sigma is very much focused on solving business issues and we believe this is the main reason why it has continued to grow in popularity over the years. As Jack Welch discovered – it is a lot more than just a quality thing (even though we know that isn't such a bad thing)!

Goal Statement

We are still working through our improvement charter, and now we can look at the **Goal Statement**. The best way to do this is to take the problem statement and do a 'mirror statement'. So, for example, if online sales are dropping, our goal is to bring online sales back on track. You will no doubt be able to develop a quantifiable goal; but it's important, like the problem statement, that this is also not fully cast in stone while you are still in the Define stage.

This can be a bit of a dilemma for leaders. You know you have a problem, you have a good business reason for tackling this problem, but how do you set a quantifiable goal at this stage?

Well you can set a challenge but it's likely that in the Define phase this would be more of a 'guess'!

What we can do is defer setting the quantified version of the goal but use a placeholder version – e.g. increase online sales to achieve a minimum of £Xk per month by <date> – and come back to this after the Measure phase when we will have a much better understanding of how things truthfully are in practice or what Lean Six Sigma practitioners call the 'current state'. One of the nice things about Lean Six Sigma is that you can (and should) update the charter as you progress through the phases and as you learn and discover more about the problem and options for remedying it.

The business case links to a wider aspect of Lean Six Sigma which is highly relevant for leaders and that is how to quantify benefits. Not just quantifying benefits but how to realise benefits; when to undertake a full cost/ benefit analysis; and how to ensure that benefits are sustained after the improvement project has been completed.

We are still in the Define phase and we are working through our improvement charter. So far, we have completed the Problem Statement, Business Case and Goal Statement which are important elements in the charter. Other elements of the charter include the list of team members, an outline timeline, and scope – what is in and out of scope?

I suggest the next aspect to consider is the 'process'. We find this is a tricky word for many managers and often kick off a workshop introducing Lean Six Sigma by asking everyone to discuss what they mean by this word 'process'. It is truly illuminating to get their reactions. In some organisations it is definitely a negative word! However, most managers see it as just the 'way we do things' and that is exactly what I want you to think it is for the purposes of introducing the next section. Don't think of process as being boring! Don't think of it as being a strait-jacket or being unnecessarily bureaucratic or tedious – it doesn't need to be.

What is a Process?

Delving deeper into the roots underpinning this kind of approach you will find a famous quote from Dr W Edwards Deming, who set many of the foundations for today's world of continuous improvement and change.

> Eighty-five percent of the reasons for failure to meet customer expectations are related to deficiencies in systems and process ... rather than the employee. The role of management is to *change the process* rather than badgering individuals to do better.

In essence, Deming is saying 'don't blame the people, blame the process'. People come to work and, in the vast majority of cases, they want to do a good job. But the way the work is organised, the 'system' of work is the barrier which often frustrates employees as much as customers. It's also where non-value waste is abundant.

Process is the word we use to describe the way that work has been designed to be carried out, the system for doing the work – or, if you prefer, the Way of Working (WOW) which seems far more interesting than 'process'.

When training executives on this kind of stuff (aka Lean Six Sigma) we ask them to think about how 'work gets done'. If we want to improve the way 'work gets done' we have to change the process, which is exactly what Deming was saying.

In Lean Six Sigma, understanding 'the process' is therefore key and we use a simple but powerful tool to describe a process at a high level: the SIPOC.

A SIPOC is really a table which lists the inputs and outputs of the process together with the process steps (at a high level so try to keep this between 4 and 7 steps) and we can then ask where do the inputs come from and where do the outputs go? In a SIPOC these are the suppliers and customers.

i.e. SIPOC = Suppliers – Inputs – Process steps – Outputs

– Customers

Its best illustrated in an example and let's look at something trivial to illustrate this like 'boiling an egg'. The example in Figure 2.3 is taken from a training workshop.

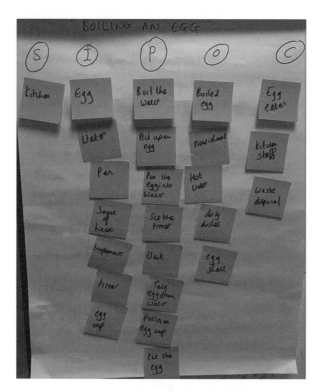

Figure 2.3   Example SIPOC from a training workshop

It may seem trivial but when you start to use the SIPOC to describe a process, and we stress this is at a high level, a lot of good questions are generated. We have seen examples where outputs are produced and go nowhere or simply get 'filed', or no one really knows who the customers are, and/or their requirements are not clear. All of these become great opportunities for improvement but it is paramount when looking at process that you are not looking to blame the people. As Deming said, *Blame the Process, Not the People*, and that is a lot harder to do in practice than it might appear.

SIPOC also provides a framework to start thinking about Measurement.

How do you measure how good a process is? In other words, how do you measure how well the work gets done? That is a seriously important question.

If you adopt Lean Six Sigma thinking then you will need to consider more than the obvious output measures. Figure 2.4 shows

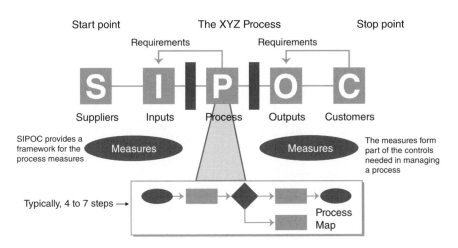

Figure 2.4   SIPOC framework

a schematic of the SIPOC and this sets the scene for us to consider exactly who are the 'customers' of this process. We define customer here as simply the recipient of output from the process, so there may well be more than one customer. An example is provided in Figure 2.5.

Each customer will have distinct requirements, and in Lean Six Sigma we talk about listening to the 'voice of the customer' [VOC] to really understand customers. This is not a trivial exercise if done well.

The SIPOC is a central tool which is developed in the Define phase of a Lean Six Sigma project. It raises all the right questions:

- What scope are we considering in this improvement project, what is the 'start point' and what is the 'end point' of the process we want to examine?
- Who are the customers of the process, and what are their requirements?
- How do we, and how should we, measure how well this process is operating?
- What are the high-level steps in the process – in other words, how is work carried out?
- How far upstream into the 'supply chain' are we intending to look? In our egg boiling process are we going as far as the hen or are we simply going as far as the fridge?

Suppliers	Inputs (use nouns)	Process (use verbs)	Outputs (use nouns)	Customer
Customer	Order (quantities, timescale, quality)	Take Order	Written Order Agreed Price and Delivery time	Customer Order Tracking IT System
Ingredient suppliers	Ingredients—water, flour, yeast, salt, Recipe	Select and Weigh Ingredients	Correct Amount of each Ingredient Prepared Ingredients	Dough Mixer
Water Utility, Bakery Manager	Selected Ingredients Work instructions	Mix to Make Dough	Dough	Dough Shaper
Dough mixer	Dough Extra Flavouring (seeds, olives, herbs)	Shape the Dough and Add Extra Ingredients	Shaped Dough	Dough Prover
Dough shaper	Shaped and flavoured dough	Prove the Dough	Proven (Risen) Dough	Baker
Prover	Proven dough	Bake at 230°	Product	Packager
Baker Packaging suppliers	Baked product Packaging	Package the Product	Packaged Product	Despatcher

Figure 2.5   A SIPOC example: Bakery process from Order to Packaging

- Who are the 'stakeholders' – i.e. people who have an 'interest' in this process, people who need to be involved, communicated with as we review the process and consider improvements. It's worth developing a list of stakeholders alongside the SIPOC as you develop the picture.

The SIPOC is one of the 'must have' tools in the Lean Six Sigma toolbag, hence the description above. It is also a great prompt for the next stage in the Define phase – understanding customer requirements.

We can take this process thinking further into a wider organisational context and look at how organisations can be regarded as a set of interconnected processes. This can form the basis for effective leadership by allocating process ownership to different leaders and teams as well as providing a framework for performance measurement and day-to-day operations. A process operating model like this can also helping you decide where to focus your energy as a leader when you are responsible for an end-to-end operation consisting of several interconnected processes.

Customers

'Customer' can be a difficult word! We have worked with organisations of all shapes and sizes – in the business and public sectors as well as in charities – and the word 'customer' can mean different things to different groups.

As a leader, you will know who your key customers are, and you will be pleased to know that these customers will be at the heart of any good Lean Six Sigma programme. It's important that you stress this and steer the programme towards the needs of your primary customers. Of course, it's also ok to have problem solving focused on 'internal' customers and ensure that the needs of the business are driving the overall direction of the programme. However, there is nothing better than improvement activity with a direct connection to real, income generating customers.

In the Lean Six Sigma world, and in the context of a SIPOC, the word 'customer' is used to mean any person or 'thing' that receives an output from the process you are reviewing. We say 'thing' as the customer, using this definition, can be another process or department, or organisation or even a system.

During the Define phase it is important to identify the customers (recipients of output) of the process and consider their requirements.

Understanding the Voice of the Customer

At first glance this seems an obvious thing to do, but in reality many people 'think' they know what their customers want and don't take the time to get under the surface and find out what they really think by involving them in improvement projects. Requirements change over time too. It can be very illuminating and surprising. Occasionally, this can make life a lot easier than you had expected as customers sometimes do not always want the service levels or quality that you thought they needed. They may also prioritise requirements in a different order than you expect.

We are beginning to see the world of Agile impacting more widely in the business world (more in Chapter 10) and the concept of the 'minimum viable product' where customers are more interested in getting a product or service earlier with basic functions working well, rather than waiting for 'perfection' or full functionality which can delay delivery. This may seem an anathema to Six Sigma thinking but it can make good business sense. As a leader, you will need to steer your improvement project teams in the direction which best meets your business needs. With Lean Six Sigma, you can make calculated decisions here.

There are several Lean Six Sigma tools and techniques which can help to understand the true voice of the customer: interviews, surveys, focus groups, sampling, Kano analysis, Quality Function Deployment to name a few. The need for these will vary depending on the business, your customer segmentation, and the improvement area. We won't cover them in this book but we have described these tools in *Lean Six Sigma for Dummies*. These all have their place and, as a leader, you will want to know that the true needs of customer(s) are genuinely investigated and understood before moving out of the Define phase.

Setting the Timescale

As a leader, we hope you can see the value of getting more involved in the Define phase, setting the direction of the improvement project, developing the business case, understanding the high level view of the process using the SIPOC and getting under the surface of customer requirements as seen from their view. The Define phase is worth the investment of your time at it sets the project up for success.

You will also need to set an outline timeline for the project and this is important. We all need a deadline. Ask me about the publishing deadline for this book! (Martin). We are all human, and without some pressure there is a risk that the project will drift and time will disappear behind you. Your improvement project team are likely to be working part time on this activity and the pressure of day-to-day operations can easily overshadow the improvement project. With all the best intentions, you are likely to experience this too and this will be a test of your commitment and this will more than likely be observed by the team.

This is one the biggest challenges facing any Continuous Improvement initiative. In fact, it is one of the biggest challenges in establishing and sustaining a continuous improvement programme of any kind. Finding the time. At a recent senior executive workshop, a senior leader made a good observation, he said 'People ask me for more time, but unfortunately it is not in my power to create more time, I am not God!'

Is this, perhaps, the ultimate DMAIC problem statement: 'we don't have enough time'?

Wouldn't it be great if we could create more time. Indeed, we all have limited time. The real issue is in how we use it. This is an issue for leaders which extends well beyond Lean Six Sigma. Think about how you prioritise your time and how people working for you prioritise their time. Optimisation of your personal time is a key issue for all leaders. We call this 'Lean Six Sigma thinking' using the principles underpinning the approach and using some of the tools and techniques to support your role as a leader.

For now, though, we will come back to the Define phase of our improvement project and the leadership needed to set the project in the right direction.

Setting a timescale in the Define phase is a real challenge for a leader. It is important to set the pace, and to some extent you need to be stating what an acceptable timescale will be from the business viewpoint.

We have seen DMAIC projects where a timeline is not adequately established at the start of the project, which then lacks urgency. It is hardly surprising, therefore, that these are the projects that end up taking too long. Time slips away. One of the criticisms of Lean Six Sigma is that projects take too long, but this needn't be the case. Before the project gains momentum in the Define stage it is important to establish the type of DMAIC approach which is best suited to the particular issue. There are a number of options –

- A 'classic' DMAIC project led by a trained internal practitioner supported by a core team. This project typically will take 3–4 months from start to end. Occasionally, these projects extend up to 6 months but we would not normally suggest you do this unless tackling a particularly difficult problem.
- A rapid improvement workshop-based DMAIC project using a series of facilitated workshops to progress rapidly through the DMAIC phases. You will need a good facilitator who is also an experienced Lean Six Sigma practitioner to lead and facilitate the workshops.

- An 'Agile' style DMAIC project. This approach differs from a traditional DMAIC project where solutions are not considered until the Improve phase. This style of Agile DMAIC approach is an important step forward in the development of Lean Six Sigma and we have asked a colleague to write a guest chapter dedicated to this approach (Chapter 10).
- A consultant or interim driven project using DMAIC as the framework. This approach involves hiring in outside expert assistance to lead the project, which will typically be carried out in a series of phases. For example, a process review using the Define, Measure, and at least part of Analyse, to ascertain the 'current state' in detail and then a 'future state options' development using Analyse and Improve to get to a 'recommendations for action' stage. Recommendations for action are then considered by leaders before moving into the implementation (Control) phase.

Setting Scope

As with any project, it is important to agree the scope of your DMAIC project and this should be discussed and agreed during the Define phase. It's essential to agree what is 'in' and what is 'out' of scope. You can review Scope again as the project progresses through the DMAIC phases. As a leader, you need to be involved in this and set the direction. Remember that projects are more likely to grow in a number of different ways as they develop, so it is better to set a restricted scope and use the 'bite size' approach rather than trying to solve everything in one huge project. If you do have a mega issue to solve then it is better to 'chunk it up' and run a cluster of smaller projects in a programme rather than one enormous single project. By the way, if we refer to a 'programme' I simply mean a collection of smaller projects, which each contribute to achieving an overall programme goal.

One of the neatest 'tools' in the Lean Six Sigma toolbag, which helps a team to discuss and agree scope, is what we call 'In and Out of the Frame'. This is so easy but so powerful to use when having a discussion about scope in a team session.

Simply draw a frame like the one shown in Figure 2.6 on a flip chart and discuss different aspects of the project scope. This could include the

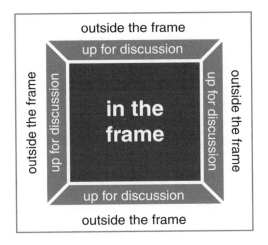

Figure 2.6 In and out of the frame

extent of the process to be considered: how far up the supply chain will the project go; which customer segments will be included/ excluded; which regions; which product groups; will IT system changes be in or out of scope; capital expenditure items, and so on. The scope discussion will depend on the project under consideration but the key thing is not to leave anything 'vague' or unclear. This is where the in/out frame tool is so useful – because it makes the discussion visual, everyone can see what has been agreed as 'in and out' of scope. The items which are unclear and which end up on the 'frame' need directing either 'in to scope' or 'out of scope' but they must not be left 'on the frame'. Simply taking a photo of the final 'in/out' flip chart is a great way to record the memory of the team discussion and avoids the situation later when people can't otherwise recall (or agree) if it was decided to include or exclude aspects from the scope. Scope is an important consideration for leaders and you'll be tempted to add to it as the project builds up momentum but do resist this temptation!

Establishing an Effective DMAIC Team with the Right People

Another key role for the leader in the Define phase (ideally before the Define phase gets started fully) is establishing the team. There are some common roles which are essential in any Lean Six Sigma project.

The Project Sponsor (or Champion)

This person needs to be a manager with a vested interest in seeing the project succeed. They act as the business sponsor. They articulate why this project is important from a business perspective. They represent the 'voice of the business'. They can access any necessary resources and budget, as well as commit the team's time needed to work on the project. It is a critically important role for the success of any Lean Six Sigma project. They need to have sufficient 'clout' to support the project and, at times, defend it from other time and resource grabbing activities. Problem solving sounds great but there is a real risk that the very problems the team are trying to solve overwhelm the organisation's day-to-day priorities which results in frantic panic measures to fix things 'at any cost'. A sponsor needs a steady nerve and whether you have genuine commitment will be tested as the project gets under way. Keep the pressure up on the team to stick to deadlines in a motivational way but support them when distractions come along and don't let yourself get diverted either. As a leader, your behaviours will be observed by the team and how you act under pressure will be a tell-tale sign of your real commitment.

Not everyone will agree with this, but in our view the project champion doesn't need to be an expert in Lean Six Sigma tools and techniques. However, they will certainly need training in their role as a champion and a one or two day course is usually sufficient to get them clear on the role and how to perform it. Of course, a number of the basic Lean Six Sigma tools will get covered on such a course and they will typically get to a Yellow Belt level of coverage but it is the leadership role which is most important. After training, for their first project or two, they will also benefit from coaching support and this is often neglected for champions. It can be a great help to talk over things with someone who has done it all before. Every project is different of course, but there will be similar challenges, particularly from a leadership perspective.

The Project Leader

The project leader will need to be appointed to the project before the Define phase gets fully underway and selecting the right project leader is clearly a leadership decision. It is usually the Champion or the Champion's leadership team who make the decision to invite the project leader to take on the project. We say 'invite' because it is much better if the project leader really wants to get involved and doesn't feel imposed upon. It is likely that the project leader will be taking this role on in addition to their 'day job' so their willingness and motivation is more important than ever.

You will have seen a lot of emphasis on leaders getting involved in the Define phase. From experience, there is good reason for this as it sets up the project for success, points it in the right direction, and gets the right people involved.

If there were just one thing to really focus on as a leader in the Define phase, we would suggest it is the *business reason*, and why it is important to be tackling this problem now.

You have to be convinced this is something which is important enough to warrant the organisation spending its valuable time on.

One thing which you will find different about using this approach from conventional project management is 'uncertainty'. Problem solving is, by its very nature, dealing with uncertainty. You won't be able to firm up on the business benefits when you start. You won't be able to direct the team to a known solution, so be prepared for some real surprises along the way when the team discover what the real issues are. There will be some 'ah ha' moments – that's for sure.

Key Points for Leaders in this Phase

- Leaders don't need to be experts in the 'technicalities' of Lean Six Sigma
- Support people in setting a clear direction for their improvement activities
- Don't jump to conclusions – focus on understanding the problem first
- Avoid big scopes. Small is beautiful
- Think 'process' not 'people'
- Place importance on the customer
- Get the right people involved

3

Measure for Leaders

THERE'S A MOMENT in the film *The Matrix* where the character Neo is offered a choice of two pills, red or blue.

> After this, there is no turning back. You take the blue pill – the story ends, you wake up in your bed and believe whatever you want to believe. You take the *red* pill – you stay in Wonderland, and I show you how deep the rabbit hole goes. Remember: all I'm offering is the truth. Nothing more.

He has to choose between security and pretence (ignorance is bliss) or the painful truth of reality. Imagine this choice – a comfortable existence where you're safe, unaware of real dangers and can continue with normal habits, or a world where you're fully aware of the difficult truth and must navigate this to achieve freedom. There's no turning back. Welcome to the Measure phase!

The Measure phase is all about finding out the truth. This is achieved by understanding how the process currently works, and then understanding how *well* the process currently works.

For leaders this can be uncomfortable, as the tools and techniques used may present findings that are out of sync with the organisation's

	Check 1	Check 2	Check 3	Total
Good	3	4	2	9
Bad	7	3	1	11
Items Checked	10	7	3	20

Figure 3.1   How good is the process?

current understanding of performance, and will often highlight waste that couldn't be spotted through existing methods

Consider, for example, the scenario shown in Figure 3.1. Ten pieces of work are being passed through a simple checking process. (Note, we'll talk more about checking later!)

On the first pass through the process, 3 items pass the quality check and 7 fail. Rework is undertaken and the 7 items are then rechecked. On the second pass through the process, 4 items pass the quality check and 3 are rejected. On the third pass, the 3 remaining items are checked again, 2 are good enough to pass the quality check and only 1 fails.

So how good is this process? There are a number of ways you could measure it!

$9/10 = 90\%$ good. After all, 9 out of the 10 items passed the quality check eventually, right?

Or…

$9/20 = 45\%$ good. Because out of 20 checks, 9 items passed. Not great? But better than …

$3/10 = 30\%$ good. Because of the 10 items being processed, only 3 passed the quality check first time.

There are a number of ways to look at performance, and Lean Six Sigma encourages a fresh look to ensure that true performance is really understood.

In this scenario, the 'first time yield' of the process is only 30%, yet the organisation might be measuring it as 90%, the 'classic' yield calculation. First time yield highlights how good the process is at delivering units right, without the need for rework. In this example, the process is not very effective at all. This is hard to swallow – a real red pill moment.

We'll look at other ways to measure a process later in this chapter. First let's focus on how the work gets done.

Picturing the Process

One of the first activities undertaken in the Measure phase is the mapping of the process in its current form. The organisation may have already documented some or all of its processes in a Quality Management System or to support consistent ways of working. However, in the Measure phase the process mapping has a different purpose, and that purpose is to capture 'what happens now' in the process. Not what *could be* or *should be*, it's a 'warts and all' representation of the process as it *really* is.

If this is to be achieved, the people mapping the process must feel comfortable about exposing the process issues and opportunities. For example, there might be things that individuals have built into their own ways of working to overcome shortcomings in systems, or things that should be done that they're not currently doing. Whatever the foibles, whatever the variations, if we don't know they exist, we can't do anything to improve the situation.

Leaders and managers often want to show their support to process improvement work by joining in with process mapping sessions. This is great, but sometimes it can have the unintentional effect of preventing issues from being surfaced. People might feel uneasy telling leaders about process failings and idiosyncrasies and may end up reciting what they think they want to hear rather than what actually happens. This is a wasted opportunity. Support for these sessions is brilliant and should definitely continue. So why not introduce the session, affirm your support and then leave the group to it? You can return at the end of the session to review the output, but leave the group to talk freely and openly while they're doing the mapping. While a panda 'eats shoots and leaves' the leader 'kicks off and leaves'!

The SIPOC that was created in the Define phase provides a good starting point for a process mapping session. The boundaries of the process (start point and end point) have already been identified and agreed. Now the team must get to grips with the steps involved, and be prepared to map them at a low level of detail if they are to surface the opportunities that exist.

For example, in a recent session, members from different functions within the same organisation were looking at the process for managing expense claims. They duly rolled out the brown paper and began to capture the process steps on Post-it notes. The first step they captured was the step carried out by the person claiming the expenses, 'Complete claim form'. The next step was to 'Submit claim form' and so on, right through to the payment of the expenses. The resulting process map looked very attractive – the team had used coloured Post-it notes, the nominated scribe had beautiful handwriting, the process steps were neatly linked together and there was no crossing out. In fact, it looked so good that it was hard to understand why the team felt so strongly that this process wasn't working for them! We challenged the group to be more specific about how each step was carried out. There was some initial eye rolling, but getting to a lower level of detail revealed some of the real 'warts' that were causing frustration. The following activities were involved in the 'Complete claim form' step:

- Log into IT system
- Reset IT system password (since this process is only carried out once per month)
- Complete claim form
- Print off claim form
- Sign claim form
- Scan signed claim form
- Save copy of signed claim into personal file

The resulting process map had a lot more steps and didn't look as pretty, but it was a lot more effective capturing the work involved in the process. The more opportunities the group uncovered, the more engaged they became in the activity. We can't do anything about these opportunities if we can't see them – so go to town!

There are a number of ways for a group to create their picture of the process. Flow charts and process maps are really effective. If a picture paints a thousand words, so does a flow chart! Using brown paper and Post-it notes makes it really easy to move steps around, and they probably will be repositioned several times as different ways of working are revealed, and details get added.

A Deployment Flow Chart is a useful format. It is sometimes called a Swimlane map because it resembles the lanes in a swimming pool. Each team or individual with a role to play in the process has their own lane, and the steps they undertake are captured within it. This technique highlights the 'handoffs' or interfaces in a process really clearly and this is important, as problems often occur at the interfaces.

An alternative or supplementary option is to develop a Value Stream Map. A Value Stream Map captures the flow of work (or information or material) in a process, and also includes process metrics. The customer is also represented in the Value Stream Map – in fact one way to develop the map is to begin with the customer and work backwards.

The data included in the Value Stream Map depends on the process. It could include the following:

Process time. The actual time taken to complete the activity. It is good practice to display the range if variation exists, with a note to explain why the variation occurs.

Lead time. The overall time, including queueing, interruptions, etc. The lead time in the Value Stream Map will be longer than the process time.

Value add time. The proportion of time spent on value added activities.

Changeover time. The time it takes to switch from one activity to another, e.g. moving from one computer screen or system to another, or switching from one product setup to another.

Demand rate. The volume of transactions at each step over a specified period, e.g. requests per day. This represents customer demand. It may vary over time, in which case it is beneficial to show the range and an explanation of the variation.

Percentage complete and accurate. This captures how often the activity receives input that is complete and accurate (from the perspective of the recipient). For example, information may be missing or incorrect.

Number of people. The Value Stream Map can record the number of people needed to perform the step or the number of people trained to undertake the activity.

Inventory. The number of items of work in the queue, the number of jobs underway, the number of items in the in-tray, etc.

IT systems. Not really a metric but useful information in a Value Stream Map to show the flow of information in a process.

Available time. The amount of time the process can be performed, or working time over a day.

A picture, like the one shown in Figure 3.2, really does paint a thousand words when it comes to process mapping, and it also prompts a thousand questions! This is a magic moment and the challenges, questions and ideas that are prompted are to be captured and valued. A note of caution however – for leaders and for all involved – don't fall into the trap of going into solution mode yet, you may be jumping to conclusions!

> Too many people confine their exercise to jumping to conclusions, running up bills, stretching the truth, bending over backward, lying down on the job, sidestepping responsibility and pushing their luck.
>
> **Anon**

There is more work to do to identify the root causes of the problems. We'll look at this in the next chapter.

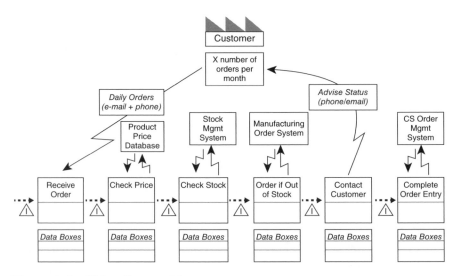

Figure 3.2   Value Stream Map

Of course, there may be some quick wins that become obvious when process mapping is carried out. It may not be necessary to wait for all the DMAIC phases to be completed before these can be addressed.

Measuring the Right Things

As well as providing us with an understanding of how the work gets done, Process Maps (including the SIPOC, Deployment Flow Charts and Value Stream Maps) can help us to identify what to measure, to understand performance fully.

From a customer perspective, what matters most to them is the output of the process which is what the customer 'receives' as shown in the SIPOC produced in the Define phase.

In Lean Six Sigma, we talk about different voices – first, listening to the voice of the customer (VOC) to help us to determine their requirements and what is important to them and what is not so important. The key requirements from a customer point of view are called the Critical to Quality requirements (CTQs) and these will need to be measurable in some way so that we can determine how well the process is meeting these requirements.

The 'voice of the process' (VOP) represents exactly that – how well the process is performing in practice. For example, imagine a customer has a requirement for a particular service which needs to be met in under five minutes. In this case the Critical to Quality requirement as specified from the voice of customer view is 'I want this service in less than five minutes'. We can then measure the actual performance of the process to discover how well it is doing against this requirement. Assuming there is no readily available data, the team will need to collect a representative sample of measurement data to determine the true performance. Let's say the data collected shows that the performance on average is six minutes. In this case the 'voice of the process' is clearly not meeting the customer requirement. The voice of the process is saying 'I can provide this service in six minutes'. There is a mismatch between the 'voice of the customer' and the 'voice of the process'. Another way of expressing this is to say that the process is not capable; and measuring process capability is a subject which is covered in Lean Six Sigma training using some statistical methods when necessary. The above example has been very much simplified to illustrate the basics of the different 'voices'.

From a leader's view, it's important that you grasp the basics but you don't need to understand the detailed technical aspects of how process capability is measured in all cases. The key questions to ask of the team are:

- Do we really understand our customers' requirements?
- What are their critical to quality requirements?
- How well is the current process performing against these requirements?
- In other words, what is the capability of the process?

In Lean Six Sigma lingo the output measures of the process are called the Y measures. This is a mathematical convention (we'll come across a small number of those as we go along, but not too many). So, the first thing to do is to develop Y measures.

The organisation may already have measures in place to identify how well the current process is meeting the CTQs, but this is not always the case! (Remember the adage, 'What gets Measured gets Done'? If the Ys of the process were being measured and shared appropriately, the process you're looking at might not require the improvement it now needs.)

Measuring the outputs sounds relatively simple but there are some potential pitfalls. One organisation measured its ability to provide on time delivery and were reporting almost perfect performance. However, a large number of customers were complaining about late delivery. How could this be? The organisation's method of measurement only focused on whether the goods were *dispatched* on time. What happened next was clearly not working, but the measurement system did not address it.

Measuring the outputs of a process alone is not enough. If you wait until the end of the process to understand if it's going to meet requirements, it may be too late! For example, if your process is the resolution of time critical incidents, counting how many incidents you were able to resolve on time would tell you about overall performance, but this method of measurement allows you no opportunity to identify if you're at risk of missing the deadline. Output measures are lagging measures. They are important to monitor because they show the process from the customer view but they are not sufficient to adequately control the process and predict its performance.

So, we need to get to grips with other factors in the process that could influence the output. These factors could relate to process inputs, and they could relate to things happening in the process. In Lean Six Sigma we call these the X factors. For the incident response process, these *could* include:

- Whether all of the necessary information has been received.
- Allocation of the incident to the appropriate person.
- The incident type.
- The status of the incident four hours after receipt, etc.

By creating a measurement plan that includes Y (output) measures and X (input and in-process) measures, it will be possible to understand not only how well the CTQ requirements are being addressed by the current process, but also to gain valuable insights into the factors which cause the performance to perform in the way it is. This concept of understanding cause (X) and effect (Y) is an important principle that threads through the Lean Six Sigma problem-solving approach.

Measuring the Things Right

Measuring these aspects of the process requires careful consideration. Everyone involved should understand what's being measured and why.

Let's think about the Incident Management process again for a moment, and imagine that you are a member of the incident management team. Imagine that someone has now asked you to capture information on the status of each incident four hours after receipt. If no one has communicated clearly why you are being asked to collect this data, you make an educated guess because you 'sort of' understand why – if the incident isn't being progressed in an appropriate and timely manner the deadline for resolution won't be met. However, you're not really certain how the information gleaned from this exercise is going to be used. You start thinking 'how does my performance look compared with other members of the team?' Is it consistent or do the incidents that you're dealing with seem to take longer than everyone else's? If so, would this influence what gets talked about at your next performance appraisal? Mmmm, this starts to feel a little bit uncomfortable. So, just to be on the safe side, you amend the status of some of the incidents in the log, from 'Assigned' to 'Pending Client' and a few of the 'Pending' incidents to 'Fix in Progress'. You feel a bit better now. But the data collected on the status of incidents is impaired, and may compromise the team's understanding of what's really happening in the process.

It's also possible (and probable!) that the requirements for measurement get misunderstood. Without clear guidelines, the requirement can be interpreted in a number of different ways.

A sound and sensible measurement system is therefore required to ensure that the data collected is valid and consistent. This is referred to as Measurement System Analysis (MSA) and there are two techniques to support this, depending on the type of data that is being used.

Types of Data

For Continuous data (data which you can put a decimal point in!), a technique called Gauge R and R is used. R and R does not stand for Rest and Recuperation (although you may feel the need for some of that by the time you're this far into the chapter on Measurement!). It refers to Repeatability and Reproducibility. Check out the definitions below:

Repeatability. A measure of variation where one operator uses the same system to measure the same thing. Is the operator consistent with him/herself?

Reproducibility. A measure of variation where different operators use the same system to measure the same thing. Are the operators consistent with each other?

Gauge R and R provides a way of checking how much the measurement system is contributing to process variation. The example shown in Figure 3.3 is for two operators measuring the first steps of the incident resolution process.

The Tolerance is calculated by dividing the difference in readings by the average of the readings and multiplying the result by 100 to turn

Process measure	Operator 1	Operator 2	Difference	Average of the Readings	Tolerance
Check necessary info	97	112	15	104.5	10.67%
Log the incident	65	69	4	67	5.97%
Generate reference number	12	11.5	0.5	11.5	4.34%
Assign incident	36	34	2	35	5.71%
Total Time	210	226.5	21.5	218	9.86

Figure 3.3   Tolerance in measurement

it into a percentage. Determining a 'good' gauge R and R depends on the nature of the process and the consequences of inaccurate data and can therefore be quite subjective. But generally, if the tolerance exceeds 10% the measurement system should be improved. If it's higher than 25% the system is too unpredictable and change is needed.

For attribute data (for example, exam grades or assessment against a segmentation or classification scale of some kind), Attribute Agreement Analysis is used. To carry out an Attribute Agreement Analysis, people in the team are asked to classify a number of items. Their assessments can be compared with one another, and also with an expert's assessment. This will highlight whether classification is consistent across the team.

Measuring Enough Things

Now let's dip our toes into the waters of Sampling. But we won't fully submerge ourselves – here's an introduction, and it's probably enough for now. If you'd like to know more about Sampling there's a lot more to explore.

Sampling (when it's done well!) means that we don't have to use a lot of data, or *all* the data, to understand enough to be able to draw valid conclusions about performance. This is useful to us because data collection can be time-consuming and costly. In some situations, the act of collecting the data destroys or damages the thing being measured, e.g. drop-testing of mobile phones.

There are 3 Rs to consider when sampling: the sample should be Random, Representative and the Right Size. (Now might be a good time to practice your pirate impression, 'Arrr!')

Random

Random means that every data point stands an equal chance of being included. If the approach is not random it could lead to bias, and this could impact on our ability to make appropriate inferences from the data collected.

Representative

The data that we collect in our sample needs to be representative of all the data. To achieve this, it is necessary to understand the segmentation factors involved in the process or population being measured. For example, to understand how long it takes to resolve an incident you'd look at a representative snapshot of incident types, incidents by customer, levels of severity, etc. Figure 3.4 provides a further example.

Factor	Example
What type?	complaints, defects, problems, products
When?	year, month, week, day
How?	telephone, e-mail, internet, letter
Where?	country, region, city, work site
Who?	customer, business, department, individual

Figure 3.4   Segmenting data

Right Size of Sample

Generally speaking you would think that the larger the sample size, the more accurate the inferences we can make from the data but the amount of variation in the data being sampled is also a key factor. After all, if you were sampling from a population of clones, you would only need to sample one to get an accurate picture of every single item in the population. Of course, there is a catch-22 here, you need to know how much variation there is in order to calculate the sample size. Thankfully there are some very straightforward guidelines and calculations to calculate sample size that can be carried out by trained Green or Black belts with the help of Excel.

And finally ...

Collecting the Data

Having identified what to measure, how to measure it, and how much to measure, the data collection activity can commence! Even if you've skimmed through the information in this chapter you'll now have an appreciation of what's involved in getting robust, reliable data about process performance (and if you've read it in detail – you'll hopefully be seeing light at the end of the tunnel!).

In many cases, it will be necessary to collect some data manually. Try not to overcomplicate things by collecting information on lots and lots of 'related conditions' – keep things simple.

Check Sheets are among the '7 basic quality improvement tools'. These have their origins in the Japanese 'quality revolution' following World War II, and indeed became a mandatory subject in business training programmes. They're an effective way to capture data in real time or 'in the field'. Tally charts and Concentration diagrams can also be helpful. These tools still have their place – but perhaps built into your smartphone App!

Some top tips for data collection:

- Start with the end in mind. How do you plan to analyse and present the data?
- Agree clear unambiguous definitions of what is to be measured (operational definitions).

- Involve the data collectors in the design and development of the data collection systems.
- Test and train the data collectors on the data collection method.
- Look carefully at the initial data collected. Does it look right? If it doesn't, it's probably down to the measurement method rather than what's happening in the process!
- Make data collection systems 'visible' – to show that they're being used and make it less easy for people to forget to collect the data.
- Data collection is a process that can be improved.
- Keep going!

Key Points for Leaders in this Phase

- Be pragmatic – especially about the amount of data being used to understand performance
- But also remember the need for reliable data – don't rush the team
- Be patient. This phase might not seem as exciting or engaging as the Define phase but it's time well spent
- Reassure teams about what the data will be used for
- Continue to 'talk up' the improvement at every possible opportunity

4

Analyse for Leaders

IN THE ANALYSE phase all the information and data that has been collected will be systematically reviewed and interpreted to give meaningful insight into the performance of the process. The team will use the collected evidence (both data and visual) to determine those critical X factors causing or influencing the identified process issues, and then drill down to the root causes allowing clear solutions to be developed in the Improve phase.

There are a number of different types of analysis possible:

- Analysis of the process maps
- Visual analysis of the graphical representation of data
- Statistical analysis of the data
- Process flow analysis
- Root cause analysis

Let's start with analysis of the process maps and apply some challenge to the steps that have been captured. Remember that challenge is a positive thing. It requires us to think differently, and this can promote powerful results. 'Accept the challenges so that you can feel the exhilaration of victory!' said General Patton.

47

Using some tools and techniques to apply challenge can make it easier to do, and easier to be on the receiving end.

Process Analysis

Value Add Analysis involves reviewing the process to ascertain which steps add value, and which steps can be removed. To do so, a common definition of 'value add' is required. And, even then, it can give rise to some heated debate.

For a step to be considered value adding it must meet three important criteria:

1. The customer has to care about it (or be prepared to pay for it).
2. The step must physically change the item that's being processed, or be an essential prerequisite for another step.
3. The step must be carried out 'right first time'.

The aforementioned debate can arise when activities previously considered to be important are deemed non-value-adding. But from whose perspective are we assessing them? Note that the customer's perspective is taken here – back to the principles of Lean and Six Sigma we talked about earlier – if the customer of the process doesn't think this activity is important, why do we?

However, there may be some activities within the process that we need to maintain: process steps that the customer doesn't care about, but that the organisation must carry out in order to meet legal or regulatory requirements (e.g. some types of record keeping and reporting). These can be labelled as 'Business Value Add' or 'Essential Non-Value-Add'.

Sometimes applying the label 'Business Value Add' or 'Essential NVA' allows these steps to go unchallenged. But don't let them go unchallenged! Okay, we must undertake these activities to be legal and compliant, but we still might be able to carry them out more quickly or efficiently!

At this point we'd like to introduce you to another Lean Six Sigma 'tool' which I find leaders particularly like. This one is called 'Assumption Busting'.

This is where there is a long-standing assumption that a step in a process *has* to be done, typically for 'legal', 'compliance' or 'policy' reasons but on challenging it no one really knows why! This is a great opportunity to challenge and hopefully bust the assumption, in a positive way, by investigating whether this really is still applicable today and the assumption holds good, or whether it is a myth which has become part of 'the way we do things' without anyone really knowing why and without anyone having the 'power' to challenge it.

We find that a lot of process steps have been added by managers over the years, with the best intentions but without really taking account of the end-to-end process and the bigger picture. The problem is that if processes are not clearly owned and regularly 'cared for' they get neglected, and start to become overtaken by time. If processes are not regularly reviewed and improved the chances are they become a burden on the organisation. As they start to fail, sporadic attempts are made to add in corrective action steps when things go wrong, extra checks are typically imposed in the mistaken belief that these will improve the process. Extra checking costs more money, delays things, and is likely to make matters worse overall.

So, do welcome the opportunity to bust those assumptions and take a fresh look at the process.

In terms of identifying waste in processes, a technique called 'TIM WOODS' can provide some good clues for identifying quick wins, as well as wastes which may require more time and a more structured approach to address. Who is TIM WOODS? Let us introduce you!

TIM WOODS

T for TRANSPORT

We're talking about the movement of things (people, materials, information) from one place to another. It can contribute to waiting times (e.g. waiting to receive a part), it consumes resources, and it can increase the risk of items being transported getting lost or damaged. Examples of transport waste include moving products from one functional area to another, moving information from a system into a spreadsheet, and travelling between sites and locations to attend meetings. As Ernest Hemingway said, 'Never confuse movement with action'.

I for INVENTORY

Inventory can take the form of stocks and provisions – for example, materials that have been requisitioned in advance to ensure that a future customer order can be fulfilled, or items that have been ordered in bulk to achieve a discounted price. While the inventory may have been amassed for seemingly good reasons, as above, it is problematic. Did we order the materials in advance because we have problems with a supplier? What if we don't end up needing the items we ordered in bulk? Inventory ties up the organisation's cash, meaning it's not free to use elsewhere, and it also takes up space. Furthermore, the items of inventory could get damaged or lost while we're storing them, or they may become obsolete.

Inventory can also take the form of 'work in progress'. Where batch work is being undertaken there will be more inventory, as batch size directly affects work in progress inventory levels

Inventory is also all the 'stuff' building up in your in-tray, your email inbox and your 'to do' list. Go ahead and look. Those things that require your review, sign off or input? They're inventory. Queues of work can impact on process lead times too.

It's no coincidence that Inventory is represented as a triangle in Value Stream Maps, it's a warning sign!

M for MOTION

This could be described as 'ergonomics' – the efficiency of people in their working environment. Inefficiency could come about because of a badly designed work area. For example, having to walk to the other side of the room to collect a printout, or having to reach up high to retrieve a file. It also applies to the way IT systems are designed and information is stored when we're using them. All that scrolling down the screen to access the information you need is motion waste. Clicking on a sub folder, then into another sub folder, and then into a further subfolder, and then into another folder? Motion waste.

Motion waste is a particular focus in assembly plants where saving even a second can have a big impact on productivity.

W for WAITING

What are you waiting for? More information, a decision or approval, the resolution of an IT issue, a delivery? If we're waiting for something it's likely that the customer of the process will end up waiting too.

O for OVER-PROCESSING

Over-processing is adding work that's not required. For example, adding more fields to a template than is really required, including more information in a report than has been requested or cc-ing more people in on an email than is necessary. Workarounds are another example of over-processing: for instance, the effort used to create and maintain a separate spreadsheet to compensate for an IT system that's not fit for purpose.

'Tampering' is another example – arbitrarily changing a process without understanding the consequences; as is control waste – the energy used for supervision or monitoring that doesn't produce improvements, such as micro managing people rather than allowing them to make decisions themselves.

O for OVERPRODUCTION

Here we're looking at producing too much or too many of something, and about producing them earlier than the customer (or the next process) needs. Lean thinkers will tell you that this is the most dangerous of all the wastes, as it contributes to all of the others, and can mask the need for improvement.

Overproduction results in increased inventory, as the output from one process builds up in front of another. It may also be a consequence of misaligned targets across an end-to-end process.

D for DEFECTS

Anything that doesn't meet the Critical to Quality requirement, anything that isn't done right first time, is a defect. It results in correction (rework) that shouldn't be necessary and is costly in a number of ways. For example, if a bond certificate was processed with an incorrect value, it will need to be destroyed and a new one will need to be printed.

This is just the tip of the iceberg – there's also an impact on materials, set up, reputation if the defect gets through to the customer and there is a knock-on effect of lost productivity elsewhere. Costly indeed.

S for SKILLS

Skills waste is about failing to use the potential of people in the process. This could relate to goal alignment – the effort expended by people working at cross purposes and the effort required to resolve it: for example, introducing a third party to make travel bookings, in order to reduce expenditure on travel.

Untapped potential is another example. As the saying goes, 'with every pair of hands you get a free brain' – let's put that brain to work. And why not the heart as well! This is a key waste for leadership – make more of the latent potential which exists in the people in your organisation. One way to do this is by giving them opportunities to get involved in continuous improvement projects, you may well be very surprised. In one company we work with, one of the most skilled Black Belts had been working as a shift leader on a production line when she was asked to get involved in their (at that time new) Lean Six Sigma programme, initially by attending awareness training (White Belt) then moving up to Green Belt and finally becoming a fully certified Black Belt working on complex cross-organisational improvement projects. She is now helping install the same continuous improvement approach into a newly acquired business which has yet to discover the Lean Six Sigma approach. We cannot think of a better advocate!

Visual Analysis of the Graphical Representation of Data

Graphical analysis translates the collected data (numbers) into a visual representation (pictures). Looking at the data as a visual image often provides insights beyond what can be seen in the raw numbers.

As a leader, always encourage people to display their data visually, don't accept a table of numbers!

- Bar charts: these capture how many items of a particular category have been measured.

- Pareto charts: these are bar charts with categories arranged from highest count to lowest.

Pareto analysis recognises that, invariably, a small number of problem types account for a large percentage of the total number of problems that occur.

The '80/20' rule at the heart of Pareto analysis is representative of this: it is typical that around 80% of all problems we encounter in our processes will be accounted for by only 20% of all possible causes.

It makes most sense to tackle the 'vital few' causes first.

When these are successfully eliminated or reduced, of course, then another problem will head the list. So, next tackle that one – and so on. Encourage your teams to try out Pareto using different categories, these charts don't just jump off the page, they need working on with some experimentation to see if you can find a 'Pareto effect'.

- Histograms: these are similar to bar charts but show how many measures of a particular size have been taken.
- Time Series run charts – to plot data in time sequence order, so patterns over time can be identified.
- Scatter plots: these relate one measurement parameter to another (e.g. height to weight: is there a correlation?). Try out and experiment, the teams may well discover things that they had not expected. By the way, correlation doesn't always imply causation – for example the fact that more ice creams are eaten in New York on days when there are more homicides does not imply that ice cream eating causes people to kill each other!

Scatter plots are very useful for identifying possible relationships between two variables: for example, when one variable changes does the other change in a predictable way?

Remember, in Lean Six Sigma we are trying to find the X factors which drive changes in the Y we are interested in; we are trying to find $y = f(X)$ so that we can change the Xs in order to bring about a desirable change in Y.

Scatter plots are only meaningful when BOTH variables are continuous data.

- Box plots: these are useful for comparing different categories of measured data with each other.

Statistical Analysis

Simple statistical analysis will look at the centre, shape and spread of data. The capability of the process, and the impact that the X factors have on the Y, can also be analysed.

Note that it's not always necessary to undertake in-depth statistical analysis. It can be time consuming – and there's a cost to that in terms of resource and momentum. Could appropriate root causes be identified without it? There's a huge variety of options when it comes to analysis, and this can have the effect of distracting the team from their primary purpose, which is to solve a problem in the process. Guidance is recommended when it comes to complex statistical analysis. This section highlights some possibilities but doesn't provide an exhaustive guide.

Measures of Central Tendency

Measures of central tendency (the mean, the median and the mode) of the data describe a 'typical' or central value in the distribution of data. These will provide a single value (or three values) to describe a whole set of data. That's clearly not enough to allow for a full understanding – yet sometimes it's used as such!

- The mean is the 'average' of the data set. It is calculated by adding together all of the values and dividing the answer by the number of data points.
- The median is the mid point of the data, when it's been set in order. If there's an odd number of data points it will be the one in the middle. If there's an even number, it's the average of the middle two.
- The mode is the most frequently occurring data point.

If the data is normally distributed, the mean, the median and the mode will be the same. If it's not they will be different. The mean is used a lot in organisations, yet it can paint a distorted picture because it is influenced by extreme values or outliers. The median can be more helpful, but it's not used as much.

Measures of Spread

Variation, or 'spread' in the process can be measured using the standard deviation. This represents the average by which each data point

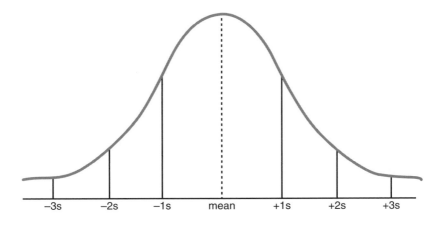

Figure 4.1   The normal distribution of data

in the set varies from the mean. It is always expressed in the same unit as the 'thing' being measured (e.g. millimetres, minutes or pounds). The smaller the standard deviation value is, the less variation there is, and the bigger the value, the greater the variation or 'spread'. A small standard deviation would result in a tall, thin curve – a big standard deviation results in a short wide one! The normal distribution of data (and quite a wide curve) is shown in Figure 4.1.

The Shape of the Data

A lot of the time, data will follow the 'normal' distribution pattern, like the example shown above. From a normal distribution the shape is symmetrical around the mean and the data has a 50% chance of falling either side of it. The 'behaviour' of the process based on the mean and the standard deviation can also be modelled if there is a normal distribution. Figure 4.2 shows the percentage of cases or data points that would fall within each band of values for normally distributed data.

Note however that data is not always normally distributed, it is likely in some processes that there will be a long 'tail' on one side or the other, particularly when looking at measures of time such as cycle time (how long the end-to-end process takes) or when looking at how long a process step or series of steps takes in practice. One of the reasons for this is that time measures cannot go below zero, although the idea of negative time would be rather useful on busy days!

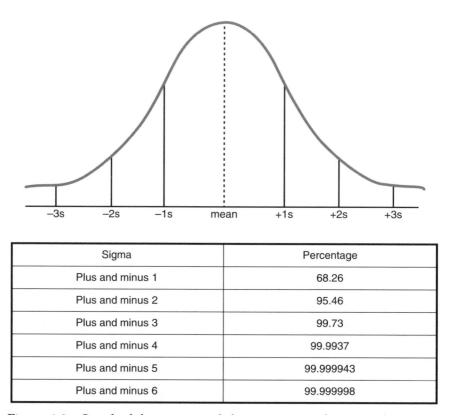

Sigma	Percentage
Plus and minus 1	68.26
Plus and minus 2	95.46
Plus and minus 3	99.73
Plus and minus 4	99.9937
Plus and minus 5	99.999943
Plus and minus 6	99.999998

Figure 4.2   Standard deviations and the percentage of cases within each band of (sigma) values

Hypothesis Tests

Hypothesis tests may also be carried out to establish if an assumption made about process performance is true. For example, you may wish to establish if there is a (statistically) significant difference between data for two different teams, or to understand if it takes longer to deliver one product or another. You need to know if there is a statistical difference between two sets of data.

Sometimes these differences are visible to the naked eye and it's not necessary to do any hypothesis testing; but in some cases you'll want to know whether the difference is real, or just the result of normal variation in the process.

Simply put, a hypothesis is a theory. In Six Sigma, two hypotheses are developed. The starting point is the development of the null hypothesis – this proposes that there is no difference between the data sets. An alternative hypothesis is then developed – this proposes that there is a difference.

Different sorts of hypothesis tests are possible. The T-test looks at two sets of data, while the ANOVA looks at three or more.

Don't forget that we're not jumping to conclusions about the reasons why – but at least we now know more about where to focus further investigation.

This chapter provides a brief overview only. It's useful as a leader to have an appreciation of this subject, but your practitioners will be trained in the tools particularly at Black Belt level. They may well use specialist software too, such as Minitab, which has become the most popular software amongst Black Belts to use for statistical analysis. It certainly makes their lives a lot easier although a proficient practitioner can do a lot in Excel too.

Analysing the Process Flow

To 'flow' means to move steadily and continuously. This is what we want our processes to do! Flow analysis looks to understand (and ultimately improve) the way work moves through the process. This includes looking for bottlenecks caused by blockages or constraints in the process; analysing queues; work in progress; and the different variety of work that the process has to cope with.

In his famous book, *The Goal*, Eliyahu Goldratt sets out the 'Theory of Constraints' and proposes an approach to help identify and deal with constraints and improve process flow. As Lean Six Sigma has developed over the years, these techniques have become another part of the overall Lean Six Sigma toolkit.

A bottleneck is a part of the process which has a capacity equal to or less than the demand that's placed on it. It has the effect of dictating the pace at which all stages in an end-to-end process can operate. Remember 'a chain is only as strong as its weakest link'? A process can only be as fast as its narrowest bottleneck.

Bottlenecks can be identified by observing a build-up of work in a queue or a backlog of items to be processed. The first step in Goldratt's process is to identify or locate the bottleneck which is acting as the greatest constraint in the process.

When you identify the bottleneck, you can then find ways to improve the processing capability at the bottleneck point in the process flow. For example, if the constraint is a machine, consider running it for more hours and service the machine after hours. Look at reducing the changeover time between different product types. Any time lost at the constraint has a big effect on the whole process. In service and transactional processes, look at the online queues and how they vary over time, use simulation techniques to experiment with different system configurations. We have found that accepted wisdom should be challenged – for example, in a medical centre which was suffering from long waiting times for calls to be answered, the solution was not a new telephone answering system but a question of removing artificially created peak loads caused by asking patients to call back at set times. Similarly, the management team of another medical centre strongly believed that the 'solution' needed to solve a throughput problem was to hire another doctor. Analysis of the flow and bottlenecks showed that the real constraint was lack of qualified nursing staff combined with an overly complex administration system. The outcome was a much lower cost solution which worked.

Similarly, Lean Six Sigma projects have been carried out in airport security, looking at the flow, bottlenecks and cycle times, and using simulation via a readily available software package (Simul8), which has been highly effective at speeding up the end-to-end process and improving the experience for passengers (and staff).

Root Cause Analysis

The methods used to identify root causes in Lean Six Sigma improvement activities are similar to those used by detectives (on TV and in real life!). Both are required to let go of preconceived ideas, and make use of data. 'Data! Data! Data!' yells Sherlock Holmes in 'The Adventure of the Copper Beeches', 'I can't make bricks without clay'. To formulate and test hypotheses, focus on the cause, and use the knowledge, skills and input of team members and subject matter experts.

To find the guilty party, a list of possible suspects is generated and explored. The 'Cause and Effect' diagram can be a very effective tool

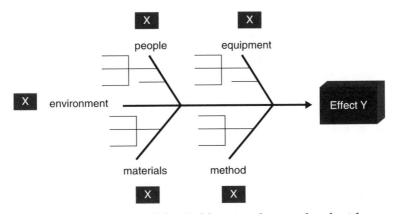

Figure 4.3   The structure of the Fishbone, to be populated with causes under each heading

to support this. Also known as the 'Fishbone Analysis' or 'Ishikawa Diagram' the approach is used to capture all potential causes so that the list can be narrowed down as suspects are eliminated from our enquiries.

You'll see from the structure of the tool (in Figure 4.3) where it gets its name from – the problem is documented in the 'head' of the fish and the potential causes are grouped and listed on a series of 'bones' that are linked to it.

The names on the bones of the fish provide helpful prompts to support the identification of causes. We often use 'PEMME' as the headings, but you can use whatever is helpful. PEMME stands for People, Equipment, Method, Materials and Environment – these are all sources of variation in a process and give us clues as to potential causes. Where they're not relevant, you can come up with your own.

Take care to write the problem clearly – phrased as a statement or a question – so it can provide an effective focus point. For example, instead of 'incident management takes too long', write, 'the investigation of incidents takes too long' – be as precise as possible. The bones can then be populated with potential causes.

Again, clear wording is required. Under the heading 'Equipment' for example, don't just write the word 'system', but state what it is about the system that slows down the investigation.

While developing the fishbone, don't get too hung up about where things should go on the fishbone (e.g. 'is it materials or equipment?'), just capture them and move on. Good facilitation and a fast scribe are required – one person for each role – is recommended.

Creating the fishbone is just the start. You can also use the 5 Whys technique to examine the causes further and get to the real 'root' of the problem.

The proverb 'For Want of a Nail' provides a useful reminder of the power of this technique. Why did the kingdom fall? The root cause appears to be the lack of a nail required to fit a horseshoe.

For Want of a Nail
For want of a nail the shoe was lost.
For want of a shoe the horse was lost.
For want of a horse the rider was lost.
For want of a rider the message was lost.
For want of a message the battle was lost.
For want of a battle the kingdom was lost.
And all for the want of a horseshoe nail.

'Why?' is such a useful question! Children are very good at asking this question, and they use it to satisfy their innate curiosity. We lose it when we get older – why?

Analyse – Summary for Leaders

The kind of analysis carried out in Lean Six Sigma problem-solving projects, combining process analysis with data analysis, looking at queues, bottlenecks and flow, together with assumption challenging/busting, is really powerful. Time and time again during the Analyse phase of Lean Six Sigma problem-solving projects, new insights are gained and 'discoveries' made which are often extremely eye-opening. How many times have we heard the expression ' … and that's the way we've always done it'? A heck of a lot!

The complexity and tools needed in the Analyse phase will, of course, vary depending on the type of process and the problem being addressed. DMAIC stays the same as the overall framework, but the tools, level of complexity, and skills needed in the practitioner team will vary depending on the problem.

A final thought for leaders: it can be tempting for the practitioner team to get carried away during the Analyse phase, wanting more and more detail – we've all heard of analysis paralysis! As a leader, you should guide them towards the improve phase as soon as sensible. Remember the business reason for tackling the problem, we do need results and they may not be able to solve the problem completely in the first DMAIC project. They key questions are:

1. Have we sufficient evidence as to the causes of the problem to be able to move into developing solutions?
2. Is the cost of spending more time on analysis going to be worth the consequent cost of delaying moving ahead?

Key Points for Leaders in this Phase

- Encourage the use of data, not opinions
- Use pictures, graphs, charts to make the process problems visible
- Challenge and ask 'why?' in a positive way
- Ensure teams are still meeting regularly and working well together
- Keep the momentum going – avoid analysis paralysis

5

Improve for Leaders

THE IMPROVE PHASE is concerned with developing viable solutions and the future state process. It should clearly build on the hypotheses and findings coming out of the Analyse phase. Remember we have always cautioned against jumping into 'solution mode' too soon? Well now it's time to dive in!

There are three stages to the Improve phase:

- Identification of possible solutions
- Selecting appropriate solutions
- Planning and testing of the solutions

The Improve phase focuses on trying to eliminate the drivers of the problem by developing solutions which directly address the root causes. Good solutions will address root causes and won't create new problems of their own!

The phase is complete when a set of impactful solutions that directly address the challenges of the project charter are ready for implementation.

Solution Generation

Where are you, and what are you doing when you have your best ideas? A recent study in the US by psychologist Scott Barry Kaufman has shown that the majority of us (72%!) have our ideas when we're in the shower.

We ask this question a lot, and lots of people do say they're in the shower when inspiration strikes. Others say they're in the bath, in bed, walking the dog, digging the garden, going for a run, etc. Only very, very rarely do people respond to this question by saying they're in a workshop or sitting at their desk! This is because of the way our brains work – they need time to decompress away from work, and when this happens, 'incubation' occurs. Activity of the attentional control network reduces, the unconscious mind takes over, we relax and. . . . Eureka!, an idea strikes. It's probably no coincidence then that Archimedes developed displacement theory while taking a bath, and that J K Rowling dreamt up Harry Potter and his adventures while travelling on a train.

It can be difficult, however, to rely on this method, and waiting for people to generate solutions when they're in the shower or in bed could slow down improvements and impact on momentum. There are, then, in the Improve phase, some tools and techniques that can be used to generate solutions and ideas. As with other tools and techniques covered in this book, they're not just for use in the Improve phase of a process improvement project but can be used at any time when some different thinking is called for.

Einstein said, 'We can't solve problems by using the same kind of thinking we used when we created them.' This means challenging assumptions, including things that 'have always been this way'. For this to work, we need to make people aware of the assumptions and encourage an atmosphere where challenge is positive and welcomed. We've already mentioned Assumption Busting as a useful tool during the Analyse phase, but it can also be very helpful in the Improve phase as it can help to generate new ideas and different ways of doing things. There are only three steps:

1. Identify the assumptions (and don't miss the obvious ones)
2. Challenge them: It can't be done? Why not?
3. Identify how it *can* be done. Asking 'what if ... ?' can be helpful here

Thinking differently doesn't always come easily, and some people find it easier than others. It is a skill that can be practiced and developed.

Negative Brainstorming is a fantastic technique for generating ideas. We talked about it in the Introduction to this book because it's one of our favourites. It's possible that you might have skipped over it, to get stuck in and begin reading the 'proper' stuff. If this is the case, go back and have a go! (What's the worst that could happen?)

Negative Brainstorming is a variation of 'traditional' brainstorming. In a traditional brainstorm a group of people identify a number of ideas and suggestions that are written up by a facilitator. This can be great where it's done well, but it gets over-used and is sometimes the *only* technique used by a group to support solution generation. Abraham Maslow, talking about over-reliance on familiar tools said, 'I suppose it is tempting, if the only tool you have is a hammer, to treat everything as if it were a nail.' In a lot of organisations brainstorming is that hammer!

Note that the word 'Brainstorm' was deemed unacceptable for a time in the noughties as it is potentially offensive to people with epilepsy. It was replaced by the term 'Thought Shower' but has slowly made its way back into the lexicon of organisations, if it ever went away. We use the words 'Brainstorm' and 'Negative Brainstorm' without any wish to cause offence, though now we know that the shower is such a rich environment for ideas we might prefer a Thought Shower, providing there's plenty of hot water.

So, instead of asking 'how can we make this better?' as you would in a brainstorm, try things a different way and ask, 'how can we make this worse?' and 'how can we really stuff this up?'.

Leaders might not always get invited to the sessions but you can encourage these ways of thinking!

Words and pictures can be very effective triggers for ideas – let's have a go at using this them.

Look at the picture in Figure 5.1. Grab a piece of (big) paper and write down the associations you have with the picture, e.g. heat, decoration, shadows, car horn sounds. Use all of your senses if you can … What would it sound like? What would it feel like? What would it smell like? Keep going and create a list.

Next, come back to a problem you have in the process – how can the associations you've listed relate to the problem? What ideas do they trigger? This technique can deliver some surprising suggestions!

Figure 5.1   What do you think of?

The technique can also be used with a random word. Pick a book, select a page number, paragraph number and word number – or just open the book and select a word at random. What associations come to mind? List these. Now look at the associations and use them to trigger some ideas.

Using archetypes is another useful way of generating ideas and seeing things differently. It allows you to 'try on' a mindset or attitude, or look at life through a particular lens. You can use whichever ones you like (for example the jester, the explorer or the lover) and consider the situation from the perspective of that archetype. What would the lover do? They might seek to build a strong relationship, give care or build a nurturing environment. What would the jester do? They might seek excitement and fun. You could even use famous people, and imagine how Alex Ferguson, Lady GaGa, Gordon Ramsay, Cher or Sherlock would address particular problems or situations.

Selection

If solution generation has gone well, there'll be a lot of potential solutions to consider. Not all of these might be suitable – some might be a bit too far-reaching for now, and some not far-reaching enough.

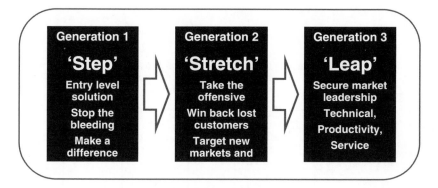

Figure 5.2   Multi Generation Planning

If solutions are considered too major for now, they can be incorporated into a Multi Generation Plan. Multi Generation Planning can support the delivery of longer term, breakthrough goals, as a series of projects rather than one big one. Figure 5.2 shows an example with three parts or 'generations' – the leap can't be achieved without the two or more generations of improvement before it. The US Space Programme is a good example of Multi Generation Planning. Apollo put man on the moon, but before this could be achieved the first generation of space rockets, Mercury, put an astronaut into space, and the second generation, Gemini, put man into Earth orbit.

A more recent example is Apple's development of the iPhone with multiple generations under development, albeit kept as closely guarded secrets!

Tools and techniques to support shortlisting and the selection of solutions can be advantageous as they add objectivity to the process, especially as they involve team members in decision making, promoting openness and transparency. Without this, there could be potential for 'pet solutions', or those that don't fully hit the mark in terms of solving the process problem to be pursued, or of individuals feeling disenfranchised from this part of the process.

Feeling dotty? The N/3 or Multivoting technique can help trim down a long list of ideas into a more manageable size. N is the number of ideas that have been generated – divide this by 3 to arrive at the number of votes each team member gets to assign across the list, with one vote per idea. They can then use a marker pen to put a dot next to their preferred options. Sticky dots can be issued to team members (which might prevent people from over-dotting). Another name

Criteria	A	B	C	Score	Rank	%
Options Weights	1	3	5	(weighted)		
Idea one	6 / 6	5 / 15	7 / 35	56	3	62
Idea two	3 / 3	7 / 21	6 / 30	54	4	60
Idea three	1 / 1	8 / 24	8 / 40	65	1	72
Idea four	8 / 8	6 / 18	5 / 25	51	5	57
Idea five	7 / 7	7 / 21	6 / 30	58	2	64

Figure 5.3   Criteria Based Matrix

for this technique is dotmocracy! Once all votes have been cast there is a reduced number of ideas/solutions to work with, making further analysis easier to undertake.

A Priority Based Matrix or Criteria Based Matrix (Figure 5.3), is a helpful next step. Here, the short list of ideas or options is written out, and the criteria necessary to support decision making are listed alongside. The criteria may include things like impact on the problem, cost, time to implement, ease of implementation and ease of modification. Adding 'Acceptance/Buy in' to the list is highly recommended. The technique is particularly powerful when the team identify the criteria (as well as the solutions), bringing transparency and supporting the ultimate 'ownership' of decisions made.

If some of the criteria are considered more important than others a weighting can be applied. Then, when scores are awarded, the score gets multiplied by the weighting to boost it as appropriate.

You can then work across or down the matrix, applying the criteria to each of the solutions to determine how well the solutions address each one. A rating scale of 1–10 can be used, or alternatively a 1-3-5 or 1-3-9 system. 1, 3 and 9 will make highly ranked options stand out more clearly and increase the differentiation between the results.

Note that we said 'work across or down' the matrix. Some matrix users like to work from left to right, considering each solution carefully and applying the criteria listed to each solution in turn. Others like to use the criteria as the starting point and work from the top down, thinking about each solution in relation to the criteria. The top downers feel that this minimises the potential for people hung up on a particular solution to bias the scoring as they work across.

As you work through, remember to multiply scores by any weightings you may have used. At the end, you'll have a completed matrix with a score for each idea and these can then be ranked accordingly.

This technique is useful for procurement, recruitment and project prioritisation as well as solution selection – just remember to adjust the criteria so they're appropriate for the type of decision being made.

Prevention

As the saying goes, 'An ounce of prevention is worth a pound of cure'. The solutions that are to be implemented to solve the problems in our process shouldn't create new problems elsewhere.

Some Black Hat thinking is useful here, to help determine if it's wise to proceed with the solution, if there are risks and weaknesses to be overcome, and whether it's likely there will be problems in the future. The Black Hat is one of six hats that represent six different ways of thinking. These were developed by Edward de Bono, the psychologist and author. As its colour might suggest, the Black Hat is cautious and careful, and exists to point out the drawbacks of ideas and suggestions. The other hats in the series provide a range of alternative ways of thinking to balance this out (the white hat is concerned with facts and data, the red hat provides an emotional perspective, the yellow hat is sunny and positive, the green hat is creative, and the blue hat provides an overview and a structured way of bringing things together). According to de Bono the Black Hat is the most valuable – it's not a 'bad hat', and using it does not make you a negative person!

Other methods for prevention can bring a more structured approach to this sort of thinking. The PDPC (Process Decision Programme Chart) is one. This looks at what could go wrong, how it could be prevented, and what you would do if it still went wrong. A framework is provided in Figure 5.4. Brilliantly simple – shame about the name!

What could go wrong?	How can it be prevented?	And if it still goes wrong?

Figure 5.4   PDPC

Failure Modes & Effects Analysis template

Process: .... Team: .... FMEA Date (original): .... (revised): ....

What?				Why? When? Where?		How?		Who?		Action Results			
Item/ Process Step	Potential Failure Mode	Potential effect(s) of Failure	Severity	Potential cause(s) of Failure	Occurrence	Current Controls and Measures	Detection	RPN	Recommended Actions	Responsibility & Completion Target Date	Action taken	Severity	Occurrence	Detection	RPN

Figure 5.5   The FMEA matrix

Failure Modes and Effects Analysis (FMEA), shown in Figure 5.5, provides a more in-depth alternative. It can be used in several situations and is a very useful stand-alone risk assessment and mitigation tool; but, in the context of our improvement project, it is used to take a solution recommendation and assesses the potential failure modes (i.e. what could go wrong) with every step in the process, as well as the potential effects of the failure, causes and current controls. For each failure mode a rating from 1–10 is applied for severity, occurrence

Rating	Severity of effect	Likelihood of occurrence	Current detectability
1	None	Remote	Immediately detected
2	Very minor effect	Very low	Found easily
3	Minor	Low	Usually found
4	Low to moderate	Low to moderate	Probably found
5	Moderate	Moderate	May be found
6	Moderate to high	Moderate to high	Less than 50% chance of detection
7	High	High	Unlikely to be detected
8	Very high	Very high	Very unlikely to be detected
9	Hazardous	Extremely high	Extremely unlikely to be detected
10	Disastrous	Almost certain	Almost impossible to detect

Figure 5.6   The FMEA Rating Scale

and detection. The scale provided in Figure 5.6 provides a useful guide for rating.

- Severity – the severity or impact of the failure mode
- Occurrence – the probability or likelihood of the failure occurring
- Detection – the likelihood of detecting the failure

Some people use 'Sod' (Severity – Occurrence – Detection) as a mnemonic to help them remember those headings, as they're literally getting right down into detail, under the surface of the process. Others may use it to describe other aspects of the FMEA!

After the ratings are applied a Risk Priority Number (RPN) is cal-culated by multiplying the ratings together as S × O × D. The failure modes with the highest RPN values then become a priority. There is no 'threshold' for the RPN values – (i.e. RPNs over 'X' must be addressed) – the team (with support from the leader) can determine what is appropriate. Actions may include the redesign of a process step (or steps), the introduction of some error detection and prevention, modification of work instructions, or modification of monitoring systems.

The FMEA leaves no stone (or sod!) unturned and can be a time consuming exercise, but it's time well spent, and is particularly useful when a process is being changed or a new way of working is introduced, as well as to support the development of new products and services.

Poka Yoke is a Japanese term for error proofing, reducing the chance of errors occurring. This technique is used whether designing a new process or improving an existing one. Poka Yoke devices either prevent or detect failures. They are often simple and inexpensive, sometimes we don't even notice they are there, but they prevent mistakes, defects, accidents and injuries.

The principle was developed by Shigeo Shingo, to support the achievement of zero defects either by making it impossible to make a mistake, or by detecting defects as they occur and preventing them from going any further.

The shape and design of fuel pumps is an example of the use of Poka Yoke – the pumps for unleaded and diesel are now different colours so the driver knows which is which, and if the driver does happen to select the wrong one, the nozzle of the diesel pump is too big to fit into the petrol vehicle, thus preventing misfuelling.

The flavour of the Nintendo Switch games cartridge is another example. The cartridges, which are about the same size as an SD card, have been given a 'horrendously bitter' taste by Nintendo, to discourage children from putting them in their mouths. (Thanks to our Lean Six Sigma Green Belt, Mark, who licked his game card for us to confirm this is correct!)

If you've ever been to Schiphol Airport, more precisely the Gentlemen's toilet at Schiphol Airport, you might have noticed another example of Poka Yoke. Positioned strategically at the bottom of the urinal, to the left-hand side of the drain, is painted a small fly. This, to put it delicately, gives the gentlemen of Schiphol Airport something to aim for, and has had the effect of reducing spillage by 50–80%, so in turn reducing cleaning costs dramatically.

So how do you 'do' Poka Yoke? Start by putting your left leg in. And then consider the risks and failure modes identified through process risk analysis, and look to 'make it easier for people to get the process right than to get it wrong'. It's easier said than done, remember that the best Poka Yoke devices are often the simplest.

Planning and Testing

The implementation of the solutions requires careful planning – remember the military adage with 6 Ps? Proper Planning and Preparation Prevents Poor Performance. You may know this as the 7 Ps and have identified that there's a P missing in our version … but then you might also remember that we dealt with that through the use of a strategically positioned fly in the above section.

The tools and techniques used to support planning are the 'classics' used in traditional project management approaches, such as Gantt charts, critical paths, and risks and issues logs. Note that the pragmatic approach that we advocate applies here as well – there's no need to use specialist project management software, unless it's already in use in the organisation, creating a plan (in whatever format that suits) and implementing the plan are what's important here.

It may be appropriate to undertake a trial or pilot to ensure the solutions are suitable and to test the approach to implementation. Piloting (i.e. implementation of the solution on a small scale before a full rollout) can reduce the risk of failure, support the 'fine tuning' of the solution and confirm that the anticipated benefits are possible. The approach is used in film making and television, where audiences are invited to viewings before a movie or television show is released, so that reactions can be tested and understood through surveys and focus groups. Responses can result in scenes being cut, titles amended or even endings changed. The 'original' ending to *Fatal Attraction* for example was a lot less dramatic, but audiences called for a more violent ending for the character played by Glenn Close, even though it meant that the film had to go back into production for an additional three weeks. In the ending originally proposed for *E.T.*, he didn't make it home!

Pilots are recommended where the scope of a change is major, the implementation costly, and where the change isn't easy to reverse. Effective pilots will highlight the consequences of solutions and their implementation in the organisation (and beyond) – whether intentional or unintentional. Pilots provide a testing ground for solutions and valuable opportunities for learning. They need to be planned carefully to ensure that full value can be derived.

It is important that pilots are run in realistic environments. One common pitfall is to trial the approach with 'our best team', as this team are most likely to be up for the challenge of making new things work. This can be effective, but it's necessary to make sure *all* of the niggles, effects and impacts are identified and captured. If the team just get on with working around these, or adapt to new ways of working that aren't quite as good as they could be (as our 'best teams' sometimes do) and issues don't get exposed there's a risk that they will cause bigger problems when the full rollout is undertaken.

Leaders supporting pilots should ensure that appropriate success criteria are established, and appropriate measurement systems are in place to capture the results. Also, be aware that pilots, their implementation and their impact, can have a bearing on stakeholder perceptions and relationships. This is also something that needs to be managed and monitored.

As in the film and television industry, importance should be placed on evaluation of the pilot results to understand how the process now delivers the Critical to Quality requirements, and to look at performance in relation to other process conditions. Did the change result in a difference? As was the case with *Fatal Attraction*, acting on the findings can be costly in terms of time, resources and momentum, but failing to act on the findings can be a lot more costly.

Key Points for Leaders in the Improve Phase

- Encourage the team to use different ways of thinking
- Challenge assumptions and support others to do so
- Ensure appropriate solutions that address the root cause – look for countermeasures, not pet solutions
- Encourage the exploration of what could go wrong
- Support decision making on solutions
- Encourage a 'true' test and a full evaluation of results where pilots are undertaken

Control for Leaders

Implement and Control?

The Control phase ensures that the selected actions or solutions are implemented as planned, that they improve the process, and can be sustained.

For those not used to Lean Six Sigma DMAIC projects, you may be surprised that this phase is called 'Control' and not 'Implement'. Remember that the Improve phase took us through evaluating different potential options, selecting the most appropriate solution, and then pilot testing that solution on a small scale. The implementation of the selected solution is not included in the Improve phase. Sounds strange but there is a good reason for this.

Once we get to the end of the Improve phase we know what the solution is going to be! We can therefore now do a sensible and realistic cost/benefit analysis. The crossover between the Improve and Control phases is therefore an excellent opportunity to review the DMAIC project before implementing the solution. This is the moment when you can calculate the gains which will result from the improved process. For many projects you can now translate those into financial benefits, and because you know what changes you are going to make you can calculate the cost of implementation.

For some organisations, for example in the public sector, this review is particularly important. For major changes in these organisations, it is likely that a senior management team will want to review the proposed solution and associated cost/benefit analysis before giving the green light to moving into implementation. This is also the final review point when the organisation's management could theoretically reject the proposal before the cost of implementation is incurred.

From a leadership view, you can see that the D M A I phases have taken you from a rather woolly problem into Define, then into Measure (establishing the 'current state'), into Analyse (uncovering the root causes), and Improve (generating solution ideas, selecting the most suitable one, and pilot testing) – before we get to the point where we know what we are going to do to solve the problem.

How formal this Improve to Control stage review needs to be will depend on a number of factors, the scale of the change, the organisation's style of management, the impact the change is likely to have, whether capital expenditure is necessary.... and at this point you realise that this is where DMAIC and traditional project management can connect together. Up until now we have not been certain about what the solution to our problem will be, we have deliberately kept an open mind, but now we do know what the solution is. This where classical project management can come into play – particularly when the solution is going to be rolled out across a large organisation. As a leader, you will need to consider the best approach to implement the solution. In some organisations, a project manager will now be appointed to take the solution forward into implementation and make it happen across the organisation. For smaller improvement projects the practitioner team under the DMAIC leader will take on the implementation. Whatever approach is taken, it's essential to work closely with the day-to-day operational organisation that will be impacted by the change. Hopefully they will have been involved before now as key stakeholders in the DMAIC project so there shouldn't be a 'big surprise' when it comes to making it happen.

Another way of looking at the cross over from Improve to Control phase is also the point in a DMAIC project when you will find you are switching from dealing with uncertainty (Define, Measure, Analyse, Improve) – to dealing with certainty and this impacts on leadership.

If you are not used to lean Six Sigma projects, this 'uncertainty' may seem strange to you as a leader. We have already drawn a comparison with a detective solving a crime and in the earlier phases, there is a great deal of uncertainty.

At the start of a DMAIC project there will be uncertainty about -

- The problem
- The solution
- How long the DMAIC project will take
- If a solution exists at all
- The complexity of the project
- Which tools and techniques will be used
- What will be 'discovered' as the DMAIC phases progress

… and you won't be able to do a full cost/benefit analysis until the end of the Improve phase as mentioned above.

This is very different from classical project management where you know, pretty well, what you are going to do right from the start (for example building a house), and you can do a pretty good estimate of costs and benefits early in the project phases when you can plan ahead the resources and timetable needed to complete the project.

So, if you have come from a project management background, then you may find this Lean Six Sigma approach a bit strange and scary until you've been through a couple of improvement projects. Take advice and tap into the minds of those that have done it before. You might benefit from some coaching yourself to guide you and reassure you as the DMAIC phases move ahead.

Control

If control elements aren't established, the full potential of the improvement effort may not be realised. People may forget about or fail to accept new methods and 'drift back' into old ways of working, then the problems will resurface – and consequently there'll be the need to deliver more improvements on the same process, and so on and so on. This was the fate of King Sisyphus, whose punishment for bad behaviour on earth was to be made to roll an enormous boulder up a hill, only to watch it roll back down and hit him, over and over again for all eternity.

To avoid an eternity of futile efforts and endless frustration, the essential elements of Control are set out here, with emphasis on the role that leaders play in establishing them.

The Control Plan

Quality guru Joseph Juran had a lot to say about the importance of control. He set out three criteria for what he called 'self control'. The self control that Juran taught was not the ability to control oneself – although Juran lived to be 104 years old, which suggests he knew a thing or two about that as well – it was about process control. It applies, said Juran, to processes in all functions and all levels, from general manager to non-supervisory worker.

Juran asserted that workers (whatever their level) are in a state of self control when they have been provided with all the essentials for doing good work. These include:

- The means of knowing what the quality goals are
- The means of knowing actual performance
- The means for changing their performance in the event that performance does not conform to goals

Knowing the Quality Goals

The quality goals are the things that the process must deliver to meet requirements. Remember the CTQs (Critical to Quality requirements) that were developed in the Define phase? The levels of performance required to meet these should now be established and clearly communicated.

The 'knowing' comes from communication about the new way of working and training on how to do it, delivered when the new process is implemented and the 'to be' process becomes the 'as is'. The new way of working, and the results attained, now become standardised.

Standardisation reduces variation in the way that the work is carried out, and it reduces variation of the output of the process. Part of this is ensuring the new process is documented appropriately and included in the organisation's framework of processes, policies and procedures so it now represents 'the way this activity is carried out'. It can't be left to languish on brown paper! But it must be updated when future changes are made to the process.

Standardisation can evoke a fearful response from people, who fear that standardisation will bring bureaucracy, or will result in a 'scripted' approach to aspects of work, removing the human spark and restricting people's ability to be flexible and apply innovation and improvement.

There is a counter argument to this: that without standardisation it is impossible to make improvements! If a process is not standardised, and a new way of carrying it out is developed, this only has the effect of adding yet another way to carry out to the task.

Acceptance of the new way of working is critical. Now is the time for people to adopt the new process, and this isn't always easy to achieve.

Human beings really are creatures of habit. Behaviours and actions repeated over time become routine and engrained – scored onto our neural pathways – so that we carry them out with very little thought. Have you ever driven to a familiar place, zoned into 'autopilot' and then looked up and wondered, 'how did I get here?' But if you drive a different vehicle, or take an alternative route it feels different – suddenly you're aware of every activity and conscious that you're putting more effort in. Want to try it? If you're wearing a watch, take it off and put it on the other wrist. Or if you're not wearing a watch cross your legs the opposite way, or hold your coffee in the other hand. It probably feels odd and slightly uncomfortable doesn't it? Changing the way processes are carried out has the same effect, and there's an instinctive pull to go back to the old way, hence the need for control.

There's also the ugly baby factor to consider. Where people feel caring and protective about 'their' processes, getting to grips with the need for change and a new way of working can be tough. These reactions are explored in Chapter 15.

Deliverables from these activities in the control phase of a DMAIC project include:

- A process map (or other appropriate format for the processes to be documented)

- Clarity on the customer focused objective of the process (the CTQs or Quality Goals)
- A communication plan which addresses the needs of all relevant stakeholders, and is developed, executed and updated
- A training plan and training materials, developed, executed and updated
- A 'live' process

Monitoring Actual Performance

Having taken a process through the DMAI phases, you will have a very good idea of the performance that should now be attained when the improved process is implemented. When it comes to ongoing performance monitoring in day-to-day operations, you can use some of the Lean Six Sigma tools to provide highly effective ongoing measurement. Measurement won't need to be as intense as it was in the Measure phase, but the same importance should be given to ensuring the measurement system is robust. The six serving men can be put to use again here! Who, Why, What, When, Where and How.

Not every aspect of the process will require monitoring – the aim is to be a 'control enthusiast' rather than a control freak! Look to monitor the outputs of the process (the Ys) but also some of the critical Xs identified in the Analyse phase, and activities that present a risk, as identified through 'prevention' tools such as the FMEA. Intelligent use of X factor measures can provide 'early warnings' of potential issues before they reach the customer facing Y measures.

Control Charts can be a very helpful tool here as they provide a graphical picture of performance over time and in real time, and highlight changes (improvements or slippage) very clearly. As suggested by their name, Control Charts identify whether the process is 'in control' or stable. They identify variation and show the 'voice of the process' so that the Process Owner knows what to respond to and what is just 'natural' variation.

Take a look at the example in Figure 6.1, showing the time taken to answer telephone calls coming into an organisation. The mean average time (in seconds) for call answering is 51.7 but we can see that there is variation around the mean and that the variation gets

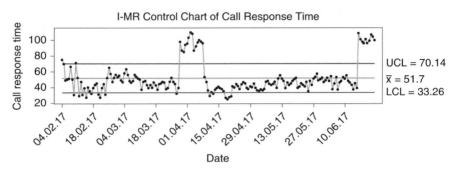

Figure 6.1   Are we in control? Using Control Charts to monitor performance. The chart shows call answering times in seconds, for week days between February and July.

more significant around the months of April and July, with some calls taking over 100 seconds to be answered. This organisation found real value from displaying the data in this format. Beforehand there had been a perception among people in the organisation that call response times were poor in general, but the use of Control Charts to monitor performance over time highlighted holiday times of Easter and summer as the problematic periods, and this was because more employees were taking annual leave at those times. These insights allowed the organisation to focus on addressing how the process was managed during holiday periods, which was definitely 'doable', whereas making improvements to general, all-year-round response times had seemed a much more daunting prospect.

Enthusiasts might be interested to note the Upper Control Limit (UCL) and Lower Control Limit (LCL) – these are calculated from process data and represent a 'normal' amount of variation for the process. If a process is performing within these limits it is said to be in control. If it isn't, like the example above, the variation is no longer normal or 'natural' and is known as Special Cause variation. Thus leaders now know where a response is required, and when to leave well alone. What a gift (Note that there are some other signifiers of Special Cause variation. Your expert practitioners should be able to tell you more!).

And it leads us nicely back to Juran's final step: *The means for changing performance in the event that performance does not conform to goals.*

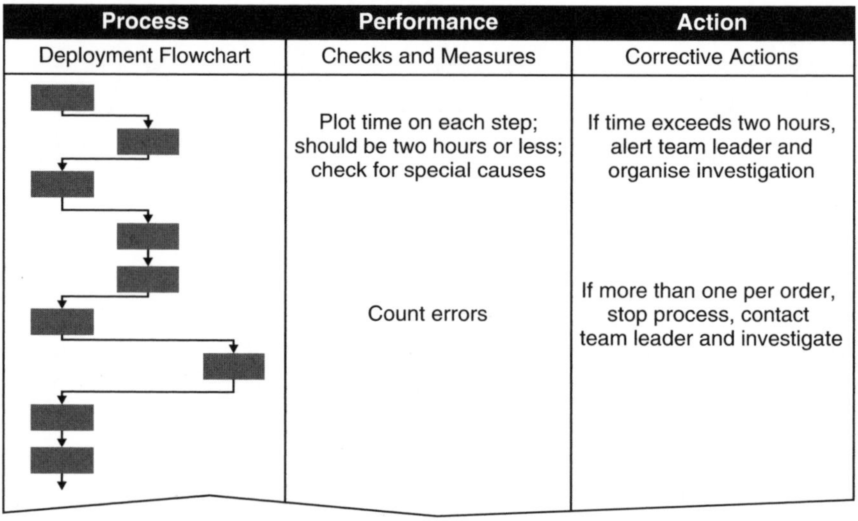

Process	Performance	Action
Deployment Flowchart	Checks and Measures	Corrective Actions
	Plot time on each step; should be two hours or less; check for special causes	If time exceeds two hours, alert team leader and organise investigation
	Count errors	If more than one per order, stop process, contact team leader and investigate

Figure 6.2   Process Management Chart

This can be achieved through the development of a Response Plan. A response plan highlights the actions to be taken when something goes wrong – if performance doesn't meet the required standards, if there is special cause variation, if there is a system failure or a shortage of other resources.

The Process Management Chart in Figure 6.2 provides a useful format for bringing all of these elements together. A good Process Management Chart will show:

- What the steps in the process are
- Who does these steps and when
- Where more detailed work instructions can be found
- Where data is taken on the process and on the product
- Who takes the data
- How (by what methods) measurements are taken and recorded
- When (how often) data is collected
- The actions to be taken based on the data
- Who takes action based on the data
- Where to find troubleshooting procedures

Monitoring must be as easy and straightforward as possible – the Process Owner must now be accountable for ensuring the controls are applied and the process is operating as 'Business as Usual'.

Transfer

Before the process improvement project is closed, it is beneficial to assess the achievements and benefits and capture the lessons learned, so that these can be applied to future improvement activities. In our experience, *every* process improvement brings lessons learned!

It's also likely that additional improvement opportunities have been highlighted, as inevitably 'lifting the carpet' on a process will reveal further issues. Documenting these and feeding them into the pipeline of opportunities for future focus can ensure they aren't overlooked.

Developing some 'sound bites' about the improvement and the successes achieved is highly recommended too. If these are short, snappy and memorable, they can be recited at every opportunity, to demonstrate the accomplishments of the team involved and the value of the DMAIC approach. Leaders' help in broadcasting these messages can be really powerful. We often talk to people about creating their 'Elevator Speech' at the outset of the process improvement journey, but it's also great to prepare one about the results achieved. Storytelling is in fact one of the keys to transforming organisational culture, as the stories that get repeated reflect what is valued in the organisation. Telling stories about improvements, then, can highlight just how important continuous improvement is.

'Storyboards' provide a helpful format for capturing information about Lean Six Sigma improvements. These capture the improvement 'journey' – from Define through to Control – and can be shared with anyone. They support the tracking of projects within the organisation and can aid a sponsor's understanding of Lean Six Sigma. Why not establish a library of completed projects to support the telling and sharing of these stories?

Oh, and one final thing to think about at the end of this chapter: are you still wearing your watch on the other side?

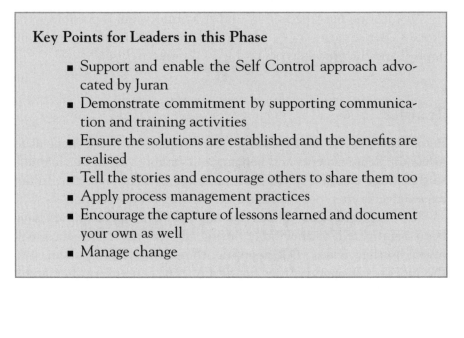

Key Points for Leaders in this Phase

- Support and enable the Self Control approach advocated by Juran
- Demonstrate commitment by supporting communication and training activities
- Ensure the solutions are established and the benefits are realised
- Tell the stories and encourage others to share them too
- Apply process management practices
- Encourage the capture of lessons learned and document your own as well
- Manage change

Using Lean Six Sigma Principles

7

Leading a Process Based Organisation

If you can't describe what you are doing as a process, you don't know what you're doing.

These words were spoken by the quality 'guru' W Edwards Deming, and we realise that this is a controversial statement and will either be accepted or not in your mind depending on your definition of the word 'process'. We know, from discussing this word with many leaders, that the word 'process' can be a problem and have negative connotations of bureaucracy and lack of flexibility. It is not universally accepted as a 'good' thing. Have you ever heard the expression from someone delivering some kind of service to you 'I can't provide what you want because the 'process' won't allow it.' This is crazy and the very opposite of what a good process should provide.

So, what is going on here? Why has 'process', in some organisations, got such a bad name? In this chapter, we are going to look at the leader's role in relation to process and why leaders should be interested in, and involved in, establishing, maintaining, monitoring, looking after and generally caring about processes.

What is a Process?

Firstly, what exactly do we mean by 'process'?

We define the word process as 'the way work is done'. You might prefer to use the word 'workflow' which is somewhat easier to grasp. That word is used in video production but we think it could have wider acceptability. For now, though, we will stick with the Lean Six Sigma accepted lingo and use the word 'process'.

A process can be complicated, for example the process for making a Commonwealth Cocktail which has 71 ingredients, or simple, like the process for making a cup of tea.

In fact, all of the work done in organisations is delivered through processes. When we refer to processes, we do not mean that every process at every level needs to be documented, flowcharted or surrounded by measures. You wouldn't do that with your 'boiling an egg' or 'travelling to work' processes, would you? Similarly, in work, we believe that common sense should prevail. It is important for leaders to have a process mindset though, to monitor, review and improve the way their organisation operates. In other words, being able to look at *how* work gets done in order to improve the *way* that it gets done. A process mindset is also helpful when it comes to measuring *how well* work gets done too, considering what are the most appropriate and sensible ways of monitoring the effectiveness and efficiency of work. Although we said that you wouldn't want to surround your non-work 'processes' with measures, you almost certainly do 'measure' their effectiveness but without consciously thinking about it as measurement. For example, how long did it take to get to work, were you on time or late and, if late, how late? Is that cup of tea too hot or cold or 'just right'?

Understanding what processes are and how we operate them is the key to efficient, effective and excellent ways of working. The principle of identifying and understanding how the work gets done is referenced many times in this book. That's no accident. Processes give you the power to understand, challenge and improve the activities (*any* of the activities) within the organisation. This chapter looks at processes from a business wide view and addresses what it means from a leader's perspective.

In Lean Six Sigma, we regard a process as being a series of activities that takes input(s), transforms them and produces output(s) for customers.

So, on this basis we can state that:

- All work is done through a series of processes
- All processes consume resources
- All processes can be measured
- All processes can be improved

Creating a Process Architecture

Every organisation, no matter what size or sector, is made up of a system of processes that fit together. By recognising this, we can understand how activities link together and where there are dependencies. Taking a 'process view' can help people in organisations recognise the importance of being more connected in wider, cross-functional teams. People can also become more connected with customers by understanding customers' experiences of the organisation's processes.

Powerful, indeed. Yet while lots of organisations have defined individual processes, relatively few will consider how the entire 'framework' of processes fits together. Try to describe your organisation on one page in a high-level picture of a set of 'processes', rather than the traditional organisational structure which describes how people are 'managed'.

This is sometimes described as the 'process architecture' and has a number of advantages such as:

- Aligning the work that gets done with business objectives. It's easier to make links between what is done and what is required when looking at the organisation this way.
- Providing a structure for process-based operational measures.
- Allocating process ownership clearly to specific leaders.
- Providing a framework and clarity for the definition of processes at a more detailed level.
- Showing where people belong in the 'big picture' and how their work contributes to organisational success. People may know where to find their team in an organisation chart, but a process view allows them to understand the importance of *what* they do rather than *where* in the hierarchy they do it.
- Enhancing induction training. Everything your organisation does, and how it fits together is shown on a page.

- Helping to understand the customer's experience. Customers don't 'see' the products and services of an organisation through its organisational hierarchy, they see the outcomes of your organisation's processes. They are not interested in who works for who.
- Distinguishing between core (customer facing) processes, support processes ('enabling' or back office processes) and management processes.
- Providing a view of process maturity and opportunities for improvement which can be used to assist in improvement project selection.

Several iterations might be required before the process architecture that best represents the organisation can be agreed upon. As with most process definition work, brown paper and Post-it notes can be helpful tools! When creating the picture, think about who to involve and engage in this piece of work. Try to make sure that wording and terminology fits with and matches what's used in other aspects of the organisation's management system. People might not recognise what they do in the model if it's called something different. There's no need for fancy terminology here, keep things simple and free of jargon wherever possible. For example, 'Manage Strategic Relationships' might be better than 'Expedite and maximise collaborative synergies'!

Using a 'verb/noun' wording convention to name the process activities is also very helpful, e.g. 'collect stock', 'issue order', 'send confirmation'. This can prevent the process picture from getting too cluttered with words and labels.

Standing back and reviewing the picture for gaps and overlaps is the next step. Considering the start and end points of the processes can be helpful in this respect.

Sharing the picture with key stakeholders is a necessary step in building acceptance – several revisions may be made before the picture is agreed.

There is no single best format for your process picture. It might change shape a number of times before the final version is arrived at. A live example is shown in Figure 7.1. It's actually how we run our own business and has stood the test of time for over 10 years.

The process architecture might be made up of different types of process.

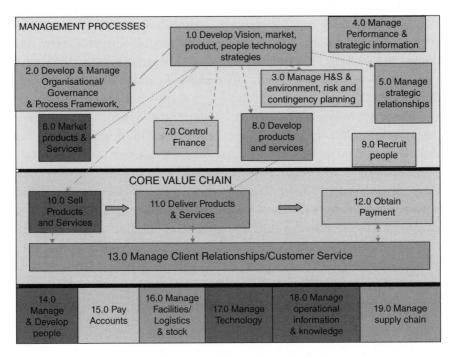

Figure 7.1   Process Architecture of a professional services business

Table 7.1   Different types of processes

Core Value Chain Processes	Processes that deliver the organisation's products and services to its (external) customers. This is why the organisation exists. Everything else is here to either support or manage these core processes.
Enabling or Support Processes	Activities that allow the core processes to operate effectively. They cannot be described as 'customer facing' but do deliver services to *internal* customers.
Management Processes	Processes such as planning and forecasting, leading business performance and managing change, that allow for effective steering and management of the organisation.

The process architecture we are describing here is 'high level' – building in exactly *how* all of these activities are carried out step by step within the same picture would result in something very 'busy' and complex looking. This might require a very large expanse of brown paper and could be extremely off-putting to stakeholders – not the desired effect.

However, now we have a high-level framework which is sometimes described as a 'level 1' picture it is easy to link more detailed process descriptions to this structure. The level 1 picture can be likened to a Christmas tree, and your processes could be described as the decorations. You might not have thought about your processes as fairylights before – but, bear with us – it's necessary to have the branches in place, otherwise where would you hang the fairylights? Without the framework it is very difficult to understand how everything fits. We'd just have a tangle of fairylights. And, if these don't get hung up and looked at once in a while we won't know if they're still working and fit for purpose.

Figure 7.2 shows a process system with three levels.

Setting Up and Using a Process Library

In creating this kind of process system, it can be very helpful to store information about the processes, the high-level process model, process

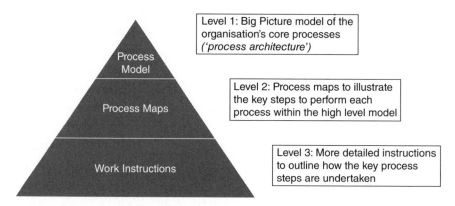

Figure 7.2   The Process System

maps, pictures and work instructions in a process library which is accessible to everyone in the organisation. The best approach for doing this will depend on your situation but we have seen this used very effectively and it brings the process world to life for everyone. It becomes a reference service which can be used for day-to-day operations and also for process reviews and improvement. Standards for work can be documented and made available for easy reference. For instance, we know of a five-star hotel who use their process library as the reference centre for storing process maps and setting standards in all aspects of running the organisation. For example, when housekeeping are cleaning a room, they can quickly access the standard by referring to photos and short videos on their iPad which are regularly updated with the latest standard so they know clearly 'this is what good looks like' for this aspect of work. It's also great for training purposes. The use of photos and videos makes life a lot easier too and overcomes language barriers which can be an issue in an international hotel.

Process Leaders can also refer to the process library to review the process they own. If you really care about something you want to look after it, regularly check it is in good health (we recommend regular health checks!). A high-level process architecture can also be turned into a cost model, looking at the cost of running each process. We have seen this used to create a graphical representation of failure cost too. This can be a real eye-opener as the amount of failure cost, caused by having to do rework and different types of waste, can amount to as much as 25% of total operating costs in certain industries before Lean Six Sigma projects start to tackle this waste. If you are a financial director and were ever in any doubt about the merits of Lean Six Sigma ask your team to look at the cost of failure in your organisation from a process perspective. You might be horrified by what you discover!

A process library can also link to process measurement systems, process dashboards and use of visual management techniques. We expect to see a growth in integrated process systems over the next few years with growth in the use of Robotic Process Automation (RPA). Developing a process based system will give you a framework to identify which processes in your organisation could benefit from RPA.

Don't Over-Process your Processes

A word to the wise. Sometimes process mapping and documenting activities get a bad name when taken too far in everyday operations (compared to when needed during a process improvement project) and literally every activity undertaken gets documented. This is not always a value adding activity, and the results – folders full of detailed process maps and documentation – can be described as 'inventory' and a cause of bureaucracy. One of the Lean wastes is 'over-processing', don't let this happen to you when you and your teams develop your process system.

When processes are documented it is useful to consider how they're going to be used, by whom and when they might be reviewed again. The 'six honest serving-men' from the Rudyard Kipling poem can be put to work to support many aspects of Lean Six Sigma. Table 7.2 shows one way to apply them.

Considering the risk associated with the activities can be another helpful focus. How high is the probability that a problem will occur? And what would be the impact on performance? Where there is a medium-to-high probability that a problem can occur in the process, and where the problem impacts on performance, extra controls (which include documenting the process) will be required.

Table 7.2   Using the 'six serving-men' to develop a process system

What	What level of detail is required? SIPOC level or lower?
Why	Why is it being mapped (e.g. to guide users, to train people, to demonstrate how a regulatory requirement is being addressed)?
When	When will it be reviewed and updated?
Where	Where (in the process architecture) does this information belong?
How	How will it be formatted? How will it be verified? How will it be reviewed once documented?
Who	Who 'owns' this process? Who will make sure the description remains up to date? Who is reviewing the process 'health'?

Definition of a Well Managed Process

Of course, documenting processes is not enough. Our definition of a 'managed process' is that:

- It's owned
- It's focused on the customer
- There's a clear picture of how the work gets done
- Data shows how well the work gets done
- Performance is stable and predictable
- It has been error proofed
- There's a control plan

Let's look at each of these from the perspective of day-to-day process management, having already looked at process improvement in Part I.

Process Ownership

Most valuable company assets are actively *looked after* on a continuing basis, typically the visible ones such as buildings, IT systems, and stocks of finished products; but *processes* – especially in non-manufacturing organisations where a visible production line doesn't exist – often become neglected. They are not 'looked after'. Processes in transactional and service organisations are often *invisible* with no one owning them in an active role. However, these *invisible processes are key assets* for your organisation, they define how work gets done! Looking after these invisible processes on a continuing basis is a less publicised secret to leading a successful organisation.

The problem is exacerbated by the pressure of day-to-day activities – operating those invisible, uncared for processes with associated failures and having to do rework in an inefficient system of work. These organisations are full of '*busyness*' ... which is not good business! A recent quote from a manager we heard was, 'We don't have time to become efficient.'

This is a catch-22 problem – how will those organisations that are most in need of becoming 'lean and efficient' find the time to do so? Making continuous improvement happen is not as easy as it might at first appear.

Clarity of roles, responsibilities and accountabilities is vital if processes are to be managed effectively, otherwise how does anybody know who's doing what, and why should anyone bother? Have you heard the story of Anybody, Nobody, Somebody and Everybody?

> An important job had to be done and Everybody was sure that Somebody would do it. Anybody could have done it, but Nobody did it. Somebody got angry about that because it was Everybody's job. Everybody thought that Anybody could do it, but Nobody realised that Everybody wouldn't do it. It ended up that Everybody blamed Somebody when Nobody did what Anybody could have done.

Starting off at the top of the 'Christmas Tree' (Figure 7.2), the role of owning the organisation's high-level process architecture is a leadership one. Similarly, each high-level process in the process architecture needs a process leader to take on this active process owner role.

Process leaders own, develop, manage, maintain and improve their given end-to-end processes. They are the 'go-to' people for the process. This is a leadership role, bringing with it accountability for performance and the continuous improvement of their process. As a rule of thumb, the broader and more 'cross-functional' the process, the more senior the process leader.

Responsibilities of process leaders include:

- Managing the boundaries of the process and coordinating with neighbouring processes, establishing process monitoring systems, driving collaboration across processes.
- Maintaining records to monitor and demonstrate performance. Producing visual reports demonstrating process performance and improvement activities.
- Defining and prioritising improvement. Contributing to the selection of improvement activities which provide maximum benefit considering overall organisational needs.

- Developing the abilities and attitudes of staff employed in the process.
- Demonstrating continuous improvement activity to increase the effectiveness and efficiency of the process.
- Formally reviewing the process ensuring it continues to meet the requirements of its customers, the organisation and interfaces effectively with other related processes.
- Controlling the collateral (policies and business rules, strategies, documentation, tools, standards, procedures, work instructions, etc.) ensuring all material associated with the process is consistent, up to date, and supports the vision and requirements of the process. Communication of these to process operators and other stakeholders is also required.
- Resolving process conflicts and removing roadblocks preventing operation of the process.
- Maintaining end-to-end accountability for the process and management of others responsible for performance of activities within the process.

For the sake of completeness, let's also look at the responsibilities of managers and process operators in the context of a process system.

Managers have an important role to play – they are the first point of escalation for people operating processes and are closer to the process detail than process leaders are likely to be. In addition to people management responsibilities, managers have some specific and important responsibilities when it comes to process management, including measuring and reporting process performance and identifying where corrective actions are required. Their contribution and the support they require from leaders is addressed in Chapter 16.

Process operators (or process users) are those who undertake the process steps. Whilst process leaders have a long list of responsibilities, the process operator also plays a vital role in process management. Responsibilities include:

- Operating the process efficiently and safely.
- Reporting and investigating any deviations from normal operating conditions.

- Dealing with basic process upsets.
- Identifying, sharing and helping to address areas for improvement within the process.
- Highlighting where there are opportunities to update or amend process documentation or other process collateral.
- Supporting process mapping and process validation activities.
- Providing information about process performance.

A RACI matrix is a tool that can help in the implementation and correct functioning of a process. Usually there are many different people involved in any process and they have differing responsibilities. RACI captures these in writing and provides a reference to be used at different stages in the process.

R is for Responsible. This describes the doers – those who are ultimately responsible for getting the work done. There could be several responsible people in a process.

A is for Accountable. This describes those accountable to oversee that the work gets done. An accountable person has the authority to approve or disapprove changes. It is essential that only one person be assigned the 'A' role. Having more than one person with the role increases ambiguity and contradicts true 'accountability'.

C is for Consulted. This describes the people who are consulted about the process or provide input at the time of a change or an exception.

I is for Informed. This describes the people who have some interest in the process and are kept informed when a change has been made.

This approach can overcome some frequently occurring problems in processes: such as duplication of effort or tasks not being undertaken at all; too much consultation or too many people being informed (e.g. where too many people are cc-ed on emails); and a lack of transparency about the level of involvement of people in the process ('why weren't we informed of this?').

So now Anybody can know what Everybody is doing, and Nobody can say that Somebody didn't define it!

Process Measurement

Now we know how the work gets done. Understanding *how well* the work gets done is another critical element of process management.

We find that organisations often create large amounts of data in an attempt to understand aspects of performance, yet we find that there are gaps when it comes to effective process measurement. Process measures often focus, for example, on volumes of work being passed through the process, or on process lead times, but don't address the aspects of the process that are Critical to Quality for process customers. Systems may support the measurement of how many items are being processed but they may not allow the organisation to clearly understand how well the process is working.

The key is to identify the Critical to Quality requirements of the customer. Unless you know what these are, how can you ever really comprehend how well your process is performing? There's a real risk that the organisation's understanding of the process will be at odds with the customers' views if the Critical to Quality requirements aren't defined.

And measure the 'average' level of performance at your peril! As we saw in the Analyse chapter, the mean or the average value is just a single value that is used to describe a whole set of data. It will describe only what's happening around the middle, and won't provide an insight into the amount of variation being experienced. There's a joke about statisticians who go hunting and come across a duck. The first one takes aim and shoots, but aims six inches too high. The second one also takes aim and shoots but he fires six inches too low. They turn and high-five each other and exclaim, 'We got him!'. Of course this is a really bad joke because good statisticians understand variation!

Measures of average are also misleading because of the effect of outliers – these can completely skew the average and lead to disproportionate results.

As this book is about Lean Six Sigma we should also tell you a little about the sigma value of a process, and what this means. Will your process be six sigma? Or 5? Or 3, or 1.7?

Our experience in working with leaders is that most won't want a long statistical explanation, so we will keep this simple. Some explanations can really put leaders off the whole subject by overdoing the statistical definition. There are plenty of books which cover this subject in depth.

A process sigma value is simply a measure of yield, how many times the process gets it right compared with getting it wrong. We all know what 99% yield is – getting it right 99 times out of 100.

However, the sigma value calculation is clever, it takes into account how much variation exists in the process data and also, most importantly, what the Critical to Quality requirement, from the customer view, is for that process. In other words – what 'good' looks like, and how well is this process measuring up against it. The detail behind the calculations is not really relevant here but look at it as a scale where 6 sigma is very good, 99.99966% good, which works out at 3.4 defects per million, and the scale drops down so that, for example, 3 sigma is around 93% and 2 sigma is just under 70%. It is not a linear scale: 1 sigma is 31%.

There are some interesting aspects of this – firstly don't be fooled into thinking that 99% or even 99.9% is that brilliant. It certainly isn't good enough if you are running a 24-hour, 7-days-a-week server system or utility. 99.9% would be 1 hour out of service every month.

Equally, we are not suggesting that all processes need to be at 6 sigma and this is one of the myths of Lean Six Sigma, that it is all about achieving crazily high quality levels. It isn't! It's the approach, method and application of the tools which is so helpful.

What the 'sigma score' does provide is a neat way of measuring how well processes match up against their requirements and it is a lot easier to see the difference between numbers on a simple numerical scale (from 0 to 6 and beyond), than it is to see the difference between, say, 99% and 99.9% – we can easily get confused by percentages.

By the way, some organisations need to go beyond 6 sigma and, as regular flyers, we're very happy that organisations like Rolls Royce who produce some of the most brilliant jet engines in the world are talking about defects per billion opportunities instead of defects per million. Coming back down to earth, we do know that the baggage handling system in a well-known airport in the UK is running at around 14 defects per 1000 passengers which equates to around 3.7 sigma.

This approach allows for comparison and benchmarking between different processes, and can also support the prioritisation of improvement projects.

A leader's role then is to challenge the way that processes are measured, seek more than a report on the average and encourage the use of measurement methods which will reveal the true 'voice of the process'.

It is also to ensure that there are links in place between the process measures used in the organisation and the critical business outcomes, so that there are clear connections between what the organisation does (its process architecture) and what it achieves. Life is a perpetual instruction in cause and effect. And so is Lean Six Sigma!

8

Delivering Everyday Operational Excellence

IF YOU'RE READING this book in order, from beginning to end, you'll know now how powerful Lean Six Sigma can be as a tool for problem solving and process improvement. If you're reading by dipping into different chapters to find what you're looking for, you probably already knew that. But now you're about to discover that Lean Six Sigma can be equally powerful when applied to the 'operational management' of an organisation – how the work gets done, and how to do it more effectively by working with processes, and the people that know the process, to achieve 'everyday operational excellence'. By the way, if you are a 'chapter dipper', good for you! John F Kennedy famously said, 'Conformity is the jailer of freedom and the enemy of growth'. We certainly believe in thinking about things differently – see our sections on the power of Assumption Busting in Chapters 4 and 5.

In this chapter you will see that the principles of Lean Six Sigma translate readily into principles of day-to-day leadership and management, and they provide the basis for an approach that is repeatable and reproducible. In most Lean Six Sigma books, you'll find Repeatability and Reproducibility being applied to measurement systems (you can find it referenced in this book in Chapter 3), but used here it describes a way of working where individuals are consistent in their own approaches, and where they are also consistent with others in the organisation.

Consistency definitely matters. Imagine going to a restaurant and eating *the* most delicious Tuna Niçoise salad you have ever tasted. Not only does it look amazing, colourful and fresh, but the flavours and textures are truly wonderful. This is an experience to savour, and you want to repeat it. You might even take a photograph of your Tuna Niçoise so that all of your friends can see it too! Now imagine that you return to the same restaurant a couple of weeks later. You've been *so* looking forward to experiencing the same luscious salad. But this time it just isn't the same. The tuna is dry, the eggs seem a bit overcooked and there is so much dressing that the salad has gone soggy. What a disappointment! It's probably the last Tuna Niçoise you'll order from this place, and you're no longer keen to recommend it. You've been let down by a lack of consistency, and so has the restaurant.

We also know that consistency is vital when it comes to family life. Children begin to understand how to approach the world when they see from others what matters most, the sort of behaviour that gets rewarded and the sort that results in admonishment. Mixed messages here can lead to feelings of uncertainty and anxiety – what will happen next? How do I know what the right type of behaviour is?

The same is true for those leading or managing people within organisations. If a leader responds to a piece of information with a knee-jerk reaction ('How could that mistake have happened? From now on *I need to review all of these orders before they go out,*'), or goes by gut feel rather than what the data is indicating, how can those around them clearly gauge the right way to approach a situation? Inconsistency can lead to a lack of clarity about acceptable ways of working. It can destabilise a working environment and impact on trust and the quality of relationships.

Let's think about famous manager Alex Ferguson for a moment. Even if you're not a fan of football, you'll know that the successes achieved at Manchester United during his tenure were unprecedented. His formula for success includes setting clear (high) standards for those in the team, and managing them to those standards. Ferguson responded when the standards were disregarded and there are some famous examples. However, he also acknowledged players who worked to his high standards. 'No one likes to be criticised', he says. 'Few people get better with criticism; most respond to encouragement instead. So, I tried to give encouragement when I could. For a player – for any human being – there is nothing better than hearing "Well done". Those are the two best words ever invented.' Ferguson applied this approach with absolute consistency.

Establishing clear standards or values within an organisation is not a new concept of course. We know that when the values are clearly defined, shared and lived within an organisation, it is easier for people to understand and align with 'the way things are done here'. But have you ever considered the links between your organisation's values and the principles behind the Lean Six Sigma approach? These things need not be separate. Highlighting the commonalities between organisational values and ways of working and the principles of Lean Six Sigma can emphasise a joined-up approach. This isn't 'yet another initiative' but a means to contribute to achieving the organisation's goals.

Let's review the principles of Lean Six Sigma with this in mind, to highlight their application in everyday operations.

Principle 1: Focus on the Customer

Being customer centric is about putting the customer at the heart of everything an organisation does. It is more than a cliché, in fact it should become a mindset.

In our world, anyone that receives an output of a process is a customer (more on this in Chapter 2). By this definition, the customers of leaders are many and varied. These range from the board, fellow leadership team members, managers, employees, partners, suppliers and customers, to regulators, unions and professional organisations, and the list goes on! As a result, it can be more difficult than it sounds to maintain a customer centric approach and balance the needs of stakeholders.

Note here we are not talking about granting all the wishes of customers at the expense of other needs. All customers and stakeholders should be considered in the mix. We are (frequent!) customers of hotels when we're out on business, for example. If someone was to ask us when we wanted our boiled eggs for breakfast we'd probably say something like, 'quickly' or 'as soon as possible', as we're fuelling up ready to get to work and we haven't got much time to spare. But, even though time is of the essence, it would be unreasonable of us to expect the egg to be served to us within a single minute. This could result in an egg that was undercooked, or an egg that had been boiled in advance, in anticipation of need, and has now gone cold – ugh! (or indeed, 'oeuf'!) – and the precooked eggs would need to be thrown away if not used. We understand this and expect there to be some waiting time, though we have an expectation as to what a 'reasonable' amount of waiting time should be.

A further challenge is that it's not always easy for customers to explain or quantify expectations. It is alleged that Henry Ford once said of his customers, 'If I had asked people what they wanted, they would have said faster horses.' The people weren't as knowledgeable as the man himself about the possibilities for production of a faster way to travel. But what they were really trying to tell him was not that the horses needed to go faster, only that they needed to get from A to B more quickly but couldn't conceive *how*. Luckily Henry Ford could.

We have seen several examples of solutions that have been implemented by organisations to solve a problem or improve a service where the needs of customers haven't been considered. One example was an organisation's response to its annual customer survey which highlighted low levels of satisfaction with the customer complaints process. The organisation took the feedback very seriously and organised a workshop with managers to identify solutions. It resulted in a series of changes being made to the organisation's complaints management system, including the ability to send emails from the system and better functionality for reporting. Lots of time and effort went into rolling out the changes. But did it improve satisfaction with the process? No. The improvements were focused entirely on 'internal' aspects of the complaints process which customers did not see or touch. Had customers been asked about what they needed from the process, they would not have talked about the database, emails and reporting capability. The happy ending to this story is that when the annual survey was carried out again, and customers said that they still weren't happy with the customer complaints process, the organisation asked customers what mattered most about the process. And what they got were some valuable insights that allowed them to rethink the process and improve satisfaction.

By thinking like customers they would have targeted their improvement effort in the right areas first time around.

Principle 2: Identify and Understand How the Work Gets Done

Thinking 'process' is also necessary. We cannot underestimate the importance of this principle!

We have looked at the power of process management and identified some effective approaches for defining and developing the framework and system of processes within the organisation. But for understanding how the work gets done, there is no substitute for *going to see the work get done*. Lean organisations call this 'Going to Gemba', as 'Gemba' is Japanese for 'The real place' – the place where the work happens. When Japanese detectives 'go to Gemba' they are going to the scene of the crime. Journalists often report 'live from Gemba' too.

There are some other Japanese words that apply to process understanding – 'Gembutsu' ('the thing') and 'Genjitsu' (the facts). Going to the place, seeing the thing, getting the facts – what an effective trio.

Or course you don't have to speak Japanese to do this, or use Japanese terminology if you don't want to! It is referred to in some organisations as 'Go and See' or 'Go, Look, See'.

It is powerful indeed, and massively illuminating. There have been numerous television programmes such as *Back to the Floor* that show what can be learnt when leaders go and see. The latest in the genre, entitled *Undercover Boss*, shows what happens when executives or owners, under an alias, go undercover in their own organisations as entry level employees for a period of time. The experience is always illuminating, and can result in promotion and development opportunities, improvements to working conditions, and changes to policies and protocols. So great are the learnings, that the programme has been franchised in several countries!

'Process Stapling' can add a further dimension to your understanding of the process. Imagine that you are the 'thing' that is being processed, whether it's a customer order, a policy paper, a component being manufactured or an expenses claim. Where do you go? Who handles you and how many times? Where are you left waiting and for how long? This can be a truly enlightening experience! In the digital age most of us have a high spec camera in our pocket – capturing the journey of the thing being processed as a series of photographs or as a video brings it to life in a really engaging way. We have seen some brilliant examples of this, where process operators have totally entered into the spirit – climbing into pigeon holes, being 'scanned', being delivered in the post cart, total process re-enactments!

If people aren't used to seeing leaders at the Gemba they may feel a little uncomfortable initially. But they will get used to it! The wise words from W Edwards Deming are worth reinforcing here,

> Eighty five percent of the reasons for failure to meet customer expectations are related to deficiencies in systems and process ... rather than the employee. The role of management is to change the process rather than badgering individuals to do better.

Looking at the process (not the people!) is a powerful habit to get into, so setting aside a few moments per week, or per day, and honouring this time can help to ingrain it. Don't over plan it – keep it simple and informal. Avoid the fresh paint syndrome – there is a saying that the Queen smells fresh paint wherever she goes – at Gemba you don't want to see the fresh paint, you want to see things as they really are.

Visual Management is a Lean technique that uses visual methods such as graphical displays, colours and shadow boards to communicate. This way of working promotes transparency within an organisation – the principle is that anyone entering a work environment that uses visual management will understand what is happening, what the standards are, and whether or not things are in control. Can *you* do this? It definitely helps leaders to identify and understand how work gets done.

One of the 'basics' of Visual Management is workplace organisation. The methodology known as '5S' originated in Japan and sets out a simple approach that supports a safe, pleasant working environment and the elimination of waste in the form of searching for items that haven't been put back in their rightful place. The approach also encourages self management *and* team working – you'll see why.

Sort. Look at the tools, materials, equipment and information needed, and separate them into those used 'frequently', 'occasionally' and 'never'.

Set (or straighten). Straighten things up, put the things used frequently close to hand. Things that don't get used frequently should be put somewhere else or thrown away. Decide how many items need storing, how they should be stored and where. These should be appropriately labelled to facilitate their easy access in the future.

Shine (or scrub). Keep the things you use, and the environment you work in, clean and tidy and appropriately maintained.

Standardise. Design a simple way of working so that your tools and information and things stay sorted, straightened and shiny.

Sustain. Keep doing it, stick to the system every day, regularly review things and celebrate effective methods of working.

Nowadays some organisations use 6S with the sixth S standing for Safety. You could argue that if 5S is done properly, safety is inherent – but it's a crucial consideration for some organisations we work with. Likewise sometimes organisations have 7S, with (environmental) sustainability added to the list.

Visual Management can be applied anywhere and has many benefits, including sharing performance information, making targets or performance levels clear, highlighting when these have been achieved or how close or far away is performance, clarifying and displaying standards of work, and providing an alert about problems.

Examples include displays of performance information, which could incorporate some Control Charts, histograms and Pareto Charts. They might even include some Booz Balls (see Figure 8.1), to show how well an item matches the criteria, or show the progress of a project or initiative in its degrees of completeness. Other forms of Visual Management include photographs or examples of performance

Figure 8.1   **Booz Balls – simple, effective indicators of achievement**

standards (e.g. standard operating procedures and pictures of how a meeting room should be left after it has been used). We have also seen colour charts used in the kitchens of organisations to communicate how strong team members like their cups of tea, and charts in the bathrooms that indicate levels of hydration!

You can see how simple and effective these methods are – and this is the principle of Visual Management. People won't have the time (or the inclination) to stand at displays for a long time reading and interpreting information – the best approaches are uncomplicated and their messages immediate. A picture paints a thousand words. Information doesn't have to be printed or look 'polished' either – some of the best ones are handwritten. The act of writing the information on the displays promotes a feeling of ownership among team members.

Visual Management can support another Lean approach – daily management meetings. These daily meetings provide everyone in a team the opportunity to discuss performance and the issues of the day, like the scrums described in Chapter 10. These don't have to be called scrums of course. Some organisations call these 'huddles' (as teams huddle around the board to review information), sand box talks and even 'morning prayers'. We've helped several teams get this process underway – focusing on getting into the habit of holding the meetings rather than perfecting the displays (this can be enhanced over time).

The meetings shouldn't take long, no longer than 15 minutes. They should be prepared for, and well organised to ensure everyone stays focused. The best meetings are stand up meetings, and they happen at the Gemba.

Sometimes there is discomfort associated with visual management, where performance becomes very visible and individuals may feel exposed or uncomfortable with this. But don't forget that the focus is on the process not the people – the point is to get processes working as well as they can, not get people working as hard as they can or focusing on volume over quality.

In a paperless working environment, or where people 'hot desk' rather than having a fixed, permanent desk, Visual Management can be a challenge ('where would the board go?', 'how can we huddle around it when we're working remotely?' and 'we're not allowed to display stuff here' are comments we often hear). But everything is possible – technology can be a powerful enabler. (You might not be at the Gemba but you can still stand up!)

Principle 3: Manage, Improve and Smooth the Process Flow

Among the things to look for when carrying out Process Stapling or going to Gemba are clues that highlight bottlenecks in the flow of the work. Are there delays at certain points? Are there high levels of work in progress or backlogs? Chapter 4 looks at the theory of constraints and how smoothing the process flow can improve process capability.

Leaders can also look to their own work areas for clues. Is there a pile of papers waiting for review or signature? What about your email inbox? Is your involvement in these matters absolutely necessary? And do you process these items in batches? Big questions. We have quoted Jim Lovell elsewhere in this book but these words might bring comfort, 'Be thankful for problems. If they were less difficult, someone with less ability might have your job'. Um, thanks Jim.

Your Runners, Repeaters and Strangers are also a useful consideration.

Runners are the items/tasks demanded or the processes carried out most frequently, say around 80% of the time. Repeaters are demanded or carried out less often but on a recurring basis, and Strangers (sometimes called Rarities) are those items or tasks that are called for rarely or may relate to a bespoke requirement.

This type of thinking can aid effective prioritisation (will a solution that we're considering improve the process for our runners or affect only a small number of 'stranger' activities undertaken rarely?); it will also support the avoidance of distractions. Should we let the strangers in? Maybe they could be taken off line or off peak, subcontracted or charged a premium for. Or could these become runners in the future?

Principle 4: Remove Non-Value-Add Steps and Waste

Where are your WOMBATs? WOMBAT stands for Waste of Money, Brains and Time. We're pretty sure you have some.

When we discussed this subject with people attending an awareness course recently they gave us some fantastic examples, citing reports that get generated and circulated routinely that don't get read, or are read only partially. One keen Wombat Slayer was required to send detailed performance updates to around 20 people in her organisation on a monthly basis. Wondering how people used this information she password protected the reports for a period of time. During that time not one of the people on her list of recipients got in touch to ask for the password. It has now been agreed that the report is no longer required, resulting in a significant time saving.

When you're tuned in to Wombat spotting you see them everywhere. Here's a challenge for you: go and find a Wombat in your workplace and do something about it.

While you're about it you might also come across Tim Woods. Tim Woods is an acronym for the different types of waste at play within processes. There's more about that in Chapter 4.

The message for leaders? Challenge and encourage others to challenge. If the steps in a process that don't add value don't get identified and challenged they'll continue to consume resources and not add any value. If we don't address Tim Woods wastes they'll cause us problems. And if we don't tackle the wombats ... we'll end up with lots of wombats.

Principle 5: Manage by Fact and Reduce Variation

Data driven decision making is at the heart of Lean Six Sigma. But the data needs to be relevant and right, and it needs to be good data! Most organisations have plenty of data and may be suffering from overload.

Alex Ferguson has some words of wisdom on this too.

> ... there have always been data hounds in football, just as there are in any sport. However, everything changed after Sky started blanketing the airways with football games. Prior to that, the only information a viewer would receive would be the result, the names of the goal-scorers and the times of the goals. These days the television coverage is drenched with possession percentages, assists, shots on goal – and what your dog had for lunch on Easter Sunday ten years ago. A manager receives all that information and a whole lot more. The statistical information was always important

and I always looked at the data, but this did not determine how I picked a team. The data was more of a tool to ensure that standards were being maintained.

This highlights the importance of seeing the wood for the trees and this is vital for leaders. 'Knowing the heart rate of a player and doing all the video analysis in the world of his opposite number is not going to help you if he loses control and gets sent off in the first minute.'

We have mentioned Edward de Bono's Six Thinking Hats in Chapter 5 and the use of Black Hat thinking to identify what could go wrong, weaknesses and risks. So now we can see the wood for the trees (not Tim Woods) and have the right data, we are encouraging use of the White Hat. White Hat thinking is concerned with facts and information. What does the data say? (And is the data reliable? See Chapter 3.) While wearing this hat we should behave like a computer, according to de Bono. The computer has no ego or agenda – it takes and presents information and is entirely neutral, and it doesn't attempt to fill in gaps with conjecture. Computers aren't emotional and they don't present an argument.

Principle 6: Involve and Equip People in the Process

We have addressed the importance of involving people that know the process in process improvement activities, and we've seen how valuable this contribution can be. It is necessary to encourage contributions and provide the means for gathering and using this input at every opportunity in day-to-day operations, not just in relation to projects. The story about the Toothpaste Factory demonstrates this very well and provides a useful reminder to leaders about the expertise they have around them.

> The toothpaste factory had a problem with boxes being shipped out to customers with no tube of toothpaste inside. Customers were complaining and relationships between the factory, buyers and distributors were becoming strained.
> In response, the CEO called a meeting with the leadership team. They decided to hire an external engineering company to solve the problem. The project was managed to ensure budget and a sponsor

was allocated, the bidding process was followed, and an appropriate third party engaged to deliver the new system. Six months (and £8 million) later the solution was implemented on time, in full, and on budget. It was considered to be a fantastic success.

The solution involved a high precision scale on the production line that would weigh each toothpaste box. If the weight of the box was lighter than it should be (no tube inside), the production line would automatically shut down, an alarm would trigger and a light would flash to alert an operative to come and remove the empty box. The operative would then re-start the line by pressing a button.

Measured data showed that no empty boxes were being shipped. Everyone was pleased with the result. When continuing to monitor the process however, an unexpected result was found. During the first three weeks of the new system, the number of defects (empty tubes) being picked up by the weighing scale were consistent and as forecasted. But following that, the number went right down to zero. No empty boxes were being picked up by the scale! The CEO asked the engineers to check that the scale was working and it was found to be working accurately.

Puzzled, the CEO walked down into the factory and looked at the line where the new £8 million solution had been implemented. He noticed that a £20 desk fan had been installed just ahead of the scale. It was blowing empty boxes off the belt and straight into a dustbin positioned below the line. He asked the Line Supervisor what was happening.

'Oh that', said the Supervisor. 'Bert, the kid from Maintenance put that in. He was fed up of walking over, removing the box and re-starting the line every time the bell rang.'

And the final principle …

Principle 7: Undertake Improvement Activity in a Systematic Way

We've covered the DMAIC approach in detail, and the value of a systematic approach should be becoming clear.

Working systematically supports consistency. Providing the principles and approaches are used it shouldn't matter who is leading the improvement work, who is involved, or which process the team is working on, it will result in an improvement. It also ensures rigour – using DMAIC means not jumping to conclusions or making assumptions about what's needed. Furthermore, a systematic approach brings transparency – there can be clarity with regards to the approach and the progress made.

We're not saying that every tool or technique under the sun needs to be applied, or that there's no room for flexibility. Remember that Lean Six Sigma is at heart a pragmatic approach. Also remember that it's much more than just a toolkit – it's a principles based way of working.

9

Winning Hearts and Minds

In This Chapter, we've taken our experience from observing many organisations, their leadership of Lean Six Sigma and their successes or failures in creating a continuous improvement culture, together with thinking from other writers under the wider leadership heading. Our aim here has been to distil for you a guide to the core subject of leadership as applied to Lean Six Sigma. This is not just theory. The case studies in Part IV have a common theme reflecting the need for a deep consideration of leadership and culture. We are indebted to our colleague in Catalyst, Chris Merriman, who is an expert in transformational leadership as well as a Lean Six Sigma Master Black Belt, for his work in researching this subject and providing his insights.

What is a Leader?

Leadership and management are often confused, and many people have both roles, but in fact they are distinctly different. Management tends to focus on efficiency and is characterised by control, measurement, consistency, standards and stability. Leadership, meanwhile, is more interested in effectiveness and characterised by providing direction, aligning, mobilising and even inspiring people. Leaders set the tone. Stephen Covey put it well when he said 'Management is efficiency in climbing the ladder of success; leadership determines whether the ladder is leaning against the right wall.' And, as Kathy Austin said, 'Managers light a fire under people, leaders light a fire in people.' We need, of course, a balance of both management and leadership in our organisations, but many focus primarily on management ... in fact we've heard it claimed recently that 'UK businesses are over-managed and under-led'!

With this understanding, we can see that it's not enough for leaders to 'get it' when it comes to Lean Six Sigma and creating a culture of continuous improvement; they need to be 'doing it'. And it's also not enough to be seen 'doing it' only on designated days, or when time is spare or when the weather suits, it needs to be manifest in a new set of habits and routines. People watch what you do. Great leaders are proactive when it comes to creating and managing culture. As Edgar Schein said, 'If we don't manage culture, culture will manage us and we may not even be aware the extent to which this is happening.'

Creating and managing culture is a prime responsibility of leaders. But there are no short cuts: as Stephen Covey said 'Quick fixes don't work on a farm'. There are natural laws at play on a farm which govern the outcome, i.e. the quality and quantity of the harvest. These laws (to do with seasons, soil conditions, nutrition, etc.) apply whether we recognise them or not. In the same way, there are principles at work which govern consequences for organisations and business, such as integrity, fairness, honesty, openness and so on. Such principles are self-evident, universal, timeless and have consequences. Whether we follow or ignore these principles, there will be consequences.

The Need for Authenticity

Great leaders either consciously or naturally work in harmony with principles. With principles at their centre, they are guided in how decisions are made, how agreements are formed, how processes and systems are designed, how partnerships are managed, and how direction is set. And the fact that these leaders consistently use such principles to guide their behaviour and actions makes them authentic, i.e. genuine, reliable and trustworthy. This is vital in enabling them to build trust in the organisation. Trust is not established through manipulative strategies or tactics. People know if you're faking it; you might be able to pull this off for a while, but eventually you will be found out. And trust, which takes a long time to build, can be broken overnight. This is true for all our relationships inside and outside of work. Trust is established through both competency and character: competency is about proven ability and qualifications to do the job, technical knowledge and delivering results, but character is about having respect for others, integrity and humility. It's character over personality; substance over style.

Leading with Humility

Humility is an endearing and powerful quality of great leaders, but has not always been promoted or encouraged. In his book *Good to Great*, Jim Collins refers to 'Level 5 Leadership', present in every good-to-great company that he found, which embodies a paradoxical blend of personal humility and professional will. Their ambition is first and foremost for the company, not themselves. Far from relying on authority, Level 5 leaders set up their successors for even greater success, they display a compelling modesty, are self-effacing and understated, and deflect credit to the team for success. 'Leading with Humility' is one of the guiding principles which underpins the Shingo Model for Enterprise Excellence, and is described as follows:

> Organisational and personal growth is enabled when leaders work to bring out the best in those they lead. They seek out and value the ideas of others and they are willing to change when they learn something new. Leaders trust others to make good decisions.

Having humility as a leader also means having the courage to seek feedback personally, and then having the emotional intelligence to act on that feedback. The humility principle has consequences. At least as much as the Lean Six Sigma tools themselves, humility is foundational for enabling continuous improvement and innovation, as it helps maximise the contribution from others. Simple ways for leaders and Black Belts to demonstrate humility are to recognise readily that they have much to learn; that they don't have all the answers; even that they don't understand the problems and that they need the help of those on the ground to make genuine progress. Humility opens the door to more meaningful conversations at all levels.

Respect for Every Individual

Another foundational principle for leaders is 'respect for every individual'. This is complementary to humility in that it is about valuing all people, looking after their health and safety, supporting their development, and enabling them to fulfil their potential. As Eric Ries, author of *The Lean Startup* said, 'respect is ensuring that every individual knows that their contribution matters to the organisation.' At Abbott Nutrition they have a short saying which is recognised and embraced by everybody, regardless of function or level, as one of their values ... 'My Work Matters'. As Tom Peters said, 'Serving our Customers brilliantly and profitably over the long haul is a product of brilliantly serving, over the long haul, the people who serve the customer.' There are various methods and techniques which can help here, and some organisations refer to it as 'Servant Leadership' or 'The Agile Leader' (see Chapter 10). Some train their executives in 'The Mindful Leader' or in 'Humble Enquiry' (see, for instance, Edgar Schein: *Humble Inquiry: The Gentle Art of Asking Instead of Telling*), but the principle of respect for every individual, in combination with leadership with humility, is at the core. Specifically, at the Lean Six Sigma level, it means recognising that problem identification and improvement ideas can and should come from everyone in the organisation, and that the most important contributions often come from those operating the process on a daily basis, not the senior manager or master Black Belt.

Focus on Process

All leaders focus on results – after all this is primarily how their success gets measured. Traditional leaders focus on results above other things, and some are only interested in outcomes! Even organisations deploying Lean Six Sigma have managers and leaders who have little regard for process. One consequence of this is a clear message sent by the leader that people and processes are of secondary importance, and while the leader might pretend these matter, the team is unconvinced. Hence licence is given to cut corners, risk quality and even compromise safety. Of course this leads to even greater process variation and degradation in overall performance in the long run. Furthermore, it renders the establishment of true standard work virtually impossible. As Toyota's Taiichi Ohno said, 'without standards there can be no improvement.' A lean management system is an effective way to counter this by encouraging (even enforcing!) a 'focus on process' behaviour and mindset from leaders. The concept is simple, containing three main elements:

1. Visual management to answer the question 'are we winning or losing?'
2. Daily accountability, to answer the question 'if we're not winning, what are we doing about it?'
3. Leader Standard Work, to answer the question 'what do we need to do today to help you win more often?'

This of course assumes that the question 'what does it take to win?' has been answered clearly, typically through a structured strategy deployment process. The Leader Standard Work element involves identifying and building into the leaders' daily/weekly/monthly calendar specific activities, often at the Gemba, which relate to assessing, reinforcing or improving standard processes. It's not micro-managing people, it's focusing on process. A simple example is that every Tuesday a supervisor is required to check that each of their team leaders has completed their 5S audit, posted the results, and has identified appropriate corrective or improvement actions with the team. This weekly supervisor activity itself might be governed by a visual T-card system for transparency through visual management. Every leader has this form of standard work developed, according to their function and level, and established visibly in their calendar.

The concept is simple, the practice is more difficult because it requires self-discipline. However, if the principle of 'focus on process' is truly understood and reinforced at all levels, then time will be found and the activity will be prioritised. And, of course, the respective teams will subsequently notice the behaviour and be encouraged to observe the principle.

Create Constancy of Purpose

The first of Deming's Fourteen Points, and a Shingo guiding principle – constancy of purpose – is also critical because 'an unwavering clarity of why the organisation exists, where it is going, and how it will get there enables people to align their actions, as well as to innovate, adapt and take risks with greater confidence.' Additionally, The Toyota Way calls us to 'Base your management decisions on a long-term philosophy, even at the expense of short-term financial goals.' Done right, this can provide the alignment to the 'higher purpose', even that burning ambition referred to earlier, uniting the whole team's energy and ambition behind a common cause, and enabling the journey of transformation to be sustainable. As Nietzsche said, 'He who has a why to live can bear almost any how.' At the Continuous Improvement programme level, this makes Lean Six Sigma project identification, selection and execution all the easier, plus the probability of project success so much higher. Fuelled by genuine desire and personal motivation for change, and confident in the direction and strategic priorities, the teams will apply more intensity, take more risks and push beyond conventional thinking and expectations.

Emotional Intelligence – The Essential Ingredient?

Managing our emotions as leaders can influence our responses and behaviours, which in turn can have a dramatic effect on the spirit of the group and the actions and outcomes that follow. Adele (2002) describes emotional intelligence (EI) as 'the dimension of intelligence responsible for our ability to manage ourselves and our relationships with others.' EI is gaining ever more focus in leadership circles, and Daniel Goleman describes it as 'The sine qua non of leadership'.

Goleman has identified a comprehensive set of twenty EI competencies grouped under four categories:

1. Self-awareness (knowing one's internal states, preferences, resources and intuitions)
2. Self-management (managing one's internal states, impulses and resources)
3. Social awareness (awareness of others' feelings, needs and concerns)

4. Relationship management (adeptness at inducing desirable responses in others)

Self-awareness, self-management, social awareness are all competencies that are not normally observable, known as 'Inner Leadership'. The social skills category contains obviously observable behaviours, or 'Outer Leadership'.

Those leaders who score highly on Emotional Intelligence know where they are heading, have self-confidence but know when to ask for help, create an environment of trust and fairness, demonstrate a strong desire to achieve, take calculated risks, have expertise in building and retaining talent, demonstrate genuine empathy and concern, and are great at inspiring and guiding others towards shared goals.

Your level of Emotional Intelligence can be assessed and improved using a mind management model called the 'Chimp Paradox' (Steve Peters, *The Chimp Paradox*, 2012). The Chimp Paradox refers to your three-part mind: your chimp, your human and your computer. The chimp part of your mind thinks emotionally and works with feelings and impressions, and is characterised by jumping to opinion, black and white thinking, irrational judgement and emotive and instinctive behaviour. Your human part, meanwhile, thinks logically and works with facts and truths. This is more rational, balanced, controlled, compassionate and with a stronger, more conscious sense of purpose. In order to live with your chimp you need to learn to manage it and take responsibility for your behaviours. Your chimp's drive won't change, but your behaviour is a choice and this can change. This is entirely consistent with Steven Covey's first habit (see *The 7 Habits of Highly Effective People*, 2004), i.e. 'be proactive', where he refers to consciously creating a gap between the stimulus (an event) and your response, in order to create that freedom to choose with those endowments of self-awareness, conscience and imagination that make us uniquely human.

Peters refers to three ways to manage your chimp:

1. Exercise (allow the chimp to 'let it all out' – either in a safe place or provided that everyone else knows that this is what you're doing – and listen to it)
2. Box (address the chimp's fears and concerns by talking to it using facts, truth and logic to calm it down and reason with it)

3. Banana (feed the chimp a banana as a distraction or reward, e.g. going for a walk, listening to music or reading a book)

When a leader gets their head in order it has an amazing effect on those around them. Your inner chimp can be your best friend or your worst enemy, so learn to live with it and become the person and leader you would like to be.

Creating a Safe Environment

Much of the above is about leaders setting the tone, and making the choice to put people first. As Simon Sinek says, when people feel safe (in the widest sense, not just physically but emotionally and intellectually) and that they truly belong, then remarkable things happen. People who feel safe, which is a natural human instinct, will naturally combine their talents and strengths to better the organisation. This is about reaching deep inside of people, at an emotional level, to engage with their hearts and souls, not just their heads or their hands. At the Newsprinters manufacturing facility in Eurocentral, Scotland, the first UK winners of the Shingo Prize in 2014, the plant manager Ross McCombe was asked if there was one key factor which had contributed most to their journey to excellence over the years, and he responded by saying 'building trust, every day'.

Leaders who focus on principles and teach them to their people are providing them the 'why', rather than just teaching practices which provide the 'what' as applied to specific scenarios. Once these principles are understood, people feel genuinely empowered to do the right thing in every circumstance, and will therefore not need constant monitoring, evaluating or controlling. A stuffed bird cannot fly!

Nobody is born knowing these principles or how to apply them to best effect. Just as DMAIC enables effective problem-solving and process improvement, every leader learns these principles and continually develops their capability through practice, trial and error, and coaching. So the good news here is that you can learn them too!

Leadership is a choice not a rank. People watch what you do, not what you say. Lead with humility rather than with authority. Leaders go first.

10

Integrating with Agile

IN THIS CHAPTER we explore the potential synergy between Agile and Lean Six Sigma, in particular the leadership perspective. What can we learn from Agile leadership?

We asked our colleague, James Dwan, an expert in Agile techniques for his views on Agile leadership and its relevance to Lean Six Sigma.

Agile started in earnest back in 2001 with the signing of the Agile Manifesto as a way to improve the way that software projects were delivered. What has followed has provided not only frameworks to revolutionise the software industry but product and services development in general. This chapter focuses not on the Agile frameworks themselves but on the new leadership and team paradigms they brought with them and the new skills and mindset required to fully capitalise on them. We also highlight the strong connection between Lean Six Sigma and Agile leadership in transforming business culture, the associated importance of inspirational leadership to establish a 'True North', and a nurturing work culture and environment of *Psychological Safety* required so that experimentation and validated learning can flourish. We think there is great synergy between the two worlds of Agile and Lean Six Sigma and there is much to be gained by understanding this potential.

For many decades, executives were expected to know how to give answers rather than how to ask questions. The culture has grown in many organisations that asking questions is a sign of weakness rather than a strength, leading to multiple dysfunctions. Just as Toyota pioneered new leadership behaviours so skillfully documented by John Shook in *Managing to Learn*, those same practices have emerged in parallel within the Agile world; fostering a community whom we develop and coach to work out innovative solutions to problems rather than leaders carrying the burden of providing the answers to everything themselves.

Self-organising Teams and Servant Leadership

One of the most popular Agile frameworks, *Scrum*, introduces the paradigm of the 'self-organising team'. This was a key mindset change in software development. Agile teams are structured and empowered by the organisation to organise and manage their own work. Hierarchy is flattened with no job titles recognised other than 'developer'. The team's role is to transform the 'product backlog' (nuggets of business value often described as 'user stories') into increments of potentially shippable product. From a leadership perspective, this brings something very new to organisations since accountability now belongs to a team rather than an individual.

This has given rise to the notion of 'T-shaped' people within teams, as shown in Figure 10.1.

Teams are designed so that they have all the cross-functional skills necessary to get the job done with people who are specialists in a field but who can collaborate across disciplines with experts in other areas. We move away from the paradigm of a 'led' team following orders to an autonomous group. We look for diversity of skillset, cross-functional so the team can get the whole job done. Jeff Sutherland refers to how research shows that having more than nine people in a team slows the team down, and that it takes significantly longer to get the same amount of work done. Everyone has to know what everyone else is doing. As teams get too big, this becomes muddled.

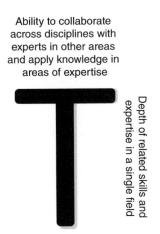

Ability to collaborate
across disciplines with
experts in other areas
and apply knowledge in
areas of expertise

Depth of related skills and
expertise in a single field

Figure 10.1   T-shaped people

Within the Scrum framework two roles exist which we may examine from a leadership perspective:

- Product Owner: sole responsibility for managing the *product backlog.*
  - o Makes sure requirements are clearly expressed
  - o Orders the backlog to best achieve the vision
  - o Ensures the backlog is transparent and available
  - o Ensures the project team understands the backlog
- Scrum Master: often described as a *servant leader.*
  - o Facilitates the team meetings when required (or asked to)
  - o Guides the team towards continuous improvement and how they can do better
  - o Removes impediments which are preventing the team from reaching their goal(s)
  - o Gets rid of blame culture – instead of blaming individuals, ensures focus is on situational topics
  - o Sets up the right conditions and framework
  - o Ensures the team has autonomy and the ability to improvise

The Product Owner has an important role to play to facilitate discussions with the consumers of value and other stakeholders to maximise the value of the work being done. The team decides how much work they can take on in each time-boxed 'sprint' of work and pulls the next most valuable work from the Product Owners backlog.

The Scrum Master acts as the 'heat shield' for the team, ensuring that the environment in which they work is conducive to success. They protect Scrum values and ensure that any impediment which is a barrier to the team reaching their goal is removed with haste. The Scrum Master also acts as the facilitator when asked, in order to provide the lubricant to the team to make good quality decisions taking into consideration the T-shaped expertise of the team.

In Daniel H Pink's book, *Drive – The Surprising Truth about what Motivates Us*,[1] he uses the metaphor of computer operating system development to describe the evolution of motivation:

- Motivation 1.0 = Survival
- Motivation 2.0 = Type 'x' behaviour – seeking reward and avoiding punishment (carrots and sticks)
- Motivation 3.0 = Type 'i' behaviour – intrinsic motivation

Pink describes how intrinsic motivation consists chiefly of purpose, autonomy and mastery:

- *Purpose*. The desire to do something that has meaning and is important.
- *Autonomy*. Our desire to be self-directed.
- *Mastery*. The urge to improve at what we are doing.

Pink describes what he refers to as the 'Sawyer effect', taking inspiration from the Mark Twain novel where Tom Sawyer convinces his friends that he actually enjoys whitewashing Aunt Polly's fence instead of it being regarded as 'work' or as a punishment, resulting in his friends wishing to pay him for the privilege of doing it themselves (see Figure 10.2). When we can reconfigure work to make it fun and embrace intrinsic motivation, we can yield superior results.

Scrum reconsiders how we think of leaders. Instead of the conventional *carrot and stick* of yesteryear, the primary function of the new leader is to create an environment where intrinsic motivation can flourish. Motivation 2.0 was suitable in an age where work consisted

---

[1]*Drive–The Surprising Truth about what Motivates Us* by Daniel H Pink

Illustration from *Tom Sawyer*
Courtesy The Mark Twain House, Hartford

Figure 10.2   Illustration from Tom Sawyer

mainly of algorithmic routines. Today's more creative and dynamic workplace demands something different. Within Scrum and other Agile frameworks, we see a recognition of this new paradigm where the way we run our business is catching up with our understanding of human psychology. This brings with it new challenges for leaders to embrace these new learnings and alter long ingrained behaviours and business practices.

Lean Startup

With Agile thinking, we take a systematic approach to product and service delivery. In Eric Ries' groundbreaking book *The Lean Startup*,[2] he describes the way to solve this by working through the problem iteratively:

- First, work out what we need to learn by creating a *value hypothesis* and decide what we need to measure to test the hypothesis.

---

[2] *The Lean Startup* by Eric Ries

- Secondly, design an experiment known as the *minimum viable product* to gather data from real customers to determine if we have a product/market fit.

Much as with Lean Six Sigma problem-solving, we expect some of our experiments will produce null results but a few will succeed. We expect our value hypothesis might be incorrect and we aim to invest the minimum effort to learn and pivot accordingly based on validated information to move on to new and/or adjusted value hypotheses.

Contrast this with a conventional portfolio management approach and we see how leadership behaviour must change for this systemised approach to work. In many ways, the former project paradigm made life easier and more comfortable for leaders since they were able to enjoy the luxury of an *illusion* of certainty and predictability:

Our people know what our customers want and all the specified value is desired by our customers.

This was a culture where leaders needed to be experts with answers to all questions; but this exacerbated the problem and the marketing team, driven by this paradigm, naturally started to present their hypotheses as cast-iron proofs. What had been the norm for many companies was then to rush to spending valuable development and operational resources in a mad dash to meet the market opportunity window. The pressure ramped, and all too often, requirements were added, deadlines missed, staff overworked and ultimately quality was compromised and delivered products and services did not meet the need of customers. At its worst, blame culture followed, leading to knee-jerk reactions, a mistaken belief that more 'up front' work was needed on requirements, and a revolutionary replacement of people in a vain hope of finding a better way.

Agile leadership takes a different approach. Whereas the conventional project manager is rewarded for delivering on time and to cost, the emphasis of Agile leadership is focus on the definition, measurement and management of specific outcomes. The leadership team sets a 'true north' for the desired outcome and empowers and trusts the team. In many ways the Agile leader's role is to get out of the away so the talent can get on with success; setting up teams to win and removing obstacles. The senior leader's role is around strategy. Instead of the belief that the project plan is a prediction of what will happen, Agile teams embrace change using an 'adapt and inspect' mindset so they can iteratively pivot based on incremental validated learning.

During Agile transformation, this can lead to some difficult conversations such as:

Leadership team	'When can we have our stuff?'
Agile team	'We don't know yet?'
Leadership team	'What will be delivered?'
Agile team	'We don't know yet, we learn that as we go.'
Leadership team	'How much will it cost?'
Agile team	'We are not sure yet but we'll let you know when it is done.'

There are similarities with a Lean Six Sigma project at the start of a DMAIC problem-solving project.

Leadership team	'What is the solution to this problem?'
DMAIC team	'We don't know yet.'
Leadership team	'What is causing the problem?'
DMAIC team	'We don't know yet, we learn that as we go.'
Leadership team	'How much will it cost?'
DMAIC team	'We are not sure yet but we'll let you know as soon as we know.'

In the Agile world, we have seen leadership teams up in arms when they first experience this approach to product development, and the project team counter arguing with quasi-religious zeal that their leaders are Luddites for not seeing the light. Often Agile transformation can begin at grassroots level with teams having dipped their toes into Scrum, and discovering a more enjoyable and fulfilling way to work, whilst at the same time producing results which the team can be proud of. However, to fully embrace the benefits of Agility, transformation of mindset needs to occur at all levels within the organisation with senior managers fully supporting their teams and living and breathing their new role within the system. This is very similar with Lean Six Sigma.

With Agile, the role of middle management is to see the whole and develop the capability of the organisation to build great products. They should help the teams and Scrum Masters with removing obstacles and making improvements. They should teach teams how to solve problems. They should *go and see* to understand what is really going on in the place of work and see how they can best help the team improve their work.

The role of senior management is still required to take the strategic decisions related to the company and its products. However, they become much less engaged in deciding the 'how' and become experts in communicating the 'why'. They are responsible for building the capability, ensuring the organisation hires, develops and coaches the right people so they can deliver. Another way of looking at this is that the value flows 'horizontally' through the organisation, directly to the team without interference of managers, whereas capability is built 'vertically'.

Whether at portfolio, program or project level, business Agility brings a new paradigm with validated learning at the heart of each cycle. In Lean Six Sigma, we teach our people to recognise and remove waste from business processes. With Agility, we teach our people to treat business models as hypotheses to be tested with minimum investment whether it be at micro or macro level. In all cases, we are applying a more scientific (through controlled experiments) method to the way business is run and supporting our community of 'experimenters' to fail early and fail often on their road to success. This means we have to create a culture where they feel safe when testing out new thinking.

Psychological Safety

Amy Edmondson at Harvard first introduced the concept of team safety defined as a shared belief that the team is safe for interpersonal risk taking.[3]

As a result of the famous 'Project Aristotle', Google measured performance to understand the attributes of their most successful teams. In all, 180 teams were analysed.

---

[3]http://web.mit.edu/curhan/www/docs/Articles/15341_Readings/Group_Perform ance/Edmondson%20Psychological%20safety.pdf

Google found five key attributes in successful teams:

- Psychological Safety
- Dependability
- Structure and Clarity
- Meaning of Work
- Impact of Work

Top performing teams often exhibited all or most of these attributes. However, psychological safety was found to be by far the most important and underpinned the others.[4]

Psychological safety can be characterised as a sense of confidence that the team will not embarrass, reject or punish someone for speaking up. It describes a team climate characterised by interpersonal trust and mutual respect in which people are comfortable to be themselves.

As Amy Edmondson states in her TED talk,[5] our sense of self-protection leads us to manage our own self-preservation by avoiding the following, though in doing so, we are missing opportunities to create a better organisation.

Ignorance – don't ask questions

Incompetence – don't admit weaknesses or mistakes

Intrusiveness – don't offer ideas

Negativity – don't challenge the status quo

Necessarily, the Agile leader fosters psychological safety and a climate of openness: we want and expect our people to speak up with concerns, questions, ideas and mistakes. Agile leaders need to live and breathe this, demonstrating it in their own daily coaching behaviour. Where work is framed as a learning exercise – a space in which we can experiment – we dramatically improve our results if we get everybody's contribution. A recognition that we are all fallible at all levels within the organisation creates a workplace striving to learn and improve based on good quality information. These generative organisations place emphasis on improving the system rather than

---

[4]https://rework.withgoogle.com/blog/five-keys-to-a-successful-google-team/
[5]https://youtu.be/LhoLuui9gX8

looking for people to blame; in stark contrast to pathological organisations and bureaucratic organisations with their respective blame and empire-building behaviours. When we withhold information, we rob our colleagues and organisation of opportunities to learn.

Agile Business Consortium

Helpfully, the Agile Business Consortium characterises nine principles of Agile leadership, which we explain below.

1. Actions Speak Louder than Words

This leadership principle is all about authenticity, demonstrating the leader as a learner, ensuring psychological safety and embodying the change you want to see in the organisation. Living Agile values involves coaching, counselling and reflection; showing yourself as fallible and as someone who continues to learn. Value people who are courageous and embolden people to seek forgiveness rather than asking permission.

2. Improved Quality of Thinking Leads to Improved Outcomes

Better conversations, better quality information, and a psychologically safe workplace lead to quality thinking and, ultimately, better outcomes. This means applying what we know from Lean; teaching people to talk to the people who are close to the reality. An organisation which strives to be better at communication, and which builds the right relationships, engenders an environment where high quality of thought can prosper.

3. Organisations improve through effective feedback

Ensure that the organisation focuses on systemic thinking; examine methods and processes rather than people when we get different results from what we desired. Psychological safety is paramount here. The pathological organisation, fuelled by fear, causes an antipattern where information is distorted or hidden. On the other hand, the bureaucratic organisation causes hoarding of information in silos. The generative organisation engenders a spirit of continuous learning and an organisation which perceives successes and failures as validated learning in the pursuit of a common purpose.

4. People Require Meaning and Purpose to Make Work Fulfilling

As discussed above, it is scientifically proven that purpose-driven organisations achieve more. This means that everyone can make a connection between the organisational purpose and their own purpose for being. This must be much more than mere profit incentive, with a mythology for the future in which individuals can become emotionally invested and which resonates with their sense of self.

5. Emotion is a Foundation to Enhanced Creativity and Innovation

The Agile leader fosters a culture where people work with their emotions to open up creativity and innovation. This involves also being given license to be negatively emotional when appropriate. We want passion to kindle the drive in people and maximise intrinsic motivation within the organisation.

6. Leadership Lives at all Levels of the Organisation

In our next generation of organisation, we recognise that leadership emerges from anywhere as appropriate. By supporting our self-organising teams, we create a culture where leadership can be appropriate to the situation. This starts with you as the leader demonstrating these behaviours and being the servant leader when the situation demands it, demonstrating to all that we can all learn from each other.

7. Leaders at all Levels Devolve Appropriate Power and Authority

The Agile Business Consortium recognises that delegation and empowerment are different things. When we devolve, we are not handing something off in the command and control sense. This is about enabling and empowering people, supporting them so that we get the very best out of our people.

8. Collaborative Communities Achieve More Than Individuals

Lean leadership looks at the extended value stream to remove waste (suppliers and customers). Collaborative communities see beyond silos and concentrate on flow of value.

9. Great Ideas Come from all Levels in the Organisation

Agile leaders demonstrate themselves to be always open to new ideas. This can be as simple as a willingness to praise and recognise contribution. Frederic Laloux describes a new paradigm known as 'Teal Organisations' where an organisation is viewed as an independent force with its own purpose, and not merely as a vehicle for management's objectives.[6]

Agile Continuous Improvement

More and more, we are seeing exciting results as we take these emergent paradigm shifts in leadership and team behaviour into the continuous improvement arena. By applying the ideas discussed in this chapter, where self-organising teams work in rapid time-boxed sprints of work, pull from a refined backlog with a focus on minimum viable product/process, we see more customer-oriented business solutions, an increased flow of business improvements with reduced lead times, along with maximised team motivation, contribution, energy, and effectiveness. The Green or Black Belt increasingly becomes a 'T-Shaped' team member rather than a leader. We dramatically increase the intensity of projects, and we accelerate the results.

Exciting times lie ahead as we rethink the way our organisations are run and capitalise on the many discoveries over the last century within psychology and business science. We are building organisations which can deliver faster and more effective results and where work is more satisfying and fulfilling.

---

[6]http://www.reinventingorganizationswiki.com/Teal_Organizations

11

Turning Strategy into Action

Can Lean Six Sigma thinking help turn strategy into action?

We certainly believe it can but this is another less well known approach, coming from the world of Lean thinking. This chapter has been written to answer this question and we have invited Dr Vince Grant who co-authored *Lean Six Sigma Transformation for Dummies* (which contains the technical detail behind this approach) to provide his extensive expertise and experience.

The Challenge of Strategy

> If you don't drive your business, then you'll be driven out of business
> **B C Forbes, 1945**

Forbes clearly had in mind that businesses need to follow a clear sense of direction, one that is envisaged in their overall strategy, and that leaders need to drive and steer it on that journey. But it's a journey that can only be travelled if everyone in the organisation understands and actively follows the plot. The challenge is arguably less the development of an organisation's strategy but rather its deployment.

Percentage of people who understand the strategy

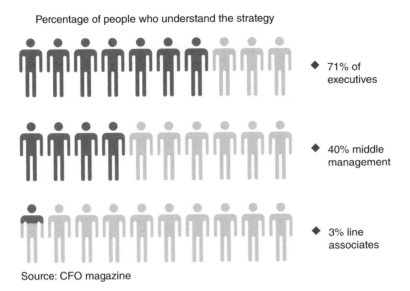

◆ 71% of executives

◆ 40% middle management

◆ 3% line associates

Source: CFO magazine

Figure 11.1   Who understands their organisation's strategy?

Surveys suggest (see Figure 11.1) that whilst 71% of executives overall say that they understand their organisation's strategy, only 40% of middle management also do, and this reduces to just 3% for front-line associates – those who are actually dealing with the customer or producing the goods and services on an everyday basis. Contrast this with outstanding performing organisations where in one European Quality Award winning organisation, over 80% of staff at all levels could meaningfully answer the following three questions:

- What do you understand to be the primary purpose and main objectives of your organisation?
- What are your individual goals and objectives in your job/position?
- How do these contribute to your organisation achieving its purpose and objectives?

The answer for that outstanding organisation is strategy deployment – or Hoshin Kanri to give it its original Japanese term. The case for strategy deployment is compelling:

- In many organisations most people don't understand the strategy.
- Many haven't been involved in developing it.

- Those who have been involved in translating it into operation have typically not done so systematically.
- As a result the downstream development and ongoing operations are often only loosely aligned with the strategy.
- The targets, KPIs and metrics used don't fully reflect the strategy, are likely to be unbalanced; and of course 'what gets measured gets done'!

A Brief History of Hoshin

Hoshin Kanri was developed in the 1950s by Toyota in Japan in order to drive strategic goals systematically and sustainably into operations. Its originator was Yoji Akao who jointly with Shigeru Mizuno also developed Quality Function Deployment (QFD), a technique at the core of Lean Six Sigma for Innovation and Design (sometimes otherwise known as Design for Six Sigma DfSS). Readers familiar with QFD will immediately recognise a strong similarity between the House of Quality Matrix and the X-matrix in Hoshin Kanri which we describe further in this chapter.

Many leading Japanese corporations, including Fuji Xerox and other winners of the Deming Prize, progressively adopted Hoshin. US companies with Japanese subsidiaries or joint ventures with Japanese companies such as Hewlett Packard recognised its significance during the 1980s and introduced the approach into their strategic planning. Adoption of Hoshin in the US was relatively slow, partly because most organisations then did not have the process management and improvement cultures on which to embed it, but also because those that did saw that it gave them competitive advantage that they did not wish to share prematurely. With the introduction of standardised processes and tools by the likes of the Danaher Corporation, the development of Six Sigma in the 1990s through pioneers such as Motorola, Allied Signal and General Electric, and the widespread adoption of Lean as knowledge of the Toyota Production System became widespread, both of these barriers were overcome. Today many organisations that are relatively mature in their deployment of Lean Six Sigma have adopted Hoshin and the X-matrix as their strategic planning and deployment tool.

The strategy deployment process is illustrated in Figure 11.2.

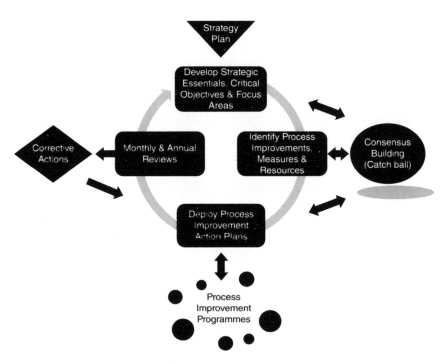

Figure 11.2   The strategy deployment process

An Example of Strategy Deployment

Let's consider an organisation – we'll call it PRU Ltd. It's a sales and service organisation obtaining products from the manufacturing divisions of its parent company. It specifies and sells specialist label and packaging printer configurations to other commercial businesses. The senior managers in the company have just finished their annual strategic planning process and have revised their strategic plan. We'll consider how they then use Hoshin strategy deployment to create their deployment plans for their new Polish regional office.

The key steps they undertake are as follows.

Step 1

Review of the strategic plan, testing it for completeness and robustness; then distilling from this the 'strategic essentials' – the critical longer term strategic goals. For PRU these are:

    a. Grow sales through emerging markets and hold existing sales in other markets;

b. Grow sales of the green (environmentally friendly) range of products;

c. Drive out waste and unnecessary costs;

d. Develop and challenge the workforce.

They have translated these goals into specific measurable targets with clear quantified outcomes for the relevant period of the plan. Those relevant to their Polish operation are:

a. Grow sales in Eastern Europe by 5% per year over next five years;

b. Build distribution network in Europe to 30%/€10m in four years;

c. Grow 'green' hi-end sales to 30% of hi-end sales over the next five years;

d. Reduce operating cost base by 5% of sales within three years.

These outcomes need of course to be balanced and comprehensive – this is one of the key tests of the strategy; if it cannot be quantified in this way then it is incomplete and certainly will not be robust.

Step 2

They then identify the focus areas which will deliver those outcomes; these are essentially development programmes. PRU lists these as including: establishing a distribution network in Poland capable in particular of selling their green products, creating capable maintenance and post-sales operations, and installing a programme of continuous cost reduction and efficiency improvement right from the outset.

Subsequently they further detail the above into the improvements and changes that need to be made in the upcoming year; these will span elements including processes, systems (or tools), people and skills, and organisation. These will typically be delivered through projects and key management actions aimed at:

a. Developing and implementing a process for identifying and engaging distribution partners in Poland, Slovakia and Hungary;

b. Designing and implementing a process for hiring and training maintenance and service technicians in Poland;

c. Developing and implementing a specific process for generating 'green' sales each year;

d. Implementing a Lean Six Sigma waste and variation reduction project process.

(It is purely coincidental here that we've illustrated four goals, four targets, and four programmes – there could just have easily been four goals, six targets and five programmes – and correlated on a several-to-many basis.)

Examples of the detailed actions and projects within these included:

- Partnering with one distributor in each of the three countries;
- Generating sales from these distributors in total worth €2m;
- Hiring and training four maintenance and aftersales technicians;
- Generating revenue from own maintenance and service of €300k;
- Training twelve sales staff and the four aftersales technicians in 'green';
- Training for and running four LSS Green Belt projects to secure cost reductions of >1% of operating costs per annum (€125k in first year).

The X-matrix, as shown in Figure 11.3, was used as their key tool to align these and gain a shared common understanding on how they interrelated. It was used in a three day workshop facilitated by experts (external consultants when the approach was first introduced into PRU).

It facilitated the tight alignment of the projects with the development programmes and the strategic goals – and quantified the correlation between all the elements of these. It showed which projects were the most critical to deliver the intended strategy. Not surprisingly aspects of it look similar to those in the QFD House of Quality Matrix as we saw above that both tools were the invention of Yoji Akao.

Step 3

Having agreed and aligned these projects PRU's leaders then went on to charter, plan and resource these projects essentially as they

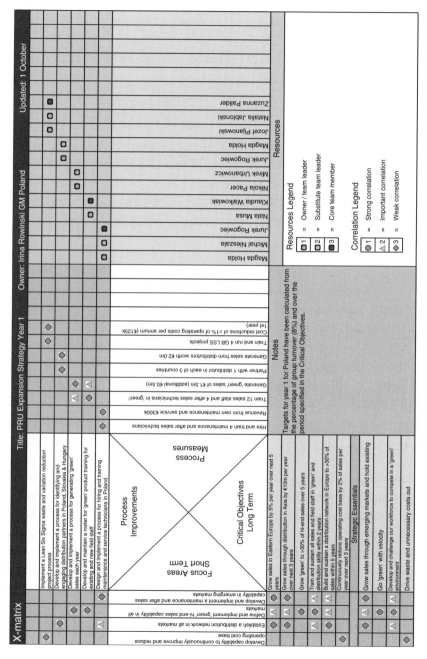

Figure 11.3 Example of the X-matrix for PRU Ltd.

143

would normally for Lean Six Sigma projects. Detailed action plans, metrics and targets were then put in place to monitor progress – and these are reflected in the Strategy Deployment Action Plan illustrated in Figure 11.4.

The individual projects were reviewed, results tested and integrated before fully deploying successful outcomes.

Step 4

Overall progress was managed through monthly reviews, taking corrective action as appropriate. A typical RAG (Red, Amber, or Green) visual tracking chart is shown in Figure 11.5.

A corrective action was planned for each and every item categorised as 'in the red' using an appropriate level of root cause analysis (Figure 11.6).

Step 5

The overall portfolio of change was then managed in an Agile manner, rippling through any necessary changes to priorities or individual elements. PRU initially learned the overall approach and then had the capability to repeat this entire process on an annual basis, or earlier if some trigger event should cause this to be necessary. Overall this system operates in a PDCA / PDSA cycle.

Further Examples

We have supported a range of organisations with the deployment of their strategies in this way. Examples include a leading five-star luxury hotels group, the European service operations of an IT company deploying a new target operating model, an electrical controls manufacturer, and an international financial payments company. In one of these deployments there were five strategic goals with nine associated targets covering all four Balanced Scorecard quadrants (financial, customer, processes, learning and growth); these spawned thirteen development programmes which then crystallised into nineteen projects plus a 'business as usual' stream of activities; three pre-existing projects were terminated as a result of the re-prioritisation

Action Plan

Owner: Jurek Rogowiec (Magda Holda substitute) **Updated:** 10 July

Process Improvement: Develop and implement a process for identifying and engaging distribution partners in Poland, Slovakia & Hungary

Process Measure 1: Partner with 1 distributor in each of 3 countries
Process Measure 2: Generate sales from distributors worth €2.0m (additional €1.0m)
Process Measure 3:
Process Measure 4:

Legend: ■ On plan ■ Off plan ■ Corrective action ■ Complete

Team Members & Initials: Agnieszka Baranowski (AB), Nikola Holda (NH), Natalia Kruk (NK), Izabela Plewa (IP), Ewa Tyrala (ET)

Action Item	Owner / Members Initials	Planned Start Date	Planned Completion Date	Actual Completion Date	Status PDCA 1234	Notes
Preparation For Kick-off Meeting						
Review X-matrix and determine targets for each country	JR	1/12	1/12	1/12	●	
Prepare agenda, invite attendees, book room and resources	MH	7/12	7/12	4/12	●	
Obtain list of potential Distributors in Poland, Slovakia, Hungary	JR	7/12	21/12	23/12	●	
Kick-off meeting						
Review X-matrix and targets for each country	ALL	3/1	3/1	5/1	●	
Determine selection criteria for Distributors	ALL	3/1	3/1	5/1	●	
Review lists of Distributors	ALL	3/1	3/1	5/1	●	
Deselect any obvious inappropriate Distributors	ALL	3/1	3/1	5/1	●	
Prioritise remaining Distributors	ALL	3/1	3/1	5/1	●	
Decide on approach to Distributors	ALL	3/1	3/1	5/1	●	
Decide who will approach which Distributors	ALL	3/1	3/1	5/1	●	
Initial Contact to Distributors						
Send initial invitation to tender letter	IP	10/1	10/1	12/1	●	
Collect and store interested Distributors	IP	17/1	1/3	16/3	●	Slow responses
Prepare information pack for Distributors	IP	10/1	24/1	20/1	●	
Prepare RFQ pack for Distributors	NH	10/1	24/2	20/2	●	
Arrange meetings with top 3 Distributors in each country	IP	3/3	12/3	19/3	●	Distributors busy
Attend meeting with Distributors in Poland	AB	10/3	10/3	22/3	●	
Attend meeting with Distributors in Slovakia	NH	12/3	12/3	25/3	●	
Attend meeting with Distributors in Hungary	NK	14/3	14/3	3/4	●	
Review meetings	JR	15/3	15/3	5/4	●	
Pre-Engagement of Distributors						
Run background checks on potential Distributors (DB, Credit etc)	ET	3/3	10/3	10/3	●	
Prepare contract for Distributors	ET	4/1	5/3	5/3	●	
Send letter and contract to chosen supplier in each country	ET	5/3	15/3	6/4	●	
Engagement of Distributors						
Receive signed contracts	ET	19/3	29/3	10/4	●	
Develop training programme	NK	2/2	1/3	1/3	●	
Deliver training to Distributors	AB,NH,NK	5/4	10/4	7/5	●	
Set-up monitoring system with Distributors	ET	1/5	1/7		◐	
Launch Distributor in Poland	AB	15/4	20/4	3/6	◐	Took longer than planned
Launch Distributor in Slovakia	NH	15/5	20/5		◐	
Launch Distributor in Hungary	NK	15/6	20/6	2/7	◐	
Standard Work for Engaging Distributors						
Develop standard work document for engaging Distributors	MH	1/6	20/6		◐	
Review and sign-off standard work	JR	1/7	10/7		◐	

Figure 11.4 Action Plan for Strategy Deployment

Tracking Chart		Owner: Jurek Rogowiec (Magda Holda sub)													Updated:15 July
Process Improvement:		Develop and implement a process for identifying and engaging distribution partners in Poland, Slovakia & Hungary													
Status Key:		On Target						Off Target							
Business or Milestone Metric	Start Measure	20XX	Jan	Feb	Mar	Apr	May	Jun	Jul	Aug	Sep	Oct	Nov	Dec	End Measure
Partner with 1 distributor in each of 3 countries	0	Plan	0	0	0	1	2	3	3	3	3	3	3	3	3
		Actual	0	0	0	0	0	1	2						
Generate sales from distributors worth €2.0m	1	Plan	0	0	0	0	0.1	0.3	0.5	0.8	1.1	1.5	1.8	2	2
		Actual	0	0	0	0	0	0.2							
		Plan													
		Actual													
		Plan													
		Actual													
		Plan													
		Actual													
		Plan													
		Actual													
		Plan													
		Actual													
		Plan													
		Actual													
		Plan													
		Actual													

Figure 11.5   Strategy Deployment tracking chart

Corrective Action

Owner: Jurek Rogowiec (Magda Holda substitute)   **Updated: 10 July**

Process Improvement:

Name:	Distribution partners in Poland, Slovakia & Hungary
Milestone Tgt:	3 distributors recruited by September
Business Tgt:	Generate sales from distributors worth €2.0m

4 Months Data Analysis (From Tracking Chart):

Month:	April	May	June	July
Milestone Plan:	1	2	3	3
Actual:	0	0	1	2
Bus Plan:	0	0.1	0.3	0.5
Actual:	0	0	0	0.2

Define (background, problem statement, current state, who is affected):

Original plan was to recruit a distributor in each of Poland, Slovakia and Hungary. Distributors took on average 3 weeks longer to respond than anticipated and the Slovakian distributor gave backward at the last moment. Distributor sales are €0.3m short to target for July.

Measure (what are the metrics and how bad is it now):

Recruitment of distributors is late by: Poland 6 wks, Hungary 2 weeks, Slovakia 3 weeks plus.
Distributor sales are €305k short of target as shown by sales log.

Analysis (root cause):

Distributors took on average 8.5 weeks to respond compared to an anticipated 3 weeks.
Slovakian distributor gave backward
2 weeks before launch. No replacement distributor was organised.

Distributor response 8.5 weeks average

Team Members & Initials:

Agnieška Baranowski (AB), Nikola Holda (NH), Natalia Kruk (NK), Izabela Plewa (IP), Ewa Tyrala (ET)

Improve & Control (corrective actions to improve and sustain) (indicate short or long term):

#	
1	Accelerate recruitment of alternative Slovakian distributor
2	Incentivise Polish and Hungarian distributors to accelerate sales ramp
3	Build additional time for hiring distributors into standard work plan
4	Maintain at least two distributors in pipeline during recruitment
5	
6	
7	
8	

Corrective Action Plan:

#	What	Who	When	Status
1	Dedicate 2 people to recruit Slovakian distributor	NH	16/5	●
2	Contact and visit 2 distributors from previous list	NH	24/6	●
3	Receive signed distributor agreements	NH	7/7	●
4	Train Slovakian distributor	NH	10/7	◐
5	Launch distributor in Slovakia	NH	15/7	◐
6				
7	Offer additional 10% commission on sales over agreed	AB,NK	20/5	●
8	target in Poland and Hungary			
9	Support distributors to increase sales ramp	AK,NB	10/7	◐
10	Update standard work for recruitment of distributors:	MH	20/6	●
11	add 8.5 weeks to timing and instruction to maintain			
12	at least 2 in the pipeline			
13				
14				
15				
16				
17				
18				

Process Measures:

Name	Before	After
Accelerate time to recruit Slovakian distributor	4 months	2 months
Recruit total of 3 distributors	2	3
Distributor sales in August, €m	0.3	0.6
Distributor sales back on track by October, €m	0.8	1.5

Figure 11.6   Strategy Deployment corrective action

of the Hoshin analysis, prioritisation and alignment. This clearly demonstrated the power of the X-matrix to manage a many-to-many correlation.

Strategy deployment is an effective way to turn strategy into action, if driven with supportive leadership. It might take a couple of attempts to learn the approach, refine it to 'fit' into your organisation, but the results will come through and we believe this is a valuable approach to help tackle the issue of 'we are good at developing strategies … but not good at turning them into action and *making them happen.*'

12

Creating a System for Innovation and Design

WE'VE FOCUSED PART I of this book on business problem-solving as this is the most common application of Lean Six Sigma using the DMAIC method. However, it wouldn't be right to leave out the use of Lean Six Sigma when a new design is required, although this is a more specialised area and goes beyond the scope of this book so we will keep this section as a brief for leaders.

> Design is a funny word. Some people think Design means how it looks. But, of course, if you dig deeper, it's really how it works.
>
> **Steve Jobs**

We used this quote in *Lean Six Sigma for Dummies* and repeat it here as it is so relevant to what we think about the subject of design.

A Brief History of Lean Six Sigma for Innovation and Design

Arguably the first organisation to consider this type of approach was General Electric in the late 1990s. In those days 'Design for

Six Sigma' (or DfSS as it was widely known) started to be adopted for the design of new processes, and the DMADV methodology, described below, emerged. Other organisations recognised that they had broadly parallel new product or service development processes and embedded DfSS principles and tools into them. With the advent of Lean's increasingly widespread adoption in the early 2000s – and its integration in Six Sigma to become Lean Six Sigma – organisations increasingly looked to incorporate Lean principles and approaches into the design space. And DfSS became Design for Lean Six Sigma. At Catalyst we prefer the terminology 'Lean Six Sigma for Innovation and Design' (LSSID) as this emphatically recognises the fusion of Lean Six Sigma and Innovation in the search for high performance major change outcomes.

When to Use the Design Approach

Maybe you have improved a process using DMAIC through a number of iterations and it just isn't possible to take it further. Sometimes you will find that improvement to an existing process is not sufficient or that an existing process doesn't currently exist in any meaningful sense to deliver the required outputs and outcomes. It could be that it is easier to start from scratch rather than centring on root causes, analysing the problems and improving the existing process. Thinking still wider we may need to design not just a process but the entire service it supports or indeed a new product.

This is when to apply the less frequently used but very useful design methodology in the Lean Six Sigma world and employ the DMADV method – Define, Measure, Analyse, Design and Verify.

Although the first three phases have the same titles those carried out in DMAIC (Define, Measure, Analyse, Improve and Control) the work undertaken in these phases is different in a Design project. We don't start with an existing problem for example – the starting point is a 'gap'. Throughout the approach, there is a strong focus on understanding customer requirements and translating these into measurable critical to quality requirements. The Analyse and Design phases move from looking at the 'what' to the 'how' and then moving into pilot testing in the Verify phase and then implementation and deployment.

Define

As in a DMAIC project this phase is focused on organising and planning the project, developing the rationale and the business case and identifying who's to be involved. Scoping and planning is also included, and there is focus on the processes, markets and customers involved. Customer segmentation is important. 'If you're not thinking segments, you're not thinking!', said Ted Levitt of Harvard Business School. 'To think segments means you have to think about what drives customers, customer groups and the choices that are or might be available to them'. Crucial considerations for design. You can't design a solution that satisfies everyone, if you try you'll satisfy no one. Which customer segments matter most? Which are most profitable? Which can't be ignored?

Measure

This phase focuses on planning and conducting the research necessary to understand the customer needs and requirements associated with the product or service. These are translated into measurable characteristics (CTQs) that become the overall requirements for the product or service. In the Measure phase targets are set and specification limits established for the CTQs. The aim is to fully understand the customer requirements and define the measures.

Key tools include the QFD (Quality Function Deployment) or House of Quality. This provides a structured approach which systematically takes the CTQs and compares them with the characteristics of the product or service. The technique draws out the 'gap' for each need and the priorities of the customers, and the goal for each need is then identified. Technical considerations are also included, along with an evaluation of the competition. It's not called a House of Quality for nothing – it has many rooms! The content is developed during the A and D phases too.

Design scorecards are also used here. This supports the prediction and understanding of performance of the service or process at implementation. It assesses the design against the requirements, and helps to highlight gaps in our understanding. As with the QFD it's a 'living' document that is used in other phases of the DMADV journey and it benefits from the input of a multidisciplinary team.

Analyse

The Analyse phase starts with the process of moving from what the customer wants to how we might achieve it. It includes mapping CTQs into internal functions and starting to look at alternative concepts.

Design

This phase takes the 'how' thinking to a deeper level by adding more detail onto each element of the high-level design. The emphasis remains on developing designs that satisfy the requirements of the process outputs. By this stage there should be enough detail to test and evaluate the capability of the design by preparing a pilot.

Verify

In the final phase the design is piloted and assessed. All the facets of project, process and change management then come together for a full-scale implementation and deployment of the new service or process.

The Challenge of Innovation and Design

When we start from an existing process the problems are usually concerned with one or two customer requirements or CTQs. When we start with a blank sheet of paper we have to consider all the customer and stakeholder requirements in the round; some of these may at first glance appear conflicting. Innovation is important to at least some degree in all improvements – remember that in the Improve phase in DMAIC we should look to consider all possible solutions before we select the most appropriate one(s); and that requires us to think innovatively. However, when it comes to a new design, innovation assumes an even greater importance as we'll inevitably be seeking a competitive edge in the outcome (or the equivalent best possible outcome in a non-competitive organisation).

But innovating and changing everything is arguably not normally the optimal path; rather it's usually more about focusing innovation and change on the vital few aspects and elements that can drive that competitive or best practice leading edge, and then sustaining good, fully capable but less sensitive current approaches to the rest. That enables the new design to be completed and implemented more quickly and efficiently without compromise to its effectiveness or competitiveness. An 'Agile' approach that quickly delivers the minimum truly viable change to assure the required customer value is delivered.

Lean Six Sigma is still very relevant to such larger scales of change – but our approach needs to reflect the different focus. We need a methodology which collects measurements focused on stakeholder requirements in the round and on comparative (and indeed competitive) benchmarks rather than on past performance; we need it also to have a different focus for mapping processes – either through process benchmarking or 'to be' options. Root-cause analysis needs to be replaced by one focused on evaluating approaches to deliver the required outcomes – forward looking rather than backwards focused.

Not surprisingly there are some important new tools and techniques in DMADV. The two we've mentioned here are QFD (Quality Function Deployment) and the Design Scorecard. These two tools more than any others reflect the multi-dimensionality of the challenge. Of course there are other new tools and those supporting DMAIC are still of value. We'll mention benchmarking here – this has a place in DMAIC projects, but is less commonly used for smaller scale incremental improvements. It is much more central here in design – outputs from benchmarking are key inputs into QFD analysis.

However, benchmarking and design methods are not the focus in this book and the reader can find excellent texts readily available elsewhere. In *Lean Six Sigma for Dummies* we describe Quality Function Deployment.

From a leader's perspective, it is important that you are aware that Lean Six Sigma is not just about DMAIC and process improvement but that there is also a well established (although far less well-known) design method, which will become increasingly important as you deploy the approach more widely in your organisation.

13

Lean Six Sigma and Agile Digital Transformation

IN WRITING THIS book we are very grateful for the contributions and support from a number of our colleagues and clients. In discussing digital transformation, it was clear that Derek Kennedy who is Visiting Professor, Ulster University Business School and Programme Transformation Director, Strategic Investment Board, Northern Ireland, not only has a great deal of unique experience and expertise in this subject area, but was very willing to contribute to this subject. We agree very much with his thinking here, which is just a little controversial!

Discovery ... Alpha ... Beta ... Sigma

Let's for a moment consider a mythical business that is currently expanding its operations and is in the process of building a new office block to facilitate its future growth. This is both an exciting and risky time in the life of an organisation as it expands to capture additional market share. The investment in the new office accommodation is considerable and in the tens of millions, representing a significant investment on behalf of the organisation's board. Shareholders will demand the investment make the expected returns.

During the life of the construction project a new opportunity arises in the market that, given initial assessments, suggests that the organisation will require 700 additional square metres in the new facility to realise the opportunity. The organisation concurrently has just restructured its product development team and the accommodation requirements of that team have also changed. Hence, they issue a client change notice as quickly as possible to the contractor who is nearing completion of the building superstructure to prevent additional costs associated with change.

Now, let's consider the impact of changing the fundamental design of the building once construction has commenced. This would result in changes that could affect the foundations already in place, areas directly adjacent to the planned change, and impact on the quality of the final product as the change was retrospectively incorporated into the existing fabric of the construction project not inherently designed into the project from the outset.

It will certainly increase the cost and time for completion of the asset. Calculated properly the cost would also incorporate the opportunity cost incurred to the organisation as a result of the asset coming online late. The change, assuming it was absolutely necessary and fundamental to the effective running of the organisation, we accept as a costly yet nearly unavoidable aspect of the delivery of an effective asset to facilitate the efficient operation of the business.

For obvious reasons the contractor never asks: what is the root cause of the change? Are you sure this change represents the best option available? We assume the board has asked these fundamental questions and, given the information it had at hand, has satisfied itself that the change is indeed a requirement of the business. The nature of business often elicits behaviours that increase the likelihood of profit or revenue being realised, and our supply chain arrangements, unless the most dynamic and mature, normally result in simple transactional and predictable responses from our supply chain partners.

But what if you were in a position to know that the change was not required at all and you could still realise the opportunity and restructure the business unit?

The reality is that most information technology projects or digital transformations face the exact same scenario as outlined above, and as stated we accept change as a costly yet nearly unavoidable aspect of the delivery of an effective digital transformation. The need for fast decisions based on the current information at hand to realise an opportunity or prevent a risk from being realised drives our decisions in digital transformation projects. Particularly when we are using the Agile methodology. After all, the methodology and very term 'agile' conjures up images of athleticism, rugby, Usain Bolt, and this is a digital transformation project … not the Olympic Games. All this and the roaring demands of a Scrum captain who requires a decision for the next sprint.

The methodology boasts and demands speed. After all, it is one of the unique selling points associated with this development methodology and assists us in realising usable product fast. But too often we do not understand the true cost of speed. The lack of a tangible superstructure coming out of the ground in the form of steel and concrete that requires significant resource and effort to change once in place, often leads us to believe that the cost of change in a digital project is somehow less, at least conceptually. This is not the case; and recent IT projects within the UK public sector have demonstrated the consequences and cost of not understanding business models and the processes that the transformation will support, with the costs of ill-thought-out changes reaching staggering amounts – into hundreds of millions of pounds. John Kotter in his book *Accelerate* offers an excellent approach as to how to structure your approach and organisation to deal with change with agility whilst clearly understanding the stakes involved. He highlights the challenges the situation illustrated above presents us with when he states,

> And that is the rub. With speed low enough and predictability high enough, certain methods work just fine in organizations. But these methods cannot possibly work when speed goes up and predictability goes down. It becomes a different game.

How do we increase predictability while operating at high speed? How do make sure we are playing the right game?

Digitisation … Discovery and Definition

As we move deeper into the digital age we could be tempted to think that simply digitising our processes into automated workflows will revolutionise our businesses. If we are not careful we could effectively be digitally encoding the inefficiencies and negative aspects of our existing culture into a very expensive digital solution. How do we avoid putting garbage into the new digital solutions and ensure a return on the significant investment of digital transformation?

Typically, an organisation will spend from 6–12 months considering its options for the best fitted digital solution. Thinking during this period focuses on the fit between our processes and 'Commercial Off The Shelf' solutions (COTS), or bespoke solutions built with the Agile methodology, and how to procure and engage with the market to extract the best value out of the process. However, too little thought is given to *what* we are actually transforming. Are we simply digitising existing processes and expecting transformative results? Have we really fundamentally examined our business models and their interrelation with our processes to ensure that our value proposition is improved by the investment of the digital transformation?

Sadly, all too often, we rely on the efficiency that digital automation brings in its potential to save resource – be it head count to save money, or speed to save time. Very often we fail to reflect upon the heart of our business models and, most importantly, our customers and how they are impacted by our processes. As a result, we potentially miss a huge opportunity to recoup not just the return on investment from the digital transformation but we miss the opportunity potentially to add to our value proposition and increase our effectiveness or profitability.

The public sector in particular is under extreme pressure to ensure that its operations are as fast and efficient as possible, as we would all expect from our public services. However, when we start to look deeper into public sector organisations we see years of organic systems development where policy and processes have developed over decades that are often built to prevent a rare event from ever happening again. A single event in the distant past, just within corporate memory, when a disaster happened. Interestingly, often no one can quite remember what exactly the disaster was. Regardless, it has resulted in the development and instant implementation of a belt and braces, fail-safe process to prevent a similar incident from happening again. Over the years many layers have been added to the system triggered by various different serious incidents. What we can observe is that we have added layer upon layer of seemingly protective measures to our systems and processes. This phenomenon is not just restricted to the public sector; many large, established private sector organisations can testify to this within their own businesses. In effect, we have built a system based on managing exceptions, and fooled ourselves into thinking that we have done it for the benefit of customers or taxpayers. In truth, we have done it to prevent future embarrassment to the establishment, and the value to customers or taxpayers is of little consideration in the organic development of our system and processes.

Enter the digital transformation … How do we peel away the layers of the proverbial onion or unravel years of protective organic systems development while maintaining business as usual whilst ensuring that the processes are actually lean? How do we make sure that, like Cortés, we effectively burn the ships and not digitise the old world into the new world?

Organisations will want to be confident that the outputs of the digital transformation will realise the benefits and the return on investment that is expected. Ironically Sigma represents a value or measure of confidence in a statistical conclusion. The complexity of the environments that businesses and public sector organisations operate in is increasing exponentially. In the face of uncertainty, Lean Six Sigma can bring real confidence in the certainty or predictability of the conclusion or the return on investment. By applying the appropriate tools and measurements during the discovery phase of an Agile project within a digital transformation, we can start to bring clarity and confidence to the outcomes we are aiming to achieve. The two methodologies are effectively evolving, to create a new species of continuous improvement tool. An exciting time indeed.

Define and Discovery

While neither Lean Six Sigma nor the Agile methodology can slow or stop time, the methodologies when combined offer organisations the opportunity to increase the predictability of the outcomes desired by a digital transformation. By introducing DMAIC in micro bursts during a discovery or pre-discovery you bring a degree of assurance that the processes you are proposing to turn into product have at the very least been sense checked.

Let's assume an organisation has reached a certain degree of maturity in the use and deployment of Lean Six Sigma (i.e. has qualified staff and runs successful projects) and is now undergoing a digital transformation using the Agile methodology. During the development of user stories in the Agile methodology, we examine the low-level process maps. At this point we introduce a DMAIC micro burst, and health check the process. In a very short time (hours not days), we evaluate the process from the customer perspective. Have there been customer issues with this process? If so, can we identify what they are? Does this process fit within the strategic vision of the organisation and does it aid or hinder the objectives of the digital transformation? We evaluate the process for waste using tools such as TIM WOODS, and understand the root causes of waste. We evaluate the data from the process and quickly validate the root causes and make the necessary changes to the process, and that is it, we stop.

Now we know what the Lean Six Sigma purists are saying at this time: 'You have not had a control period to evaluate whether the improvements have indeed worked!!' 'Do you even know if the process is in control?' 'What if you have destroyed our business by the changes you have made?'

Relax, we have assumed that the organisation has reached a degree of maturity, hence our data and knowledge of our processes brings a degree of assurance. But let's assume for a minute that there was an issue with the process improvement. We simply run all the evaluated processes through a control phase and evaluate the real implications through the scrutiny of hard data at a 'control tollgate'. We have then effectively introduced quality management into the design of the digital transformation by introducing a critical stop point into the Agile methodology. We agree with our Agile partners a time within the Alpha phase of the digital transformation, for us to run a tollgate on all the processes. If processes require further change you can now do so, at no additional cost. From there you can adjust the user stories and workflows prior to development work commencing.

Benefits Realisation

The added benefit to the evolution of these two methodologies is that we will, as a result of the micro burst DMAIC, have data sets allowing us to measure the benefits of the digital transformation, proving that we have indeed sped up processes, or saved money, and improved the customer experience and ultimately added to our value proposition. Most importantly proving to our shareholders and stakeholders that we will be providing a return on our investment.

This approach is also finding favour within public sector organisations, who by their very nature have to clearly demonstrate value for money for the investments they have made. By introducing micro burst DMAICs we can assist in preventing the waste of public money that has been seen in historic IT related projects within the public sector.

This means that we prevent the need for contractual change within the design of the digital solution; unlike the organisation building a new office, we have incorporated the change into the initial design, not appended it onto the system as a reaction to new information or opportunity. We have introduced more predictability while operating at speed, or a higher measure of confidence in a statistical outcome ... Sigma.

PART

III

Involving Everyone in Lean Six Sigma

14

Learning and Development – The HR Perspective

SPOTTED IN THE office of an HR professional, a sign saying, 'Have you hugged an HR professional today?'*

Lean Six Sigma has the potential to impact on all aspects of an organisation – it's not just about making ad hoc improvements to processes in isolation. Therefore, joining up with the organisation's HR team is necessary – though hugging is optional and clearly depends on what is written into the organisation's policy handbook!

The Belt System

There are several aspects of Lean Six Sigma that are relevant to the HR sphere. First of all, let's tackle this business of 'belts', certification and training, and what this means from an HR perspective.

The use of belts to describe the hierarchy within Six Sigma originated in Motorola, and it was Mikel Harry who originally

---

*Please note that this workplace does not sanction or condone actual hugging.

described practitioners using the 'belt' convention applied in martial arts. If you're not particularly fond of it, you may wish to know that Harry initially described Six Sigma trained people as 'process characterisation experts' which you must admit is less appealing!

As in martial arts, different coloured belts are used to represent different levels of experience and achievement, from white up to black.

Whilst the system is subject to some variation, and some organisations use additional colours, an overview is presented below. It is perfectly normal to upgrade from one level to the next. Indeed we recommend this, particularly from Green Belt to Black Belt.

White – White Belt training provides an awareness of Lean Six Sigma, an introduction to the approach and, importantly, the principles. It aims to demystify it and tackle some of the jargon that Lean Six Sigma brings. Depending on the requirements of the organisation White Belt training can last from an hour up to a full day.

Yellow – Yellow Belt training takes up to two days. It uses the DMAIC approach as its structure and includes the vital few tools and techniques used in the majority of projects. Yellow Belts can also apply the learning to make small scale improvements within their business, areas running mini-DMAIC projects.

Green – Green Belt training can take between four and six days and covers more of the tools and techniques than Yellow Belt training. The focus is on applying Lean Six Sigma to lead and deliver an improvement project. Green Belts will typically be expected to spend between 10% and 25% of their work time on process improvement activities alongside their normal operational 'day' role.

Black – Black Belt training can take up to 20 days. It includes further tools and techniques and more focus on the use of statistical and analytical tools to measure and interpret the performance of processes. It also includes additional training on change management as this is fundamental to making process improvement successful. In some organisations, Black Belts work full time for two or three years on process improvement projects, tackling the more complex issues. In other organisations they take on the role as a part-time responsibility alongside their 'day job'. They also coach and mentor Green Belts.

Master Black Belts – Master Black Belts (MBBS) are a little different because this is more of a professional role seen as a full-time career option which a Black Belt might aspire to if they are particularly enamoured by the idea of becoming a 'professional change agent'. MBBs will have been Black Belts and have several years of practical experience. They attend further training depending on their situation. MBBs can coach Black Belts and carry out Lean Six Sigma training. They also carry out a strategic guiding role, working closely with the senior executives in large organisations on the deployment of Lean Six Sigma.

Organisations using Lean Six Sigma do not have to adopt the 'belt' terminology of course – some organisations have eschewed it, preferring instead to talk about their trained resources as guides, practitioners or champions. The 'belts' system is widely known and used however, and the knowledge and experience gained from learning about and applying Lean Six Sigma is highly transferrable. At the time of writing this chapter, an internet search for 'Black Belt jobs' for example brought up literally thousands of opportunities.

In addition to learning about and applying Lean Six Sigma there is the opportunity for people who have been trained to become certificated. It is subject to some variation among providers in the marketplace, but for a recognised, accredited certification (the BQF standard for example) for Yellow, Green and Black Belts there is typically a simple three step process to follow.

1. Complete the relevant training programme
2. Pass the exam
3. Present evidence of the application of Lean Six Sigma

Certification to Lean Six Sigma Master Black Belt takes a different route and is based on assessment of the experience of the applicant and their portfolio of evidence.

The benefits for the individual 'belt' include recognition, consolidation of the training experience, and the development of confidence and competence that the opportunity brings. For the organisation there are also numerous benefits – as well as being on the receiving end of the financial and operational benefits that process improvement brings, organisations can exploit the development and recognition opportunities and build on these as maturity increases. For leaders and the HR function, consideration can be given to the fit with existing approaches used for professional development. The same goes for recognition – certification to Yellow, Green or Black belt level is not mandatory, but it can provide appropriate recognition for the achievements of the individuals involved.

Making the Most of your Trained Practitioners

So now the organisation has a group of people with a strange names (belts), a different way of thinking about problems and working on improvements. What do you do with them, how do you manage them and how do you give them the best possible chance to apply their knowledge?

We've mentioned Jack Welch in another chapter of this book – how he embraced Six Sigma and put it to work across GE to overhaul operations and drive real quality. At GE under Jack Welch *all* employees were required to take a Six Sigma training programme and *all* were expected to put it into practice by delivering an improvement project within a designated timeframe. We are not proposing that *all* of your employees get involved to the same extent, but where they have been trained, putting the approach to use through practical application is a perfectly appropriate expectation. Note that involvement does not necessarily mean the initialisation of a project – there'll be a limit as to how many projects your organisation can support. But what about applying Lean Six Sigma using the rapid improvement approach? Or asking every person with an awareness of Lean Six Sigma to tackle a wombat (Waste of Money Brains and Time! – i.e. waste)?

It is worth noting, however, that many factors can impact on a practitioner's ability to apply Lean Six Sigma to deliver an improvement, and that some but not all of these are down to the individual practitioner. We have seen many such instances in our capacity as coaches and mentors to practitioners. Here is a list – but be aware this is not an exhaustive list.

Lack of a time and space to devote to process improvement work.
This is the number one reason we are given when progress is lacking. Yes, at times this can be down to the practitioner, their use of

time and how they choose to prioritise it. It can also be due to the focus and attention afforded by the project sponsor or champion and the practitioner's manager – if Lean Six Sigma work doesn't appear to be a priority for them why should it be a priority to anyone else? The willingness of a manager to allow the time is an important factor. In Chapter 16, The Manager's Perspective, we mention a manager who asks his practitioners to work on their projects 'in their own time', i.e. in the evenings and at weekends. This is not a suitable approach – process improvement, as we have seen, is a contact sport and requires the input of people who know the process, so it's not something that a person can do on their own at night. Neither would that approach be endorsed by an HR professional.

It's a new way of working, with new tools and a new methodology. Sometimes of course it's not completely new and different, and people might have adopted similar approaches or techniques before, but there are likely to be aspects of process improvement that the practitioners, and those working with them have not tried before. This can mean that things take longer than expected, as time is needed for planning and preparation, and if people are uncertain about things, we've seen that those are the things that are likely to be pushed down towards the bottom end of the to-do list.

There's no deadline in place. As much as some people love to hate them, deadlines do have a motivating effect on people; and, up to a point, an individual's motivation increases as the deadline approaches. (If you're interested in this, look up the Yerkes-Dodson Law – you never know, it could be the answer to a question on University Challenge one day!) If the practitioner has not developed a plan for him/herself or agreed a timeframe with the sponsor/champion, the motivation isn't as likely to increase as there's no 'end' to work to, and the work can take far longer to address and complete than it should.

There's a deadline in place! Alternatively, if the practitioner is overwhelmed or stressed out by the deadline, their productivity will also suffer. A fine balance here!

Unrealistic planning. If you loved learning about the Yerkes-Dodson Law (see above) you might also relish reading about the

Planning Fallacy – the thing which makes us prone to underestimating how long things will take to complete. Putting together a plan of action with dates against key deliverables is a good habit for Lean Six Sigma practitioners to get into – and it provides managers and sponsors (as well as coaches!) with the means to understand if plans and expectations are actually realistic, as well as on track.

This piece of work is no longer a priority. Something to watch out for and something that can be identified and discussed with sponsors/champions (and underlines the importance of the sponsor's role). Has something changed? Now we know a bit more about the problem is it as significant as was initially believed?

The availability of data. Getting the data required to understand the aspects of process performance that we need to know about can take time, as it may require the development of a new measurement approach and the manual collection of data. The Measure phase of a project generally takes the most time to complete.

Other people unreceptive. We've seen how daunting new ways of working can be to practitioners. This is also the case for those they'll need to work with – people might be hesitant if they've heard that the approach uses lots of jargon, statistics and uncomfortable brainstorming exercises for example (not that it does!) and this might be the reason they decline a meeting invitation or answer as 'tentative'. They might also be fearful about bringing data and measurement information to the table if they're unsure about how it's going to be used or if it paints a picture of poor performance.

Fortunately, there are remedies for all of these reasons, and these can be influenced from the HR sphere.

Coaching

Coaching for Lean Six Sigma practitioners, their managers, their sponsors and their team members can be extremely beneficial and can impact positively on progress, on learning, on development and on confidence. Your organisation may already use coaching as a means to support its managers and its people, or this may be something completely new, but it definitely has an impact when it's done at the right time and in the right way.

Some organisations who already have 'seasoned' Lean Six Sigma practitioners who are experienced in coaching can draw upon them to support those more recently trained. Engaging an external coach can also be considered.

Equipping Sponsors/Champions and Setting Appropriate Objectives

In Chapter 17, The Practitioner's Perspective, you will see what is required from sponsors in supporting Lean Six sigma projects. From an HR perspective this means that, like practitioners, sponsors/champions themselves will also need to be afforded the support to get this work done.

The responsibilities that leaders have with regards to improvement and to supporting members of the organisation who contribute should be duly reflected in their objectives. If objectives are geared entirely around day-to-day operations then these aspects will take priority at the expense of improvement and development activity associated with Lean Six Sigma. Achievements will not be recognised and the appropriate discussions will not take place in performance reviews. Where leaders and managers are sponsoring practitioners and supporting activities outside of their functional areas there's a risk that this gets missed in performance reviews. A re-focusing away from an entirely operational focus into a more strategic sphere can overcome these risks. Experts within the HR function can help to ensure this focus is reflected within their systems and approaches for setting objectives and reviewing performance.

Making Progress Visible

There are a number of ways to share information on the progress being achieved. These range from inclusion of Lean Six Sigma measures or metrics within the organisation's performance measurement system to visual displays within organisations, etc.

The object is to demystify the work and make involvement desirable, rather than put people under the microscope and make them feel under pressure.

Awareness and Involvement

As we've seen, demystifying Lean Six Sigma and introducing people gently to the subject can have a beneficial impact. Those involved in improvement activities will be more receptive and less fearful; and those with ideas and opportunities for things to be improved will know that there is a route for tackling them. Awareness sessions that we have run in organisations often generate volunteers who want to support activities and have great enthusiasm for doing so.

The 'pitch' and focus of awareness raising communications need to be carefully considered however. If your organisation has an internal communications function it could be advantageous to draw on their expertise here.

Including some information about Lean Six Sigma and how it's used could also be included in the organisation's induction training approach, so that new employees can understand more about the organisational culture and attitude to improvement, the methods used and the way that they can contribute within their new role.

There are some 'do's and 'don't's to consider, as shown in Table 14.1.

In Chapter 16, The Manager's Perspective, we look at the challenges associated with nominating and involving people in Lean Six Sigma activities, and the opportunity to identify people with the potential to thrive. HR experts in the organisation can support managers in this as part of the 'talent management' approach to ensure consistency and the best possible outcomes. They can also recognise that Lean Six Sigma can provide a clear development route to those that have been recognised as the organisation's top talent. Recognising high potential employees and maintaining their motivation and engagement contributes directly to the effectiveness of the organisation.

As we have seen in this chapter the potential investment in developing individuals to become Lean Six Sigma practitioners is high. We have also seen that the benefits this can bring to the organisation will

Table 14.1   The 'Do's and 'Don't's of Lean Six Sigma Awareness

Don't	Do
Use too much jargon	Use the language your organisation already uses, to show how Lean Six Sigma fits in with what you already do
Go into too much detail	Keep a pragmatic focus. It's not an academic exercise
Raise expectations too high	Position Lean Six Sigma as an ongoing approach rather than a one-off
Say '*your* process is so bad that we have to do Lean Six Sigma'!	Encourage people to challenge current ways of working and consider what customers need from processes
Position Lean Six Sigma as just another initiative	Show how Lean Six Sigma can support the delivery of the organisation's goals, not present a whole load of additional ones
Let the consultants run the show	Listen to guidance and the voice of experience, but be clear about the messages you want to share and about what works well in your organisation when communicating
Leave others to get on with it	Attend awareness sessions, or top and tail them to show your support. Your presence sends a powerful message and so does a lack of presence
Let the dust settle afterwards	Follow up with action and share the results and impact of that action in a timely manner
Just do it once	Take all opportunities to reinforce key messages and make it 'part of working here'

outweigh the investment with sound leadership. We still hear from time to time concerns about retaining the trained Lean Six Sigma talent, 'What if we train them and they go?'. And the answer to this question is a more eloquent version of, 'What if you don't train them and they stay?' Richard Branson expressed it more articulately when he said (and in fact tweeted), 'Train people well enough so they can leave, treat them well enough so they don't want to.'

15

The Employee's Perspective

LEAN SIX SIGMA brings with it some jargon and, FYI, plenty of acronyms. One to get to grips with when considering the view of the employee is BOHICA. It stands for 'bend over here it comes again' and was a phrase used by US armed forces in the Vietnam War, when an unfavourable situation was about to be repeated and compliance was deemed the most judicious course of action. It is among a number of potential reactions when an organisation starts to use Lean Six Sigma!

The voice of the employee is one of several voices that should be heeded by leaders. In fact, the same voices might also represent the voice of the customer if you consider that the people in the organisation are customers of the Lean Six Sigma approach. The importance of involving people in continuous improvement and equipping them to do so has already been looked at from several perspectives – this chapter addresses how employees might react to Lean Six Sigma. It takes a broad view and does not attempt to analyse and explain human behaviour – there are plenty of other books on that subject. There is no panacea, but some approaches that could be considered by leaders to support effective responses are also outlined.

It is important to note that responding in a way that is not 100% positive to the news that the organisation is about to begin a new programme, initiative or way of working does not mean that the individual is a negative person. We are complex creatures. Indeed, when Jack Welch (chairman and CEO of General Electric between 1981 and 2001) first came across Six Sigma he was wary about it, and had a deep dislike of fads and 'flavour of the month' quality initiatives. Initially cautious, he became a convert and can now be described as a poster boy for Six Sigma. This is not intended pejoratively – during his tenure at GE its financial value increased by 4000%.

You'll see some representations of the bell-shaped curve elsewhere in this book. In many situations data follows this distribution; in fact it is described as 'normal' distribution. When measuring things like the heights of people, blood pressure readings, the sizes of snowflakes or exam results, the data will fall into this pattern. In fact, asking people to arrange themselves by height is something we often do in training courses. When we do this, most delegates are bunched up in the middle, as normally most of the people are of 'around average' or average height. There are smaller numbers of taller people and shorter people, and these form the edges. There are sometimes some 'extremes', though there are even fewer of these. (The authors of this book are generally standing at the extreme ends of the line when we do this exercise together!)

When data is normally distributed, the 'likelihood' of data points falling where they do is easy to understand and predict. About 68% of the data points (or 68% of the training delegates we ask to line up) will be in the middle, and some 15% will be at either end. It would probably be the same if we asked people to line up to illustrate their responses to changes, such as the use of Lean Six Sigma to improve ways of working. (This is something we don't do in training courses!) It might look like the picture in Figure 15.1. It's good to know who the innovators and early adopters are as these people can help build critical mass for acceptance. It's also important to look at late adopters and resisters and address concerns and questions clearly and honestly.

Note that the shape of the curve can change in environments where there are lots of initiatives and changes. A 'skewed' curve could develop, with few innovators and early adopters and a larger tail of resisters.

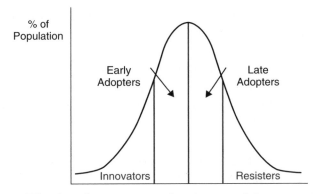

Figure 15.1 The distribution curve showing people's responses to change

The responses are shaped by many factors (personal, environmental, etc.). Those outlined below do not represent an exhaustive list, but have been defined from research with our clients and colleagues and from our own experiences of working with people in organisations and *being* people in organisations. It is necessary to understand these to be able to plan and communicate effectively about Lean Six Sigma, so let's have a look.

'BOHICA' or Initiative Fatigue

Change is constant in work and in life. While this latest new way of working represents an innovation, it's worth noting that a number of others may already be underway and in the pipeline, each requiring time, effort and emotional energy. 'No man is an island' wrote John Donne, and neither is an organisational initiative. No wonder then that people are talking more and more about initiative fatigue and its impact.

If people feel this way about Lean Six Sigma, these questions or comments could emerge:

- Last time we tried something like this … (it failed to live up to expectations/it was frustrating/it fizzled out, etc.).
- Another new framework is being adopted, how many more will there be?
- How does this fit in with the other things going on?

- I hope it doesn't impact on me/my team/my department, we're too busy to get involved in anything else.
- More consultants nosing about!
- How much money is being spent on this?
- If I keep my head down long enough it will all blow over.
- Why did the business 'choose' to do this now when there is so much we 'have' to do?

If, as already seen, people's time, resource and emotional effort are already being exerted to the max in other areas, there will be little left to apply here.

Anxiety

Some of the responses from those feeling anxious or apprehensive are captured here:

- Is this because they think I can't do this on my own?
- Aren't I/we good enough?
- Things in the process aren't all perfect – will I be judged on this?
- Who will all the findings be fed back to?
- What's the driver here? Is there a financial imperative?
- Will I have to change role?
- Will I lose resource when the benefits have been reckoned? Am I at risk?
- What's wrong with the current way of doing things?

The focus that Lean Six Sigma puts on data and measurement, the close examination of processes and the use of words like 'waste' and 'non-value-add' can be extremely off-putting (and even, inadvertently, insulting) to people who work in the areas where it is being applied. It can be described as 'ugly baby syndrome'. When people work hard to develop their way of doing something it becomes, in a way, their 'baby'. This brings with it the feelings of a parent – being caring, nurturing and protective. Imagine the feeling when someone comes along and says your baby could be better. Ouch.

Words like 'efficiency' can also drive fearful responses, if people think that headcount reductions and organisational restructuring will result from the work being done to improve processes.

Excitement

Some may respond with excitement and enthusiasm.

- I'd really like to get involved
- Who gets picked to support this activity? Why not me?
- It's a great opportunity to learn and progress is my role/career
- This will solve ALL my problems at once!
- How will they decide the areas of focus? Let's look at the 'X' process first!
- I can get a qualification to put on my CV

Such responses are a real positive, but they also need to be managed, to ensure that expectations are realistic and the enthusiasm can be maintained. People who respond in these ways are likely to be 'early adopters'.

Disillusionment and Switching Off

When people experience what is more like 'fatigue' than 'initiative fatigue' they may comment as follows:

- It'll take ages for me to get all the data they need
- How will I get the bandwidth to support this?
- I can't see this working
- I see that Brenda's involved. I don't like or trust her
- People who don't understand the work will be crawling all over it. No thanks!
- I'm too tired for this

This happens when energy is low, and the reactions may be manifested in absenteeism, demotivation or transfer requests. Raising the energy level to allow people to become participants rather than 'victims' is necessary and requires focus on managing change.

So, What do People Need from Leaders?

Or actually, if we're honest, we're talking first about what leaders need from people.

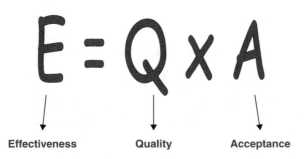

Figure 15.2   George Eckes's 'formula'

Leaders can address the responses outlined above in several ways, but address them they must in order to build Acceptance for new ways of working within the organisation.

Why the capital A for Acceptance? Acceptance with a capital A is a critical component of the invaluable formula for managing change developed by George Eckes, $E = Q \times A$ (see Figure 15.2). In the formula E represents the Effectiveness of the implementation; Q represents the Quality of the solution; and A, of course, represents the level of Acceptance of the solution.

The formula highlights how an ideal solution may have been identified, but that its effectiveness will depend on how well it is accepted.

To illustrate this, let's imagine a scenario where a good quality solution is implemented that has the potential to impact positively on performance. This is common – we place lots of importance on high quality solutions, it's what project teams generally do best. If you like, you could award this solution with a score from 1 to 10, with 10 being the highest possible score and 1 being the lowest. We'll score it 8 for Quality. But let's now imagine that in this scenario, little attention was paid to gaining acceptance, so we'll score it as 2 out of 10. The Effectiveness rating that results ($E = Q \times A$) is 16, because $8 \times 2 = 16$. Considering what a great solution it was, this can hardly be considered as effective. What a waste! And it had real potential too! We have seen this happen, and we've also seen how leaders respond. 'That didn't deliver the expected benefits', leaders will say to project leads, 'go back and enhance the solution. That way we'll get the results we expected!' But, alas, even if we get to a 9 out of 10 for Quality, unless we do something to increase the Acceptance score, we'll still only get a grand total of 18 for Effectiveness.

The issue is that if the project team are focused completely on the 'technical' quality of the solution – as they may think they should be – they will be 'blind' to considering what is needed to gain acceptance. In fact they may believe that 'this is not my job'!

What leaders need to know is that it's the Acceptance that needs to be worked on. A team could have a truly amazing solution, but if no one buys into it, it will never deliver the results deserved. Project leads also need to know that it's okay to ask for leaders to support them in increasing Acceptance. This way, with a 9 for Quality and, say, a 7 for Acceptance, the score for Effectiveness increases to 63. A dramatic difference.

The 'standing only' experiment at Holborn Tube Station provides a real-life example. Users of the London Underground will know that when using the escalators at Tube stations, the convention is that people wishing to stand still and ride the escalator do so on the right-hand side and those wishing to walk up or down do so on the left-hand side. (If you're not a regular user of the Tube and you don't know this convention – someone will soon tell you!)

In 2015 an experiment was run whereby the station's 'up' escalators became standing only, with the aim of reducing congestion and improving the flow of people through the station. This seems counter-intuitive, but filling up the escalator with people standing on both sides at the busiest parts of the day meant that queues were reduced and as many as 30% more customers could get on. The experiment was repeated in 2016 in order to understand which type of message, signage and information was most beneficial in changing Tube users' behaviour. So technically this was a good solution but why hasn't the 'standing only' convention been implemented definitively at Holborn, and why haven't all other stations adopted it? Yes, it's down to the 'A' – a lack of Acceptance. People refused to stand still. Talk about voting with your feet!

Acceptance can take several forms and there are a number of definitions. Acceptance can mean the action of taking something that is offered. It also means agreement with, or belief in, an idea or an explanation. Another definition might be the willingness to tolerate a difficult situation.

Understanding how people in the organisation will respond to Lean Six Sigma (or any change, for that matter) is necessary as it allows leaders to plan and make decisions on how it is to be introduced. This takes time and effort but, as highlighted by Eckes, Acceptance is vital to effectiveness. Now let's look at what leaders can do to build it, and get back to what employees need from leaders.

Listen

We talk about a lot of 'voices' that should be heard using the Lean Six Sigma approach, the voice of the customer, the voice of the process, the voice of the business, the voice of the employee – it really is a listening approach. We're not talking about an annual staff satisfaction survey here, we're talking about eliciting true, timely, actionable information from the organisation's people that can be used to shape the way things are done. Going to the Gemba is a great way to start to do this, as we saw in Chapter 8.

Are you a good listener? It takes practice! Some tips for good listening are as follows.

- Use 'open' questions to promote discovery and stimulate thinking, they can get people talking ('I'd be interested in hearing more about ... ').
- Use 'follow up' questions to gain further understanding ('In what ways could this impact the team?').
- Use clarifying questions to make sure you're clear ('What you're saying is ... ').
- Closed questions can help you to check facts quickly, but they're less helpful for trying to get a conversation going ('Do you measure this?').
- Listen actively – try to quieten your mind by putting aside other matters or concerns.
- Don't interrupt or be tempted to finish someone's sentences.
- Try to control the environment if possible, for example by removing physical barriers and stopping interruptions.
- Listen carefully to what's being said. Focus on the speaker, shut out your thoughts and reactions, and give the speaker your full, unbiased attention.

- Use some positive non-verbal signals such as nodding, smiling, an interested facial expression and eye contact.
- Use positive verbal signals ('ah ha', 'that's interesting').
- Don't be afraid of pauses, these are natural and allow time to absorb and reflect. Resist the need to fill them. Don't hurry the speaker.

Respond

Planning how new ways of working (or other changes) are to be introduced requires time and careful consideration. Can the questions, comments and concerns outlined at the beginning of this chapter be addressed clearly? What's the best way to go about it? Are there any key words or phrases that people respond well to and are there any to avoid at all costs?

A structured approach to communication is recommended. 'One swallow does not a summer make' – and one email does not an effective communication make!

Honest, simple communication is required but it's not always easy. In fact, 'genius is the ability to reduce the complicated to the simple', according the oft quoted CW Ceran.

David Kusnet, former speechwriter to Bill Clinton, points out that Abraham Lincoln's Gettysburg Address took only two minutes and 246 words, most of them one or two syllables. The speaker before Lincoln spoke for two hours and used 13,607 words. Simplicity makes for memorable messages!

And we're not just talking about communication, we're talking about influencing too.

The three Greeks provide a useful reference point when it comes to effective influencing. They are *ethos*, *pathos* and *logos*, and they represent three standpoints to be used to maximise the impact of communication. We can thank Aristotle for this model.

- Ethos is concerned with guiding beliefs and ideals (think 'ethics'). This brings authority and credibility to the communication. Why should someone listen to you? What qualifies you as an expert in this area?

- Pathos represents an appeal to the emotions. Can an emotional response be evoked? Why would people care about this?
- Logos denotes logic, reason and analysis. What are the facts and what is the logic? This is the Greek that we tend to use the most (without knowing it!) as it helps us to reason.

Using all of the Greeks is key. Only deploying one or two of the triumvirate can undermine credibility. Imagine for example listening to a renowned expert in the field of Lean Six Sigma tell you all about it. They are undoubtedly well qualified to talk on this subject and they also have data galore to demonstrate the impact and benefits of the approach, in measurable terms. But sadly … they are also extremely dull and uninspiring! What a shame. It's hard to connect and engage from the heart. This speaker forgot about *pathos*.

Now imagine hearing about Lean Six Sigma from a wonderfully engrossing individual. This person has brought the subject to life in a way that is very real to you. You are feeling Lean Six Sigma! This person also has lots of data and information, but … did we mention he is nine years old? He hasn't got a 'belt' or any experience on the subject. Yes you like him, but can you trust him? How credible is this? You get the picture.

There's an 'order' of deployment to consider in addition. Listen out next time you hear someone present a case for something in your organisation or deliver a communication. They'll probably start with *logos*. But why should you care about that? Always start with *ethos* to establish trust, then *pathos* to engage the heart, followed by *logos* to engage the mind. Thanks Aristotle!

Join Everything Up

Using Lean Six Sigma to lead is a theme of this book – and we've seen how effective Lean Six Sigma can be to support the attainment of an organisation's plans and strategies.

The Forcefield diagram can provide a useful technique not only for identifying the 'forces' for and against change but also for understanding the context of a change or new way of working that is being planned or implemented. It can help to capture what else is happening, and whether these projects, schemes and initiatives will

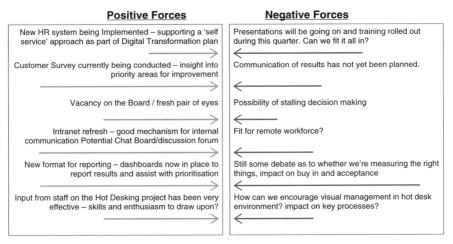

Figure 15.3 Forcefield Analysis

provide positive drive to support change, or negative forces that will present a barrier to it.

A Forcefield Analysis begins with a brainstorm of the factors working for and against a change. The example in Figure 15.3 is for an organisation beginning to use Lean Six Sigma among a number of other initiatives. Positive forces, things that could support the use of Lean Six Sigma are captured on the left-hand side. Negative forces, things that could hinder it, are captured on the right-hand side. The 'strength' of the forces is then determined. Sometimes a score is used here, or sometimes different sized arrows are used to represent the strength of the force (the longer the arrow, the stronger the force).

As Isaac Newton taught us, 'for every force, there is an equal and opposite force' and this is true in a Forcefield Analysis. A positive force often has a negative opposing force, as shown in Figure 15.3. Discussing and agreeing what can be done to build on positive forces and maximise their potential, and reduce or remove the negative forces comes next.

Manage the Change

Managing change effectively increases the chances of success. This is true no matter what the change, or how experienced you are in that area. It is equally true when using Lean Six Sigma and you will identify it as a theme in the case studies and stories from leaders in Part IV of this book.

Understanding the key elements involved in managing change are essential. The Elements of Change model originally based on work by John Kotter but adapted for Lean Six Sigma projects, outlined in Figure 15.4, supports a considered and effective approach and provides guidance on how to address the requirements.

Let's look at these elements in turn.

The first step is to *establish the need for change*. Without this, people will give little importance to the change, and why should they? They can't see the need. It is essential to communicate this need clearly – note that communication is at the centre of the Elements of Change model as it applies to every element.

Building stakeholder engagement is the next consideration. As we have seen, it is vital to involve and engage people as early as possible in the delivery of a change (or the improvement of a process) to build Acceptance. Having established the need, communication and influencing becomes easier.

Developing the vision and the plan is vital. If there's a clear need for change but no roadmap for delivering it, people can become anxious and frustrated. The forward plan should include all of the

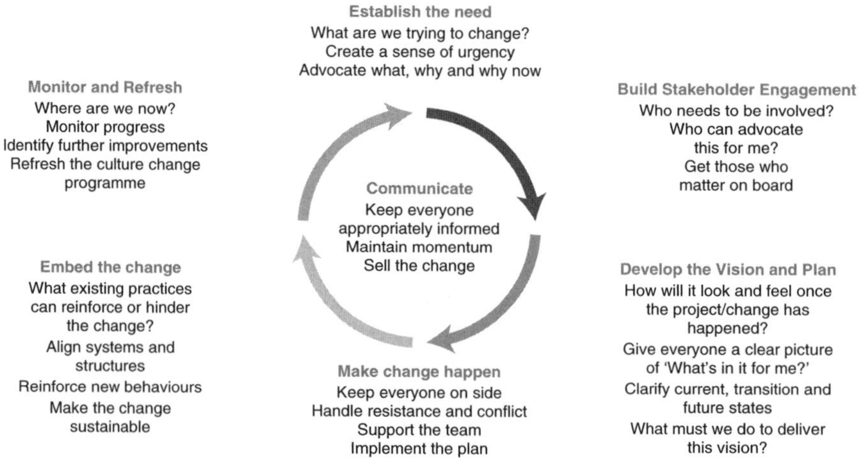

Establish the need
What are we trying to change?
Create a sense of urgency
Advocate what, why and why now

Monitor and Refresh
Where are we now?
Monitor progress
Identify further improvements
Refresh the culture change
programme

Build Stakeholder Engagement
Who needs to be involved?
Who can advocate
this for me?
Get those who
matter on board

Communicate
Keep everyone
appropriately informed
Maintain momentum
Sell the change

Embed the change
What existing practices
can reinforce or hinder
the change?
Align systems and
structures
Reinforce new behaviours
Make the change
sustainable

Make change happen
Keep everyone on side
Handle resistance and conflict
Support the team
Implement the plan

Develop the Vision and Plan
How will it look and feel once
the project/change has
happened?
Give everyone a clear picture
of 'What's in it for me?'
Clarify current, transition and
future states
What must we do to deliver
this vision?

Figure 15.4   The Elements of Change

steps necessary to achieve the vision – this is about knowing where you're going and how you're going to get there. Essential!

Then of course the change should happen, and the approaches outlined in Part I of this book could be used to support the delivery of the change.

And it doesn't end here. If you've already read about the control phase of a DMAIC project you will know how important this is. Some people call this the stickiness of change! The 'new way' needs to become *the* way, so building new approaches into the organisation's management system is key. It's also important to note that nothing is cast in concrete – monitoring the implementation and integration of the change should be undertaken and steps taken to refresh and continuously improve things as necessary. And so the circle starts again! As Winston Churchill wrote, 'To improve is to change; to be perfect is to change often.'

So as change is interwoven into the core of organisations ('Change is inevitable, except from a vending machine!' – Robert C Gallagher) change management is an intrinsic part of the leader's role.

16

The Manager's Perspective

MANAGERS PLAY A significant role when organisations use Lean Six Sigma but their needs are often overlooked, with the primary focus given to the requirements of leadership team members and practitioners. Often unflatteringly referred to as the 'meat in the sandwich', managers must support the layer above them, manage and motivate the layer below, and must bridge the gap in between. This chapter considers the manager's perspective, looks at the importance of their contribution and suggests how they can be engaged and equipped to make the essential connections between those leading the programme and those impacted by it.

Managers have the responsibility for directly managing the people *and* the processes within a particular function of an organisation. Both of these, as we've already seen, are critical aspects of Lean Six Sigma's scope – hence the need to consider managers as a unique group within the organisation with considerable 'skin in the game'.

On the people side they:

- Manage the team(s) of people that execute business processes
- Act as an advocate and role model for ways of working within an organisation (e.g. 5s, visual management)

- Recruit team members
- Train and support team members
- Communicate team, department and organisational goals
- Appraise and feed back to team members about performance
- Engage with managers and leaders across the organisation
- Provide people resources for process improvement activities

And on the process side they:

- Report process performance
- Are responsible for ensuring process collateral is up to date
- Support process improvements
- Address the findings of audits as appropriate
- Are the first escalation point for decisions
- Identify the need for corrective actions
- Ensure quality standards are met

Information and Understanding

Many items on these lists are impacted by, and can impact on, the use of Lean Six Sigma – therefore it's vital that managers are equipped with information, understanding, capability and capacity to allow them to do this positively. They are likely to be the first point of contact when their people have questions or queries about the approach, its application, and its impact on them and their team or department. Managers therefore require *more* information and more *specific* information about Lean Six Sigma than that which is cascaded universally.

The principles of Lean Six Sigma have been described in terms of 'Every Day Operational Excellence' in this book – this is not just the domain of leaders but of anyone with influence within the organisation. Managers as well as leaders must bring these to life through behaviours and actions to influence the way others in the organisation experience and perceive Lean Six Sigma.

One manager we talked to recalled a past continuous improvement programme that was launched in his organisation. The same messages were shared with everyone in the organisation by way of a 'town hall' style presentation (and the programme leaders no doubt felt that they were doing a comprehensive job). After the presentation, several questions were raised by the manager's team about their potential involvement, impact on resources within the team, and the possible overlap with a systems project that was being run in parallel. The manager had no further information to provide to the team and had not had time to digest the messages for himself or consider the answers to the questions. He referred to the programme leaders for information, but felt disenfranchised from the programme and consequently cautious and unenthusiastic about what it was doing.

Managers won't require the same detailed and practical knowledge of Lean Six Sigma that practitioners will, but an understanding of the language, methodology and approach, as well as the principles, allows managers to translate Lean Six Sigma into real life, business-as-usual activity for their people and address questions in a timely manner. This has the effect of keeping the focus on, in between the activities of the programme, town hall meetings and whole company communications.

It also builds consistency and continuity within the organisation – managers can support their team members by encouraging them to find the root causes of problems for example rather than jumping to conclusions, and can promote the importance of customer needs. After all, people in teams may not have the opportunity to engage directly with the leadership team or practitioners on a day-to-day basis, but they will do so with their managers.

Providing Practitioner Resources

Where resources are required to support process improvement activities, leaders and practitioners will look to managers to provide them. We've seen that Lean Six Sigma is definitely a 'contact sport' and that involvement and engagement of people is key to shaping and embedding new ways of working. This clearly provides an opportunity for managers and those involved but it also presents a challenge, as resource is not necessarily available.

Think about it for a moment. Who are the go-to people within your organisation? Imagine you require a key piece of data to answer a question on financial performance, or need an IT fix asap, or need to know the status of a client relationship. Who would you ask? The chances are you have identified one of a small number of people within the

192 INVOLVING EVERYONE IN LEAN SIX SIGMA

organisation with subject matter expertise who are known as the people who get things done. These people (who may very well be managers themselves) are generally well known within the organisation, and as well as being *your* go-to people they're also *the* go-to people because their effectiveness is recognised by others. But it's probably quite likely that the go-to people are already involved in a number of projects, programmes and activities, as well as being such a valuable asset in their day job. So, are these the right people to involve in Lean Six Sigma activity? The adage goes, 'if you want something done ask a busy person'. However, there is a limit to what can be achieved by a mortal, and managers must face the challenge of determining who to call upon to get the best result both for the programme and for their own team or department.

Managers should consider looking beyond the 'usual suspects' in their selection of supporting resources, to allow others an opportunity for involvement. This could come from unlikely places, but we have seen lots of instances where people have thrived when they've been given the chance to shine. Remember the note that was made by a casting director at MGM when he first met Fred Astaire? 'Can't act. Can't sing. Slightly bald. Not handsome. Can dance a little.'

Involvement presents a great professional and personal development opportunity. Knowledge of the way things work now, and the ability to work collaboratively with others to challenge this and shape an improved alternative should be among the selection criteria.

Note that the people selected, as well as the projects selected, make a big impact on the likelihood of success. In our experience of working with many organisations in many different sectors we have undoubtedly seen people flourish given the right opportunities. We have also seen, but thankfully rarely, instances where the wrong people have been put forward, because the boss doesn't know what else to do with them. The term 'special project' is sometimes used. Let us state firmly here, 'Lean Six Sigma is not a special project' and funny as the Monty Python scene might be, it is not an opportunity to 'bring out your dead'.

Let's look at the characteristics of a good Lean Six Sigma contributor now:

- Knowledge of the current process – what works well and what doesn't work well
- Honesty about what's working and what's not

- The ability to work with others
- Able to have an open mind and let go of preconceived ideas
- Willing to try new ways of working
- Keen to learn and adopt new tools and techniques to support process improvement
- Able to translate some new theories and concepts into real life
- Able to influence others
- Able to contribute the time

Those involved need to be afforded the time to undertake the work required. One manager we came across nominated some resources but instructed them that they must undertake the work out of hours, causing considerable stress and a detrimental impact on the progress of the improvement project.

Managers will also have the opportunity to put new skills to work within the team and should be encouraged to provide a forum for those involved to share information and practice approaches, tools and techniques with their team members.

Adopting New Ways of Working

Managers also have a crucial part to play 'when the rubber hits the road' and new improved processes are implemented. They must understand the changes, the reasons for the changes and be ready to encourage team members to adopt them.

It's likely that they'll also need to adopt new ways of monitoring process performance, and this may put aspects of the process that haven't been measured before under the spotlight. This can represent additional work, if the things being monitored are new additions to the existing suite of team, department or process measures. It may also mean the adoption of new monitoring methods (e.g. use of control charts) to display performance results. Managers will be required to interpret these and take actions on the findings as appropriate.

Following the launch of an improved process, managers should be on the lookout for:

- Impact on team members
- The use of process documentation and standards

- Impact on stakeholders
- What performance looks like now
- Realisation of benefits
- Unforeseen effects (unexpected benefits, unexpected drawbacks and perverse results or 'back fires')

Realising the Benefits

Whilst managers clearly have a significant role to play and important responsibilities to fulfil, let's also remember that managers will benefit from business problems being solved, from processes being improved and from work being made easier.

For example, as a result of removing non-value-adding steps, people in the process team (the process operators) are freed up to focus on other steps that *add value*, e.g. there are fewer administrative steps to complete so more quality time can now be spent on building relationships with customers.

However, benefits can fall short of their full potential if managers aren't clear on how team members are now spending their time. The time saved could easily be absorbed by other non-value-adding steps in another suboptimal process. Parkinson's law states that work expands to fill the time available. He was right!

Managers should be ready to account for the savings made by improvement activities, otherwise can we really say that a saving has been made? Encouraging those who benefit from time saved to use that time (or at least some of that time) to explore and deliver further improvement opportunities is a way to maximise the value of the savings made.

Feeding the Pipeline

Focusing on a process almost always results in the identification of further improvement opportunities. Managers should be feeding the pipeline continuously with further opportunities and considering how their people who have been 'exposed' to Lean Six Sigma can be involved further in improvement work.

Managers can also support smaller scale improvement activities in their 'local' area (sometimes called local Kaizen). This requires an ongoing, everyday focus on improvements, at workstation level or team level – like 'just do it', but using a considered approach to support the doing. Sometimes small changes are enough to make a big difference. Trusting those that know the processes, products or services, empowering people to make changes, delivering small improvements and doing lots of them is key.

Management's job is to convey leadership's message in a compelling and inspiring way. Not just in meetings, but also by example.
Jeffrey Gitomer (US author and business trainer)

17

The Practitioner's Perspective

THERE IS A fantastic quote by Jim Lovell that reads, 'There are people who make things happen, there are people who watch things happen, and there are people who wonder what happened. To be successful you need to be a person who makes things happen.' Jim should know, he was the commander of the *Apollo 13* mission which was recovered safely in 1970, and one of only 24 people who has been to the moon.

Successful Lean Six Sigma deployments require people to make things happen – practitioners.

Practitioners in a Lean Six Sigma deployment are those who bring the principles, approach and toolkit to life. Activities undertaken by practitioners might include: delivering improvement projects or running rapid improvement events; providing coaching, training and support to others; managing a 'pipeline' of potential improvement projects or opportunities; guiding the selection of projects; communicating about Lean Six Sigma activities and results.

These individuals have an important part to play. Not only because of the importance of the activities they are undertaking but because their work (as well as the input from leaders) helps to 'position' Lean Six Sigma within the organisation and influence perceptions. Is Lean Six Sigma seen as important to the success of your organisation, division or department? Are others inspired to get involved?

Clearly then, the support and infrastructures that leaders provide to practitioners are vital. The sections below set out the needs of practitioners in detail, and focus on how leaders can address them.

An 'Infrastructure' to Support Lean Six Sigma

Infrastructure refers to the structures, systems and approaches in place to support a Lean Six Sigma deployment. In some organisations these may already exist, and in others some development may be required, to give the deployment the best chances of success and allow practitioners to make things happen.

1. Executive Sponsorship

If the full potential of Lean Six Sigma is to be realised, and if practitioners are to succeed, executive sponsorship should be established and should be effective. This requires those who lead the organisation, department or division to make clear exactly how Lean Six Sigma will be used to contribute towards the attainment of key objectives and the delivery of plans – thus aligning the approach to the organisation's strategy.

Providing active and public support is also required. Executive sponsors are required to communicate the importance of Lean Six Sigma through their words and also through their actions, for example, by getting involved in reviews and in recognition events. Personal communication by leaders, and their open support for Lean Six Sigma is hugely influential. When the alignment is in place, and when leaders are personally seen to champion Lean Six Sigma, it is far easier for practitioners to gain the input they need from others in the organisation to make things happen.

Imagine, for example, a practitioner asking other members of the organisation to spare the time to attend a project workshop or contribute to a rapid improvement event (and not only to attend it, but to prepare for it in advance and deliver on the actions raised). If they don't regard it as significant, if it is not seen to be important to leaders, and there are no perceived benefits of participating, the practitioner is unlikely to get the support and input they need.

If, on the other hand, it is clear how the improvement activities contribute towards delivering what is important to the organisation, and if leaders are actively interested, the input required from within the organisation is easier to come by. Indeed, an invitation to get involved may become desirable and prestigious!

In addition to providing strategic alignment and establishing direction, the executive sponsor should ensure the budget and resources are in place and agree the scope for Lean Six Sigma.

2. Project Sponsorship

In addition to executive sponsorship for Lean Six Sigma at a 'programme' or 'deployment' level, it is strongly recommended that each individual project or improvement activity undertaken within the programme is sponsored or championed as well.

The project sponsor should have a level of authority within the organisation that is equal to, or bigger than, the scope of the project or improvement being undertaken. This allows for the effective decision making and clearing of roadblocks that practitioners will require.

Clearly defining the role and responsibilities of the sponsor or champion is important so that practitioners know, and others know, what can be expected. It also provides a means for monitoring and appraising performance. Responsibilities of the sponsor may include:

- Providing strategic direction for the project team
- Developing and agreeing the improvement charter for an improvement project and ensuring that the scope is stretching but manageable
- Keeping informed of progress and taking an active role in reviews
- Helping the team overcome roadblocks
- Facilitating the identification of resources as needed
- Keeping the team focused on the desired results
- Spreading the message

- Sharing information with others, e.g. leadership team members, steering committees etc.
- Ensuring appropriate reward and recognition for practitioners and their teams
- Providing budget/resources
- Being prepared to stop a project if it is necessary

In some projects, a situation could arise in which it may seem appropriate to appoint more than one sponsor, for example if the process that is being improved cuts across the organisational structure and includes two departments (e.g. the marketing department and the sales department) and there are two 'heads of department' involved. Joint sponsorship may seem in theory to be a fair solution, allowing equal importance to each role holder. However, this approach can be problematic in practice, particularly when it comes to decision making. Are both sponsors in agreement? Who has the final say? Practitioners or project leads managing two or more sponsors can find that decisions are hard to achieve, delayed or avoided. Clearly defining who is going to decide what, and how they are going to decide, is crucial. Agreeing a sole sponsor is advised.

3. Tollgate Reviews

Carrying out a tollgate review at the end of each DMAIC phase of an improvement project is important to take stock of progress and ensure activities are on track.

Listed in Table 17.1 a to e are the deliverables of each project phase, to make clear what can be expected, and a list of questions that sponsors can ask. In addition to those listed, there are some 'basics' which can be asked at tollgate reviews, or at other points, to support open and value adding discussion, e.g. how are things going? Are things on course? What has been learnt so far? What's going well and why? How can I help?

4. Suitable Projects and Improvement Opportunities

Crucial to practitioners' success is the selection of appropriate projects and improvement opportunities. You might be surprised to read in a

Table 17.1(a)   A Sponsor's Guide to Tollgate Reviews

Define Phase Deliverables	Key Questions for Project Sponsors
■ A draft improvement charter that includes a business case, a problem statement, a goal statement, the project scope, milestones and roles and responsibilities ■ The CTQs ■ A SIPOC diagram, providing a high level map of the process ■ A stakeholder analysis ■ An understanding of the risks to the project ■ A communications plan ■ A storyboard	■ What is the purpose of this project? What are we trying to do? What prompted it? ■ How will customers be affected by the successful completion of this project? ■ How will we know if things improve? ■ Does everyone know their roles and responsibilities? ■ What data or information is missing? ■ Have you started the storyboard?

(b)

Measure Phase Deliverables	Key Questions for Project Sponsors
■ Confirmed CTQs ■ Current state process map, value stream map or deployment flow chart ■ Agreed output (Y) measures ■ Identified in-process and input measures (Xs) ■ Agreed data collection plan ■ Baseline measure of performance possibly using process sigma ■ Updated improvement charter, storyboard and communications plan	■ Has a process stapling exercise been carried out? Has what really happens in the process been identified? ■ Are there any non-value-added activities? ■ Where in the process do the symptoms of the problem appear? And when? ■ Are the measures showing any of the Tim Woods wastes? ■ Who is involved? Who isn't involved? Who else needs to be? ■ Have the improvement charter and storyboard been updated?

(continued)

Table 17.1(c)   (*continued*)

Analyse Phase Deliverables	Key Questions for Project Sponsors
■ Identified waste and non-value-added steps ■ Understanding of process flow, and identification of bottlenecks ■ Identification of possible causes ■ Validation of root causes ■ Updated improvement charter, storyboard and communications plan	■ What are the possible causes of the symptoms of the problem? ■ What are the possible deeper causes? (keep asking 'why?') ■ How can these possible causes be verified? What measurement data is needed? ■ How has the data been presented? What is it showing? ■ Can all the root causes be addressed? ■ Who needs to be working on the project now?

(d)

Improve Phase Deliverables	Key Questions for Project Sponsors
■ A number of potential solutions that genuinely address the problem ■ A 'future state' process map, value stream map or deployment flow chart ■ Pilot experiments conducted and evaluated ■ Outline cost benefit analysis ■ Evidence of a systematic solution selection process using e.g. a priority based matrix ■ Documented rationale that the solution selected will address the root cause ■ Updated improvement charter, storyboard and communications plan	■ What are the possible solutions? ■ How did you generate these ideas? ■ Which possible solutions seem to best address the root cause(s) identified? ■ What are the advantages and disadvantages of these? ■ Which of the possible solutions is the most effective in meeting our selection criteria? And is it viable in terms of cost benefit? ■ How did the results compare to what you expected? ■ Which tools did you use in making your selection? And how did you choose the selection criteria? ■ The solution may appear to be the best option, but is it good enough? Can it be improved?

Table 17.1(d)   (*continued*)

Improve Phase Deliverables	Key Questions for Project Sponsors
■ Where appropriate, a more comprehensive pilot that helps confirm the suitability of the proposed solution ■ An agreed implementation plan ■ Evidence that the team has tried to error-proof the implementation by building in prevention	■ Are we sure we have the right team membership? Do we need to involve anyone else in the project? ■ What's the implementation plan? And who needs to approve it? ■ How will the plan be communicated? Has everyone who needs to know the changes been informed? ■ Are the handover responsibilities clear and agreed? How will the results be measured?

(e)

Control Phase Deliverables	Key Questions for Project Sponsors
■ A control plan showing the new process map, key measures, and actions depending on the results ■ Statistical data that the new process is 'in control' ■ Evidence that the solution has been integrated into day-to-day work ■ Evidence of process management in place, including an agreed process map, a clear customer focussed objective reflecting the CTQs, an agreed data collection plan with an appropriate balance of X and Y measures, a response plan ■ An updated improvement charter, communication plan and storyboard	■ Following any adjustments from the pilot, what is the new standard method, process, product or service? ■ How have the changes to the process documentation been standardised? Are there any implications for internal or external audit? ■ Have all the people who do this work been trained? ■ How will the measures you've put into place help you monitor ongoing results and prompt further improvement actions? ■ Has the handover process worked so that roles and responsibilities are clear?

(*continued*)

Table 17.1(e)　*(continued)*

Control Phase Deliverables	Key Questions for Project Sponsors
■ Key lessons learned identified ■ Recommendations or ideas about further improvement opportunities ■ A project storyboard ■ Evidence of success including actual costs and benefits or at the very least an estimate of when these will be available	■ How well do the results match expectations? ■ Was the cost benefit analysis accurate? ■ How well did the plan work? ■ Were there any unforeseen effects of the change, and what is their impact? ■ How can the solution be improved? ■ Have you identified opportunities for prevention? ■ What should be done in terms of recognition?

book about Lean Six Sigma that, in some circumstances, Lean Six Sigma is not the right approach for project delivery or getting some things things done!

Putting into service a new piece of equipment or phone system, building a bridge, or rolling out new modules of an IT solution are examples of 'classic' projects that are delivered using project management approaches such as PRINCE2. Such projects focus on implementing known solutions whilst Lean Six Sigma problem-solving projects start with a problem that doesn't have a known solution – this becomes clear when DMAIC is used! That's not to say that Lean Six Sigma can't be used for design and development of new products and services as mentioned in Chapter 12.

As we have seen, identifying issues that are aligned with the needs of the organisation is important. After all, if this piece of work doesn't help the organisation achieve the things that matter most, why should we bother?

That said, care should be taken to ensure the Lean Six Sigma projects are of a suitable size and scale, 'not too big to be manageable, but not too small to be meaningful'. It may be tempting to try to use Lean Six Sigma to address the organisation's big, ongoing problems when the programme is initiated, but trying to do too much will often result in failure to deliver. The saying goes, 'when eating an elephant take one bite at a time'. By the way we mean an elephant sized challenge – we love real elephants! Imagine presenting a practitioner with an elephant sized project, and consider what happens when someone bites off more than they can chew. The practitioner could easily feel overwhelmed or intimidated by the task, they could lose sight of what they are trying to achieve, unrealistic expectations may have been set, and the practitioner is unlikely to enjoy the experience or be left with an appetite for more. Breaking down elephant projects into manageable chunks is highly recommended. As a rough guide, projects should be achievable within 3 to 6 months.

Care should also be taken to ensure that the number of projects being undertaken at the same time is appropriate. The availability of resources needs to be considered, as well as the demand for leaders' time.

It makes good sense for leaders to be involved in selecting the first projects undertaken. Once the deployment is underway and a supporting infrastructure is established, a 'pipeline' of potential projects or opportunities can be developed. For the initial projects however, it is recommended that leaders work together to identify the process problems that are important to the organisation and its customers.

5. Importance Placed on Benefits

Placing importance on the benefits to be realised through Lean Six Sigma activities is a motivating factor for practitioners. If the improvements are being made in the right areas, and where their success contributes to the achievement of the organisation's goals and objectives, then the delivery of specific, quantified benefits is surely important. Leaders can support practitioners by being interested in what the benefits are, and when they will be delivered.

Benefits are identified, quantified and confirmed at specific points in the improvement project. In addition to tollgate reviews the Lean Six Sigma improvement journey includes three specific benefits reviews.

In the Analyse phase, the opportunity can be quantified when the current level of performance is understood with measured data, and waste has been identified. Leaders can support this activity by ascertaining the assumptions where the potential savings from eliminating waste have been identified. They can also support a review of the project goals. Is this opportunity too small, does it justify widening the scope of the project, or a phased approach?

The second review takes place at the end of the Improve phase, where the deliverables from the project can be confirmed, and there is confidence that the chosen solution will address the root cause of the problem. In this review, any costs associated with the solution and its implementation should also be confirmed.

The final review is a post implementation review. Were the costs and benefits as anticipated? Were there any unexpected benefits or costs?

Leaders should participate in these reviews so that they may provide direction and guidance, monitor progress and motivate practitioners.

6. Methods for Reporting and Monitoring Progress

In addition to holding tollgate reviews, establishing methods for reporting progress provides practitioners with a method for sharing updates, and sponsors and leaders with a way of keeping informed. 'What gets measured gets done' is an oft-used adage – what gets reported gets done is another general truth!

Progress updates need only to be brief and to the point – the sort of update that can be collated and consumed quickly, but succeeds in its dual purpose of keeping practitioners driven and keeping stakeholders up to date.

The 'Kipling Questions' (from Rudyard Kipling's *Just So Stories*) can be put to use in a number of situations in a Lean Six Sigma project or in general deployment. The poem goes,

> I keep six honest serving men
> (They taught me all I knew);
> Their names are What and Why and When
> And How and Where and Who!

Table 17.2   **Using the Six Serving Men (again), to report on progress**

What	What are the things we need to include in the report? E.g. overall progress, milestones and issues
Why	Why is this information important? (helps to filter out any less important content)
When	When will the reports be completed and submitted?
Where	Where will the templates be kept? Where will the completed reports be sent to?
How	How will these be submitted? How will they be reviewed?
Who	Who needs to provide the content and who will input the details? Who will they be sent to?

The questions can be used here to help determine the frequency and content of progress reports (Table 17.2).

Top tips for leaders monitoring progress:

- Don't ask for too much information.
- Accept bullet points as it helps to keep the reports brief.
- Make sure the structure and format of the report is easy on the eye and easy to read and digest.
- Beware of subjective RAG ratings relating to the 'health' of a project. Consideration could be given to developing some criteria to help practitioners determine whether their project status is Red, Amber or Green.
- Use the information! Progress reporting is not just an exercise in reporting – use the content to share information and shape discussions.
- If issues are being identified within the report, make sure that they are dealt with. Look out for issues that keep appearing on reports.
- Get used to using these methods for progress reporting and embed them within the deployment and maybe even elsewhere in the organisation.
- Review and refine the structure and contents when required.

7. Methods for Recognising Successes

Appropriate reward and recognition approaches motivate practitioners to perform, and they also communicate to others the importance of the

Table 17.3   Some 'Do's and 'Don't's for recognition and reward

'Do's

- Make the reward/recognition immediate, or it will lose its impact
- Make sure the reward/recognition reinforces the actions and behaviours that are important within the organisation
- Make the criteria for rewarding and recognising clear to everyone
- Specify why an individual or team is receiving reward or recognition
- Be consistent in the application of reward and recognition

'Don't's

- Don't underestimate the impact of a simple, personal thank you
- Don't allow recognition or reward activities to turn into an expectation
- Don't single out individuals. 'Employee of the Month' style approaches aren't effective when people perceive that it is someone's 'turn' to get recognition
- Don't forget to do it frequently and regularly

activities being undertaken. Leaders should consider how this can be applied within a Lean Six Sigma deployment to encourage those that make things happen, and also to reinforce the actions and behaviours that are desired across the organisation.

Reward and recognition can take several forms, and these aren't all related to financial gains or material rewards. Examples of reward and recognition activities include saying thank you in person, thank you letters or emails (with a copy in the practitioner's employee file), team breakfasts, messages in company newsletters, certificates, ice cream van visits and opportunities to attend conferences, seminars or networking events. Some do's and don'ts are listed in Table 17.3.

8. And Methods for Dealing With Lack of Progress

On the other side of the coin, dealing with a lack of progress is also important. This is something all leaders and managers must do at some point in their work, though it is sometimes missed from Lean Six Sigma deployments where leaders or managers may feel they don't know enough about the methodology being followed or the tools being used, and therefore steer clear of this aspect. Failing to deal with poor performance, and perceptions that those doing a mediocre job are getting the same treatment as those doing a good job, can be a significant cause of demotivation.

Progress reporting and the use of tollgate reviews provide the means to understand progress and identify performance issues, but these should promote action. As the saying goes, 'weighing the pig won't make it fatter', but acting on the information will.

Time and Space

'I need more time and space' is a common claim by Lean Six Sigma practitioners. While physicists and geniuses are working to define time, physics, the universe and our very existence, requesting that leaders make 'time' for Lean Six Sigma practitioners seems like a big ask! However, specifying exactly what practitioners need from leaders in this respect makes it easier for them to provide it.

There are guidelines as to how much time practitioners spend on Lean Six Sigma activities, for example that Green Belts will devote around 20% of their time to project work, and Black Belts will work full time on Lean Six Sigma. Leaders can support this by working with managers to ensure that practitioners are able to allocate their time appropriately, for example by reassigning responsibilities to others in the organisation. This could very well provide development opportunities to those affected, e.g. if a Black Belt has previously been responsible for managing and maintaining aspects of the organisation's quality management system, and this is taken over by another team member, and it could even be classed as a benefit arising from a Lean Six Sigma deployment.

In some organisations an employee's time is formally 'booked' against projects or activities. Where this approach is used it is essential that practitioners have a code against which to book the time they spend on Lean Six Sigma activity!

On a different point, it may also be appropriate to identify if practitioners are spending *too long* on particular activities and are overworking. In today's world it is possible to connect and communicate from anywhere and at any time, and working long hours (either to resolve critical issues, to address deadlines, because of a sense of duty or because they think it is expected) is a widespread phenomenon. As well as impacting negatively on health and wellbeing, overwork can result in a diminished output.

Resources

Leaders play a key part in ensuring that the resources required by practitioners are available and adequate. Resources include available team members, access to mentors or coaches, and tools for the job such as software licenses and space to work in.

9. Team Members

Involvement of people is a key Lean Six Sigma principle – working with people involved in the processes that are being improved and the stakeholders affected is crucial when it comes to building acceptance for change and the adoption of new ways of working. Practitioners will require these people to contribute to projects as team members or subject matter experts. Expecting them to work alone or even 'out of hours' to get things done is not an option.

The qualities of a good team member include being enthusiastic about the project being undertaken, being willing to apply DMAIC principles and use the appropriate tools and techniques, being honest about what's working in the process and what's not, and being an effective representative of the 'voice of the people'. A good project team member isn't just along for the ride, but contributes to the project.

Leaders can support practitioners by communicating the importance of involvement and participation and ensuring that managers can free up the appropriate team members.

10. Mentors or Coaches

As seen, a lot is required of practitioners, and where Lean Six Sigma is aligned with what is important for the organisation to achieve, much is placed on their shoulders. A coach or mentor can be a useful source of knowledge, encouragement or challenge for practitioners, helping with problem solving, understanding and applying certain techniques or tools and building confidence.

Whilst a leader may be highly effective in the role of executive sponsor or project sponsor, they may not be able to provide the 'technical' guidance that a professional would. For example, where a practitioner may be using data and statistical tools and techniques to analyse aspects of process performance and may require guidance on which statistical test to apply or how to interpret the results. Likewise, support may be required to determine if enough analysis has been done to identify the root causes of a problem, or if further investigation is needed (particularly where the organisation is looking for results!).

Coaching and mentoring can be arranged on an ad hoc basis or more regular interventions can be arranged. This could come from within or outside the organisation.

11. Space to Work, the Obeya Room and Support Tools

Involvement and engagement of people is a key principle of Lean Six Sigma and practitioners will require input and support from subject matter experts. Much of the work done to achieve the deliverables listed in the tollgate review section, in this chapter, will be undertaken using a 'workshop' approach – it can't be done by practitioners working alone. Having appropriate space to support this approach is therefore a requirement. It may sound obvious, but momentum can suffer if a practitioner is unable to find suitable available spaces for holding workshops and getting project work done.

If available, a meeting room dedicated to Lean Six Sigma can be set up, in the style of a 'War Room', or 'Mission Control' room. This can be used to display process maps, gantt charts, storyboards and progress reports, and hold project meetings, reviews and communication sessions. Anyone entering the room should be able to understand progress quickly and easily, which supports programme communication, and also provides a demonstration of visual management in action. Some organisations call this an Obeya room (Japanese for 'big room' or 'great room'), where individuals involved with the planning gather to achieve fastest communication and shortest decision-making processes. This also helps to remove barriers that may have been created over time; in a certain way Obeya can be understood as a team spirit empowerment tool at an administrative level. If it isn't possible to allocate physical space, creating an intranet page or shared drive for essential project information is recommended.

In a distributed work space environment over many sites, you can set up a virtual Obeya in the cloud, with shared folders, whiteboard space, regular webinars/online meetings, and online visual charts.

More down-to-earth practitioner tools for the job may be quite basic – including, for example, flip charts, brown paper and Post-it notes, and a smartphone with a camera is ideal for 'process stapling'. Don't forget the need for personal protective equipment – hi viz, safety boots, ear plugs which might be needed in some workplaces. Practitioners may also need access to, or licenses for, systems or software, such as Visio or Minitab.

Decision Making

At key points in a Lean Six Sigma project or in managing the programme, leaders are called upon to make decisions, including for example, determining which projects to undertake, establishing the scope and focus of projects and agreeing which solutions are to be implemented.

Understanding how decisions will be made, and who they'll be made by, is vitally important to practitioners, as this impacts on how they'll engage people within their project teams and how they will establish expectations with stakeholders.

For example, in the Improve phase of a project, a project team will identify a number of potential solutions, and will prioritise these. If a leader or project sponsor then vetoes these, and insists on making the decision about the solution to be implemented, the consequences could include disenfranchised and disgruntled project team members, solutions that don't properly address the root causes identified by the team, discrediting of the DMAIC methodology and wasted time.

Crucially, leaders or sponsors should act as the 'voice of the business' for practitioners and project teams, representing what matters to the organisation and its stakeholders. This should support the practitioner in understanding how the programme, project or improvement activity contributes to the achievement of the organisation's goals and objectives, but also keep them abreast of changes, challenges or opportunities that might arise over time.

Trust

> The only way to make a man trustworthy is to trust him; and the surest way to make him untrustworthy is to distrust him and show your distrust.
>
> **Henry L Stimson**

It is vital that leaders place trust in practitioners, and that they trust that the DMAIC approach will lead them to the root causes and the appropriate solutions. Starting a project with a problem and not a solution can be a big challenge for leaders who are used to people in the organisation looking to them for answers. In this respect some may find it necessary to increase their appetite for uncertainty. The good news is that 'managing by fact' is a key Lean Six Sigma principle. This means making decisions based on reliable, measured data, rather than on opinion, guess or gut feel, so uncertainty should not last beyond the first phase of the project! Leaders should support the use of evidence-based decision making (not decision-based evidence making!) to understand the causes of problems before solutions are identified.

Leaders can support practitioners in the Measure phase by understanding that the activity is important, but also helping them to avoid the trap of trying to measure too many things or measure for too long. It is also helpful for leaders to understand that project progress may not be as 'visible' during the data collection phase as it was in Define.

Focusing on the customer is another principle of Lean Six Sigma, and another aspect of the practitioner's work that requires trust. Delivering the best customer experience requires a clear understanding of their requirements and expectations and to achieve this it is necessary to listen to and understand the voice of the customer. Customers may be internal (e.g. other members of the team or department, or members of other teams or departments) or they may be external to the organisation (clients, consumers, service users, etc.). Leaders should allow practitioners access to process customers wherever this is possible, rather than encourage them to assume the requirements. This may require input from customer relationship managers or other personnel from the organisation and the client organisation, but is essential if an accurate, up-to-date understanding is to be achieved.

Visible, Public Support

The importance of visible support has been highlighted throughout this section of the book through a number of channels including:

- Using existing communication mechanisms, e.g. messages in the business briefing about progress and achievements, intranet, social media and newsletters.
- Using corridor conversations (leaders doing this so they can 'talk up' practitioners and their projects at every opportunity).
- Visual management – a place to post key information about the deployment, the approach, particular projects or even to share information on the performance of a particular process, in the form of control charts, etc.
- Recognition events.
- Being seen and heard but most importantly, being seen to listen.

PART

IV

Stories and Case Studies
from Leaders

No, no! The adventures first, explanations take such a dreadful time.
Lewis Caroll, *Alice's Adventures in Wonderland*

So, you could say we've gone about it back to front, but now we've explained it all (and we hope it hasn't been too dreadful), we'd like to share the details of some adventures in Lean Six Sigma!

We're privileged to work with some amazing leaders who've shared their stories with us, and have been incredibly honest about what's worked and what hasn't.

These are captured as 'stories from the front', and as interviews and as mini case studies, so you can hear the voice of experience directly and clearly. You'll see that leaders from a range of sectors have contributed, including a five-star hotel chain, a UK government department, one of the world's biggest banks, and the world's second largest contact lens manufacturer, demonstrating the applicability of the principles and approaches described in this book just about anywhere.

Kevin Barrett – CooperVision

Kevin Barrett is responsible for CooperVision manufacturing operations across Europe, including sites in the UK and Hungary, manufacturing contact lenses and lens care solutions.

Kevin talks about getting Lean Six Sigma started – being clear about the need and using the approach to support the delivery of key business outcomes. He outlines for us how infrastructures and frameworks were established to make Lean Six Sigma happen, and what the organisation did to gain acceptance for it. This included not calling it Lean Six Sigma. What's in a name?

Mike Baddeley – Ricoh

Mike is the Head of Innovation and Strategy at Ricoh UK, and is responsible for Business Excellence across Ricoh UK, leading teams to deliver Strategic Change and Transformation and Managing Continuous Improvement and best practice in Ricoh UK Quality Systems, including Health & Safety, Quality, Information Security Management and Business Continuity.

Mike's story focuses particularly on working with people in the organisation, on managing change and on providing people with the skills and support to take on Lean Six Sigma. He also considers what the future holds for his organisation and the validity of the approach in a changing world.

Derek Kennedy – Forensic Science Northern Ireland

Derek Kennedy's leadership is making a big impact in Northern Ireland. He is currently working on a programme to reduce the running costs of the Northern Ireland Central Government property estate. In his role at Forensic Science Northern Ireland (FSNI) he led a project to achieve a 10–15% increase in capacity and a 10% improvement in turnaround times.

Here he describes how FSNI applied Lean Six Sigma to improve the speed of forensic science activities by getting his ducks in a row and levering the culture of the organisation to get things done. He talks candidly about his successes, what he'd do differently with hindsight and what advice he'd pass to other leaders.

A range of shorter case studies have been provided in addition.

Aegon/Sky – Wayne Fisher

Barclays – Beau Ormrod

UK Government, Central Government Department – Lorraine Daly

Homes and Communities Agency – Mark Canning

5 star luxury hotel group – Business Transformation Project Manager

Vanderlande – Alec Gibert

If history were taught in the form of stories, it would never be forgotten.

Rudyard Kipling

The purpose of a storyteller is not to tell you how to think, but to give you questions to think upon.
Brandon Sanderson, American fantasy and science fiction writer, in The Way of Kings

To hell with facts! We need stories!
Ken Kesey, American novelist, essayist, and countercultural figure

Kevin Barrett, SVP, European Manufacturing, CooperVision

A Personal Perspective from the View of the Leader

CooperVision is one of the world's leading manufacturers of soft contact lenses sold in over 100 countries around the world. This case study takes the form of an interview.

Martin Lean Six Sigma, why did you start it? What prompted you to get going?

Kevin I think for me Lean Six Sigma has always been a toolkit that adds value. Throughout my career I've been involved with it and used it as an engineer, so for me it is an obvious tool to help us improve and develop the business. It was a natural progression to move into that really to move into that Continuous Improvement approach.

Martin You had discovered it quite a while ago?

Kevin Yes, I remember probably back in the late 70s early 80s doing SPC courses doing SPC courses and structured problem solving etc which then became parts of the Lean Six Sigma toolkit and the Toyota Way. I've probably been steeped in it all the way through my career really.

Martin And how did you get started?

Kevin   Moving into the leadership role in UK manufacturing, there
was a very clear need and I think that's one of the things I
would say to anybody: there really must be a clear need i.e.,
an imperative for improvement. That imperative will then
lead to a commitment for improvement. For us there was a
very clear need, as there were a couple of product lines at
least that were facing some challenges to perform at the
required level. They hadn't been designed well, especially
from the manufacturing process perspective, the lines hadn't
been designed for continuous 24/7 production needs. So,
there was a very clear need to improve and there wasn't
really an improvement structure or an improvement process
in place. To get things going we started with the senior
management and getting that team together and talking
about 'hey, we have a clear need to improve here, what
methodology, what approach are we going to take?' It was
pretty clear *what* we had to do, but what wasn't clear was
how we were going to do it? So that was the initial
discussion that I brought to the team; what approach are we
going to take in order to achieve some of these
improvements that we really need to achieve?

Martin   How did you get them to buy in to taking on this kind of
Lean Six Sigma approach?

Kevin   It was an interesting journey actually, we had a whole mix of
people, some who had never heard of it, some people who'd
tried it before and didn't have a good experience with it and
therefore didn't feel it was a good approach and then we had
other people who had used it and who were very
enthusiastic. It was a long discussion in the end, lasting
several months rather than weeks. We didn't just jump in
and all agree it was Six Sigma. In fact, in the end we didn't
even call it Six Sigma, we called it the CooperVision
Improvement Framework, although the basis was Lean Six
Sigma. We came to the conclusion 'what's in a name?' It
doesn't matter what you call the approach, it's whether you
commit to it and execute it. That was one of the quirky
things that I wasn't expecting when setting off on the
journey, that people would have issues with the name, but

there were clearly people who did and I wouldn't move it away from the senior team until we had agreed it, because without that commitment I felt it was going to fail.

Martin   And how would you describe the style of leadership that you were using there?

Kevin   It wasn't directive leadership in any way, I suppose I could have just mandated the approach in a very directive style by saying, 'we are going to do this, guys, we have no choice'. I was always very clear about the need to improve, but wanted much more of a collaborative discussion, trying to reach consensus around *how* we were going to approach and execute the strategy. And I guess that is the general style that we use a lot, our leadership style is to make clear to people *what* needs to be done but give them the space to determine how to do it. That is the style I generally adopt i.e., a very collaborative style for determining how we were going to approach this but pretty direct in terms of what we needed to do. We needed to improve, we absolutely had to get this product to a manufacturable level.

Martin   Once you'd agreed on the name, the CooperVision Improvement Framework, what happened next, what was the next step?

Kevin   We had a business improvement plan running by that time, based on a VMOST cascade model (Vision, Mission, Objectives, Strategy, Tactics), and we had a very clear picture of what things we had to do and we then married it to the CooperVision Improvement Framework which was the toolkit we then used to execute improvement activities. We were using the DMAIC approach, using Six Sigma Tools and other quality tools like Total Productive Maintenance as well which then led onto a full OEE (Overall Equipment Effectiveness) system implementation. Really starting to say to people 'OK, you know what you've got to do but you've got to do it in a very structured way' so we sold it to people as 'people often tell you what to do, but they don't very often tell you how to do it. We are going to tell you how to do it as well, we are going to teach you and train you how to do these things well. That is when we brought you guys in and started to invest in training the organisation, putting the first Green Belts in place and the first Black Belt training. We started reasonably small, we put quite a bit of money and commitment behind it but we were conscious that we didn't try to 'boil the ocean' all in one step. We started with a reasonably small number of activities and grew it from there.

Martin   What were the biggest barriers that you found on the way?

Kevin   I think the biggest barriers were: first of all there had been some attempts at Lean Six Sigma and Business Improvement Techniques at shopfloor level before I arrived. Something like 250 people had been trained in Business Improvement Techniques, however there was no framework to support it so when people came up with ideas or they wanted to improve things there was no framework to allow that and that had left a pretty bad legacy behind. People said, 'we've heard of all of this before' and 'we tried it and it didn't work' and 'we came up with improvements and they were never implemented so we are not going to do it again'. There was a sort of – I wouldn't even say it was inertia – there was a resistance because people just didn't want to go through all of that again. However, we fairly quickly got over that by demonstrating on a few successful projects that improvements could be done and we were taking it seriously this time. We also showed that we weren't just sheep dipping everybody through a training programme and expecting results, we were putting a framework and a structure in to back this up and sustain it. So, I think that was one of the things. I think there was an initial inertia in that people thought it will be a flavour of the month and it'll disappear; that we'll do all this work and we won't get supported. Again, we demonstrated that very clearly with the investments we made. Bringing the coaches in from your team, seeing it through and being very tenacious and consistent about the message 'we are very committed to this, we are going to do it'. And I think it is that initial, probably 6–12 months, where you have to do that and if you don't do that, that is where it will probably wobble and really get you into difficulties. There's a point at which it tips and it is pulling you rather than you pushing it. And while you are pushing it, you have to keep pushing it and, all of a sudden, it's like getting to the top of a hill and you start going down the other side. It's a strange feeling because you have been pushing it for so long and then all of a sudden, the weight goes away and people start pushing you for stuff and asking you for things and it's a very nice feeling but you won't get that without pushing it up the hill first.

Martin   You mentioned the need for a framework a couple of times, what kind of framework did you set up?

Kevin   You really need to think of the things that will be needed to support people; if they need money or if they need resources or they need expertise in order to achieve the improvement they are working on you have to back your words up with that money and you have to back up with your support and resources.

One of the problems, for instance, is if you train 250 people in Business Improvement Techniques, they are going to come up with say 3 ideas each. That gives you 750 ideas for improvement. To try and resource 750 ideas and to try and get the money behind that and to get the engineering support or whatever you need to do that is an impossible task, so you end up creating an impossible expectation. If you limit your ambition initially, to, say, 10 ideas, you can put the money behind it, you can put the commitment behind it and you can demonstrate then to people that yeah, the company is prepared to put the money where its mouth is and then all of a sudden things start to move; I call it organise for success rather than for failure. You need to put an infrastructure in where ideas can be logged, they can be understood and they can be prioritised. And be prepared to say to people, 'yes it is a great idea but we are just not going to do it now, it doesn't fit into the priorities, it doesn't fit in the scheme', or, 'we cannot resource it today'. This is because it is just as important to tell people what you are not going to do as well as what you are going to do, in order to keep that credibility of the system. So, you have to have the framework, you have to be able to capture ideas, you have to prioritise them, you have to be able to put resources behind the ones you are going to do so they have a chance for success. There is nothing more demotivating than coming up with a great idea, being told you can progress with it but then not being given any money or any resources or anything to back you up; it very quickly demotivates people. They'd rather hear 'great idea, but we are going to park it for now because we just can't resource it.'

Martin How much involvement did you have personally in the governance of it – the leadership of it – once you got it going?

Kevin Initially I was very heavily involved, people saw it as my idea and it was my passion and it really was! I think every leader is recognised for something they are passionate about and that they drive as their own personal agenda. It was my personal agenda, it was my passion so I was involved a lot. I was involved in all aspects of it, from the set up, to the financing, the review of progress, the visibility and celebrating success. I was there a lot but I wasn't there alone, I had all of the senior managers who were initially mandated to participate and support and review the progress, where they very quickly became converts and key leaders. Very soon, the reivews actually became part of our normal management process in our normal management cycle. We asked the question, 'how do you know you are on the right road?'. We said we'll know when we are there, when it is 'just what we do around here'. You talk to people and say, 'are we successful, yes or no?', 'are we improving? Do we use Six Sigma?' People say 'of course we do, what else would we do!' So over time, I think we have come very close to achieving that culture in a lot of areas. I wouldn't say that we are completely there, I'm not sure that you ever get completely there but it's when people say that's just the way we do it, there isn't another way.

Martin You can't be complacent, though, can you?

Kevin Oh no, it's like every system, it needs maintenance, it needs support, it needs energy and drive. So, we put a lot of that in there and what we see now is that it is more pulled from us than pushed by us. However, even then, if you don't support it or you take your eye off it, it'll start to deteriorate. So, you have to keep the momentum but it's great to see some of the progress now. If you see some of the OEE systems we've got now and inbuilt statistical process control – where the machine is monitoring itself effectively and sends us an email to say 'I think I'm out of control here, you'd better come and have a look.' It's incredibly powerful. But the other watchword I would say – and for me it was very important, is that it was a journey of many years – there are no quick fixes and no shortcuts. People see the shiny new OEE systems and the Lean Six Sigma tools and they think in a year's time we are going to be fantastic. It doesn't work like that, it's a long-term investment and it's a long-term commitment and I think most organisations get into it with the naivety that it can be done pretty quickly and it can't. They treat it like a project, 'we'll run this project for six months and then it will all be done and we're good'. It's not a project, it's a lifestyle.

Martin   What were the great successes as you look back on it?

Kevin   I think the great successes were, in terms of actual numbers the productivity improvements that we made, the performance improvements that we made. We turned ourselves from probably being a bit of a business liability to being one of the business's key strengths.

But the one underlying mantra in it all for me is, it is all about people' and we set ourselves this objective of developing confident and competent people across the whole organisation. I use 'competent and confident' because one word doesn't cover it and we've got competence everywhere in the business but competence without confidence is a bit like you get what you get, but the people don't improve because they don't have the confidence to try something different. If you have confident people who are not competent, and every organisation has a few of those, they are truly dangerous people. But if you've got confidence *and* competence across the organisation what you see is an organisation that believes in itself and drives for change and drives for improvement and I think that is the greatest success. When I walk around this organisation now I see a huge number of confident and competent people who are, every day, finding a way to do it better, finding a way to improve the business and it's the people side of it I think that you get the most satisfaction from. So, the 75% improvement in productivity, the 70% reduction in quality defects, all of those things I think are fantastic numbers but they were achieved by building a fantastic team, full of confident and competent people.

Martin   What would you do differently in hindsight, if you were to do anything differently?

Kevin   What would I do differently? It's hard to say really, I think like all journeys there are things along the way that you say, 'well, we could have done that differently, we could have done that better', but I think with any journey you sometimes have to go off track in order to learn. So, I think there are always ways I'd look back and say I could have done it more efficiently or done it with a different kind of spend but I don't really regret anything we did.

I think one of the mistakes we made was, at one point, we created a Continuous Improvement Department and we very quickly realised that what happened then was people devolved continuous improvement responsibility and accountability to the department and it suddenly wasn't their job any more to do continuous improvement because there was a Continuous Improvement Department who handled that. So, I think we ran with that for probably about six months and then we disbanded it realising that this is sending the wrong message. We needed people, if you like, who could be the champions and the catalysts for continuous improvement but actually calling it a Continuous Improvement Department proved to be the wrong thing because it sort of made it someone else's way of working rather than ours.

Martin   I guess you needed someone to coordinate it all for you and manage the kick off, didn't you?

Kevin   Yes, so we did appoint someone and he did a huge amount of great work at the start but actually by creating a department and giving him some resources and a department name actually took us backwards a little bit as well.

Martin   So starting it up was like a project, with an end, kick it off, get it started but run it from operations …

Kevin   … yes, this is 'just what we do around here'. I keep coming back to that, you know, it has to become just a lifestyle, it's the way we do things.

And it's interesting, the two additional factories that I take care of now obviously didn't go through the same journey, so we are working to give them support to get to the same level, and initially they would say. 'we'll never get to this point, there's Minitab in every presentation, there's facts everywhere, how in hell did you get to that?' Well you get to that by going through the journey and developing that confidence and competence in people so that they know the data does the talking. Very few decisions now made across the UK organisation are based purely on opinion, whereas in the two other factories they are still on the journey and still have some decisions made on opinion. The new factories hopefully can use what we learned in the UK plant to accelerate their progress.

So, I think, yeah, looking back we went down a couple of blind alleys, usually they were organisational rather than technical blind alleys. But I think having the vision in the end – that it's got to be embedded within everything we do in every person – became the right mantra to carry us through, and if we did go down a cul-de-sac then we would change it. But I think anybody that starts this journey has to expect that it's not going to be a straight road, you're going to take some wrong turns and you're going to get some of it wrong.

I'd say another important thing is when we got it wrong we held our hands up and said, 'you know what, sorry guys, we got this one wrong, we went down the wrong track'. And we did that right at the beginning with the Business Improvement Training (BIT), I stood up in front of the whole organisation and said, 'we've given a lot of you BIT training and we've got you all excited about being able to improve the business and I'm really sorry about that, it's going to be quite a while before we can use those skills'. I was very honest with people and I guess it is that openness, honesty – the clarity is what helps us to create the environment for this to be able to thrive.

Martin Would you say humility as well?

Kevin Oh yeah, I think we are quite a humble organisation. People give me feedback regularly and one of the words they use a lot about me is relentless. Relentless drive to change and relentless hunger to improve, and that for me is based on the fact that I am always convinced we are not good enough. We'll never be good enough. I guess that links to a humility that we'll never be at the end of the journey, its as simple as that. We have to be humble, we have to understand that we don't know everything, we don't understand everything and every day's a school day.

Martin You were clearly central to this whole thing and its success but one of the things I find is that senior executives get changed around quite frequently and sometimes you get good staff with a great advocate and then that person gets moved into a different role somewhere and ...

Kevin I agree, I agree absolutely! And that's why it was so important for me, that I wasn't going to introduce it to the organisation until the whole senior management team understood it, and was behind it, because you could then lose one and it would carry on. And it was very interesting, when I knew I was going to be moving on and I was working with my replacement, ready for him to take over my position, I talked to him about a lot of different things and one of them was about how we keep the continuous improvement momentum going. And he said 'well, nothing's going to change, it just isn't going to change. We just keep on that journey'. And he was so intrinsic to that journey that he just didn't see another way of doing it 'Yes, of course we'll carry on and do exactly what we have been doing'.

So, trying to understand that you need a champion, you need a person who is going to be the absolute leader of that and has the passion for it, but it can't be them on their own. You've got to build the rest of the team, build onto that. If they don't then you're exactly right, you take the leadership light out and the whole thing will flounder.

Martin   Any advice to give to other leaders?

Kevin   My advice is, be clear about the need, and if the need is not an imperative that you have to do it, don't start. If you don't feel that it's an absolute must to do it, you'll probably fail, so don't bother. But, if you really believe in it, and you say this is something we have to do, then realise it's a journey and set out on the journey.

We use a chart showing that we need to stabilise, then improve and breakthrough; don't try and improve and make breakthroughs before you're stable. You have to follow the recipe. It's like DMAIC, don't jump into Analyse if you haven't defined your problem, you have to follow the recipe.

Martin   Anything else?

Kevin   I would just say to everybody it's hugely rewarding. It's not just great for the business, it's great for the people and it's great for yourself to lead a team through that sort of development. It's our job and when you do your job and you do it well the rewards are immense.

Martin   I don't know whether you wrote notes before or whether you just had time to think about it but I have to say that was really superb. Thank you.

Kevin   Well I just jotted down a couple of things, I was just trying to pull my thoughts together but for me it's been a journey that I've quite clearly followed in my mind for ten years so I pretty much live and breathe this stuff. It's been a great journey.

Leading Change at Ricoh UK Limited – Mike Baddeley

Start with the Big Why ...

To lead real, embedded change in any organisation doesn't necessarily start with great leadership but it often starts with consciously recognising the reason for change, the '*Why* are we doing this?' Leadership personally for me, is merely understanding the big 'Why', creating a vision of the future desired state and making this into a reality by creating a movement of like-minded people across the organisation.

Change and leading change (and more importantly embedding change) has always been a challenge for large organisations and there's a very good reason for it, one which many leaders recognise. Simply put, 'we do not like change'. We (this advanced breed of monkeys on a minor planet of a very average star, in the words of Stephen Hawking) are hard wired and get comfort from doing the same things we've always done, in the same place at the same time.

I realised this very early in my Process Improvement career. Originally I came from a technical background, fixing electronic and mechanical equipment. This was simple, find the faulty component or parts that didn't work, replace, reassemble and 'hey presto' it all works.

As I embarked on my Process Improvement journey I assumed that processes are exactly the same as fixing machines. Simply understand what's happening, find the faulty or ineffective 'bit', fix it, reassemble and 'hey presto' it works ... This is where I was completely wrong.

The 'hey presto' moment didn't work, often perfectly designed process fixes had no effect, random things occurred or new solutions would magically appear which didn't work. The reason, as I'm sure you've guessed, is that processes include people and people are unpredictable. In fact I would say that they are the main factor in Process Improvement (or in fact any change project) success (or failure). As we are hard wired to resist change, when change is placed 'on us', we just continue to do what we've always done.

This is not because we want to sabotage or resist, it's often because we don't understand the need for change or are more concerned with the impact on ourselves rather than understanding the bigger picture. This is a critical (if not *the* critical) point for successful leadership in any change situation.

Leadership during change or transformation personally is about creating a vision, finding early champions or adopters, creating critical mass and embedding the change into the very fabric or culture of the organisation. This is only achievable if all those involved genuinely understand the big 'Why' and can invite more people into the new 'movement' as change gathers momentum.

Ricoh's Big Why

Ricoh, if you're not familiar with the organisation, was established in 1936 and provides document services, consulting, software and hardware to businesses around the world. From its early days in photocopier and printer manufacture to our current focus on bringing people, technology and processes together for business transformation, innovation has always been at the core of the business and it's one of our critical strengths.

Ricoh UK, specifically, had been on a tremendous change journey over a number of years, deploying a completely new system across its organisation, integration of a number of organisations through acquisitions. This occurred in this period of time where unprecedented change is occurring, particularly in the technology sector.

The deployment of new systems combined with integration of people, process, technology and space did mean that the business had become unnecessarily complex. Relating back to my previous point, people resist change and therefore during integrations it results in multiple ways of doing the same thing as each function carries on the way it's always done, often despite standardisation attempts.

Secondly, we had a new ERP (Enterprise Resource Planning) system, so effectively this is also added another way of doing things. Combine all this together and we have a massive opportunity to simplify our business, improve our processes and reduce duplication.

In tandem to this (and probably more importantly) the world is changing, our place in the technology industry is changing at an increasingly rapid rate and disruptive approaches and technology are constantly accelerating this.

Technology has literally transformed the world in the last 20 years. It has created more disruption than we have ever seen, given rise to a new breed of organisation (the Millennial equivalent at an organisational level), one which was born with technology, its products are virtual and its speed and agility unprecedented when compared with traditional legacy businesses with their inherited processes. The changing world of work, the digitisation of the office has fundamentally changed the landscape and this has driven the need to change across many businesses and marketplaces.

When you combined our situation at Ricoh – following the integrations of our acquisitions along with a rapidly changing marketplace and rapidly changing customer needs – this gives us a huge reason to change.

The core principles for our change are Agility, Efficiency, Adaptability, Innovation and Simplicity to prosper and grow in the technology space in this fast-moving world. You could argue that this is relevant in most marketplaces.

This was our big 'Why' and this is critical to driving change. It wasn't simply deploying and growing Lean Six Sigma because it works and it's the right thing to do. Our deployment was the start of a journey to change the organisation's culture. To create a culture not of continuous improvement, but a culture where we combined speed, adaptability and simplicity with innovation enabling us to prosper in this rapidly changing world.

The Practical Steps to Leading the Deployment

Lean Six Sigma was to become one of the foundations for our organisational change, a practical approach to solving many of our challenges and supporting increasingly faster and larger change across Ricoh.

As a leader responsible for embedding Lean Six Sigma (creating a culture where change and continuous improvement isn't the responsibility of a chosen few, but is part of everyone's role!), we had a vision and understood the big 'Why'; next was practically starting the change.

I have to say at this point: why Lean Six Sigma?

Lean Six Sigma has really had a mixed press recently when it comes to its effectiveness in making improvements, particularly the time taken for project completion and its place in an agile organisation.

It is important to recognise that, alone, Lean Six Sigma is not a magic wand, it cannot fix problems effortlessly and instantly without hard work. When it comes to leading change, I find it extremely helpful to deal with these perceptions head on and set expectations – which I'll go into in more detail later.

Lean Six Sigma is a tool set. Much like a workshop does not make a great carpenter, the Lean Six Sigma toolset won't make excellent Continuous Improvement professionals or deliver rapid change. This is where I believe the responsibility of the leader is to enable individuals, create teams supported by the organisation, which ultimately results in a movement towards a change culture. How we use the tools in the environment we create in organisations can deliver huge improvements, rapid change and tangible results. However, this is only possible with a clear strategy, hard work and leadership. Let me describe the practical steps we took in Ricoh.

When I reflect, driving the change across our organisation was split into six key sections, and I believe these were critical to our overall success in creating robust and sustained cultural transformation and the foundations for future (increasingly rapid and disruptive) change.

I would suggest these are the six key factors for leadership to a differing mindset, creating an agile continuous improvement culture.

The Six Steps

1. Getting 'real' buy-in
2. Selecting the core team
3. Creating the structure and development team
4. The tools and methodologies.
5. Leadership development and training
6. Integration and future developments

Personal Leadership Perspective – Derek Kennedy, Forensic Science, Northern Ireland

Derek Kennedy, former Transformation Director, Forensic Science, Northern Ireland (FSNI), now Visiting Professor, Ulster University Business School and Programme Transformation Director, Strategic Investment Board, Northern Ireland.

1. Why did you start it – what prompted you to get going?

Context

Society in Northern Ireland had normalised, and crime associated with the 'Troubles' had diminished. Crime trends are now more like those elsewhere in the UK with similar populations. Forensic Science Northern Ireland (FSNI) had to be both accurate (which it always was) but without the luxury of time (it always had as much as it wanted) in order to meet society's expectations and those of the NI criminal justice system (CJS). The judiciary were demanding that the speed of the forensic activities be improved as a justice system awaited results from forensic analysis that traditionally was afforded all the time it needed to get the results correct. The Police Service Northern Ireland working now under new budgetary pressure demanded that forensics be commercially competitive with the private forensic market elsewhere in the UK, effectively demanding value for money. The Department of Justice (DoJ) above all had to ensure that the confidence in the justice system was never compromised while working within a new budgetary environment that was never before imposed on Northern Ireland.

We had to address the urgent need to achieve results with the same or diminishing resources. In effect, we had to succeed with what we had or with less than we had (both money and people) and we needed a methodology that would protect the effective portions of our processes and not compromise on the quality of our science. You can imagine the paramount importance of maintaining quality during a period of reform in a forensic environment within a criminal justice system such as Northern Ireland. In short, change was urgently required as the people of Northern Ireland expected more, and the Exchequer expected us to do it with less.

2. Before you started what did you think/what previous experience had you had?

Before we started I avoided Lean Six Sigma like the plague. I had studied it during my post grad but promptly discarded it as something that would benefit manufacturing, not service or public sectors. I had a breadth of experience in continuous improvement activities and was certain that the appropriate tool for effective change would emerge naturally as I understood the organisation better. In regards to Lean Six Sigma, I wanted to discard it as an option ... but something niggled me about it. The reliance on data within the methodology sat well with me and the culture within the forensic environment. As much as I wanted to, I knew it might have a part to play. Then having been invited to go to the Netherlands national forensic lab to see how they approached a similar challenge I arrived to find them in the second year of their Lean Six Sigma journey, and the thing I wanted to dismiss became apparent as the correct tool for us as it was already proven to drive results in a forensic environment. With my own cognitive bias overcome, I realised it was 'hard to kick against the goad', and that

Lean Six Sigma was the perfect fit for FSNI. In fact, I was determined to use a methodology that fit best with the culture of the organisation and, to that end, I expended a considerable amount of time and effort to understand the culture to find that Lean Six Sigma sat perfectly as the right tool to produce sustainable results.

3. How did you get started?

Imagine a team of ducks who have lived their natural lives for the past 21 years on a river because the pond they enjoyed over 20 years ago was destroyed by a man-made disaster. Having been used to the consistency of the former pond they had been thrown into a new river, a new and strange environment. Daily they live their lives at any one time swimming against the current or indeed with it. Needless to say the effort required to just swim was considerable. Challenges around keeping the young ducklings safe, and teaching methods on how to survive on the river got passed down through the generations of ducks, all the time the memory of the old pond became talked about in legends and songs. How did I start? I wanted to know how the ducks functioned, thought and felt about their environment, what they believed was possible, did they fly and, if so, how far were they willing to go?

I got started by clearly understanding the culture of the organisation. One of our goals was to improve the culture in a real and meaningful way. If we were to improve the culture in FSNI then this had to, at the end of our journey, be tangible, visible and felt. My fear was that words like 'culture' are often (over)used in the workplace but never clearly defined, hence we defined culture. For the purposes of our transformation it was imperative that FSNI defined the existing culture in order to move towards a further improved state. For our purposes, we defined culture as noted by Edgar Schein, an accepted expert in organisational culture. He formally defined culture as:

> the pattern of shared basic assumptions that was learned by a group as it solved its problems of external adaptation and internal integration, that has worked well enough to be considered valid and, therefore, to be taught to new members as the correct way to perceive, think, and feel in relation to those problems

I had observed culture at the various levels within FSNI, and by assessing the cultural Artefacts, Espoused Beliefs and Values and Underlying Assumptions that existed within the organisation was able to better understand what improvement methodologies might be most effective. They were defined as follows.

Key Cultural Artefacts (the visible organisational structures and processes). Those discovered were:

- FSNI was located in a disused tobacco factory.
- FSNI is based in a very litigious and adversarial criminal justice system.

Espoused Beliefs and Values (the strategies, goals, philosophies and espoused justifications). This is in the context of the impact of the preceding 21 years after the lab was blown up and the staff were promised a new lab. In the meantime they carried out the highest standard of science from what was supposed to be a temporary solution (for 21 years after the Newtownbreda Bomb). They were:

- The belief existed that the environment that staff worked in was not important to senior management and a new lab was not a priority for them.
- The belief existed that stakeholders within the CJS were not able to move at the same pace of change as FSNI and as a result would become a barrier to change in FSNI.
- The CJS did not facilitate or want change.
- FSNI as an organisation believed it had to continually defend its position.

Underlying Assumptions (the unconscious, taken for granted beliefs, perceptions, thoughts and feelings of groups or individuals which form the source of their values and actions). These were that:

- The new lab would never happen.
- Change in general and changes in processes would be limited.
- Even if change did happen it would have a very limited impact.
- FSNI senior management and the DoJ did not care about the work environment or the quality of the science of the FSNI team.

So what does this have to do with Lean Six Sigma?

This meant that we were not simply forcing the organisation to adopt a new methodology, but rather we were developing a new way of working that best fit with the way they already operated, as well as working to reduce the impact of the negative aspects of the existing espoused beliefs and underlying assumptions by aligning the approach with the culture of FSNI.

Back to the ducks...

Effectively what I am saying is that scientists took to the data driven approach offered by Lean Six Sigma like ducks take to water. While I would not say it felt natural to them, I knew that if they could find a way to exert the same or less effort in an environment that was familiar to them, they might just see that ducks don't have to just live on a river ... there were other waters available to live on.

4. What were you trying to achieve?

Hard Deliverables:

- More for less (15% improvement in time and 10% reduction in costs)
- Culture change (tangible, visible and felt)

Soft Deliverables

- Less tired ducks

5. How did you go about it?

We started with the culture, then developed a change management strategy based on Kotter's 8 Steps (now using Kotter's XLR8). I ensured the change management strategy had real hard actions designed to start, sustain and maintain the changes (48 actions, to be exact, all with timescales, ownership and accountability assigned ... no easy feat in a public sector environment).

Then we needed to train ourselves in Lean Six Sigma ... we had to become the new way of working. We selected a world-class partner to assist us and we picked who we thought were the best suited ducks for the challenge. Some ducklings were suited to Yellow Belt training, others were already flying and could really use the tools a Green Belt would have. Some ducks we mistakenly gave the training to who should have just focused on their important roles in the team and not Lean Six Sigma. One duckling just stood out ... there was something special about her, she could relate to all the other ducks but also speak with authority to the Big Flockers. She never wavered, trusted the direction and the methodology and the data that came out of it and stuck to it. She also had a good friend who did not come from the river. A strange bird that migrated from somewhere in French-speaking Europe but that did not matter because everyone was able to understand her. She was able to inject energy, and hope that a better way of living was within our grasp.

We never gave up. There were times when the needs of the CJS would have led you to believe that there were other things more important but we were relentless. No matter what came against us we just kept going ... Define, Measure, Analyse, Improve, Control, Define, Measure . . . .

6. What were the biggest barriers?

- We learned that not everything that swims on the river is a duck ... we had to deal with some cormorants, who insisted they were ducks but they always seemed to be disappearing under the surface (where did they go? what were they doing and who exactly were they talking to down there because their data never seemed to completely add up?).
- Celebrating success in the environment of public sector austerity was challenging.
- The constant tension between business-as-usual and the need to change was at times hard to manage.
- The top level of middle management ... these are the ducks who are tasked with the doing of BAU and the leading of the change ... and some of them just would not get in the water. They thought their role was to quack loudly from the river bank but never actually get wet.

7. What were the greatest successes?

■ Drugs project (award winning).
■ The reporting project sped everything up by nearly 50%.
■ Lean Six Sigma made the organisation believe that it could change itself ... that they were capable of solving the problems it faced ... that more money and more people were not the solution to the problem.
■ The Big Flockers learned that the tool, while it could be very sophisticated (because we all know that Big Flockers like to be Big Sophisticated Flockers!), did not always need sophisticated solutions. Some very simple management actions as a result of the data could achieve remarkable results and improve the performance of individuals and teams with very little action required.
■ Lean Six Sigma assisted to make the culture change tangible (something real we could attribute change to), visible (our performance was now transparent, bringing accountability to teams and individuals) and felt (people started to enjoy their jobs and work environment again).

8. With hindsight, what would you do differently?

■ I would have thought more strategically about the initial project selection. Our projects initially were selected using a bit of a scatter gun approach. As we became more confident in the methodology projects naturally emerged.
■ The selection of capable Green Belts and Yellow Belts is critical. Don't select any cormorants passing themselves off as ducks!
■ Our special duckling ... I would have had two of her ... so she would have had more support. I know these are very rare and special ducks but if you listen to the entire team you will see there are a few special ducks and when you get them working together it offers each of them support and builds in contingency and builds the confidence of the Big Flockers looking for results.

9. What advice would you give to other leaders?

- UNDERSTAND THE CULTURE OF THE ORGANISATION!!! USE IT AS A LEVER TO ENSURE SUSTAINABLE CHANGE.
- Have a strategy ... not just a plan. If you only have a plan and it goes pear-shaped how will you know what direction to continue in? A strategy acts as a compass in the stormy environment of change and lets you know if you are making progress when you are too close to the detail.
- A lot of little wins can seem insignificant but, don't worry, they can and will soon add up to an overall significant change.
- Not all projects will yield something ... don't fret ... keep going.
- Choose your team carefully.
- Find a special duck or two.
- You live under a microscope ... everything you say and do is recorded and will be played back to you by people in the organisation. You need to live what you are talking.
- Get someone outside the organisation to support you ... it is lonely and you will need someone to encourage you ... like the strange European bird or a wise Welsh owl.

10. Anything else you'd like to say that might be helpful ?

I could start but I would not stop!!!!

Personal Leadership Perspective Mini Case Study – Sky UK and Aegon

Wayne Fisher, Process Improvement Manager at Sky, and former Head of Process Excellence at Aegon has, and shares experiences of leading Lean Six Sigma deployments here.

First, Wayne explains the deployment at Aegon:

1. Why did you start it – what prompted you to get going?

I started our Lean Six Sigma programme due to a business need. There was a requirement to help the operation to become more self-sufficient when it came to conducting their own incremental change and continuous improvement. Change resource was being fully utilised on the larger Transformational Change at time and the organisation was spending over £20m in Change, contracting consultants and other resources to assist in projects.

2. Before you started what did you think/what previous experience had you had?

At the start of our journey we had some strong sponsorship in place both from the CEO and Change Director, so I had confidence that

242

I had good backing for the programme. At this stage, I had experience within the process improvement arena, but had never performed the role of a Deployment Champion and set up a company-wide programme of this size.

I was also aware that the skills and knowledge that I had in my process excellence team were mixed and many were not necessarily experienced change professionals or indeed the right people to perform the role. I had inherited the team shortly before the decision to start up the Lean Six Sigma deployment programme. This made me nervous because my team would be deemed the experts when many were quite new to this themselves.

Expectations were also very high to ensure that we delivered benefits from the programme very early on. The organisation was going through a massive transformational change on the back of the financial crisis and employees were nervous about the reason that our team was in place.

3. How did you get started?

The first area for me was to ensure that I had the right sponsorship in place to support the programme. Luckily I had the support of the CEO and Change Director and my advice would be to establish a senior executive to endorse the programme for you.

I realised that I needed some support to help set up a deployment programme of this size and magnitude and sought consultancy support. I assessed the current capability of the Process Improvement Team, we had currently only aligned the Customer Services division and were then due to face off to the entire organisation. Key priorities at this stage were to understand our key stakeholders across the organisation and understand their level of engagement.

I also had to review the current capability of the process improvement team that I had inherited. Many of my team had not been trained in Lean Six Sigma and were going to be viewed as the experts when in fact they were just learning too. For me, we had to make some difficult decisions and move some people who did not necessarily possess the softer skills such as good communication, relationship building and effective stakeholder management. The team went on the Green Belt training first and each was given a project to help them achieve their own certification. A coaching framework was put in place and regular surgeries with our consultants were put in place to provide additional support to the team.

We also built in a solid communication plan and framework to help us promote the programme and the team. Regular updates were cascaded via the CEO, and we took a thermometer/pulse check at the start of the programme to assess the organisation's awareness and if they had heard of Lean Six Sigma. Figures were initially low, but six months later awareness had moved up to over 80%.

I also linked in with HR to look at ways in which we could incorporate the Lean Six Sigma principles into the behavioural framework of the organisation and started to add Lean Six Sigma experience to all jobs advertised moving forward within the company.

4. What were you trying to achieve?

Our main aim was to cut out the annual £20m cost of hiring external project resource to complete problem-solving projects. It was also key to equip people across the business with the skills and knowledge to manage their own small change agenda and make process improvement a way of working.

5. How did you go about it? (see question 3)
6. What were the biggest barriers?

We faced a number of barriers which included:

- The organisation was going through a massive transformation and many saw our programme as a means to make people redundant.
- The organisation had used Lean Six Sigma before and the approach did not land well. People had been sheep dipped and the training was not used to deliver change. This was seen before, but not driven from the top, with no real sponsorship. We therefore had an uphill battle to change perception.
- The Process Improvement team had been forced to downsize just before the programme started and some key experience had gone, leaving a largely inexperienced team in its place. The team were deemed the experts when they were still only learning.

- Aegon operated in silos, and departments up and down stream did not work well together, this did not help when trying to improve end-to-end processes that stretched across a number of departments.
- There was a real lack of a provision of good data across the company, that made data collection more challenging and often more time consuming and manual.

7. What were the greatest successes?

The successes included:

- We certificated over 50 Green Belts within an 18-month time frame. Projects landed were across HR, Customer Services, Finance, Marketing, Sales, Risk and Compliance and IT.
- Certificated 3 Black Belts and 2 LSS Champions Belts.
- Set up our own in-house Yellow Belt training programme, becoming self-sufficient in our own training delivery at this level and trained 200 individuals across the business.
- Stopped the annual cost of £20m on external contract resource.
- Paid back the cost in training investment on the Process Improvement team within the first six months.

8. With hindsight, what would you do differently?

I believe that the deployment model used in Aegon was an ideal approach that I would replicate elsewhere again. The early stages of the deployment were key and that included individual face-to-face meet and greets with the executive team to help gauge their level of support. Having the CEO as the programme sponsor gave us the best platform of support and helped to overcome barriers. Allowing the executive team to volunteer their areas to go through the training and start working on areas of improvement worked well. We used the pull effect.

Two key areas that we engaged with early on were both HR and Finance. These areas were key in the development of our deployment: Finance from a benefits perspective, who helped to put a structure in place for the confirmation and sign off of benefits; and HR from a people perspective. HR helped by feeding some of the key LSS principles into the DNA and behavioural framework of the organisation.

One area that I would consider doing differently is to ensure that anyone attending the Green Belt training had a project identified with a supportive sponsor in place and commitment that the individual would get time to work on delivering their initiative. Often the projects where a sponsor wasn't engaged or in place were the ones that fell by the wayside.

9. What advice would you give to other leaders?

Some advice I would give includes:

- Have patience, embedding a culture such as this does not happen overnight. Identify your supporters early on to help you on the journey, don't do this alone. Not everyone will see things the way you do, use those that get you to bring others along.
- Start small. Rome wasn't built in a day! Identify a strong area and supporter and use them as partner to prove the concept works. Once you have a success story to share it makes the journey so much easier.
- Join Process Improvement networks. This is a great way to share best practice and speak to others who have been on a similar journey. I have picked up so many good hints and tips along the way from this kind of channel.
- Get yourself a mentor or coach qualified in this arena that can help guide you and give advice to build your own expertise.
- Set up a robust governance structure that includes a programme board which is attended by senior champions and meets regularly to discuss progress in terms of project delivery, benefits, training plans and sharing best practice. Your governance structure should include a clear plan of initiatives in progress, a mechanism for tracking benefits and an active communication plan.
- Work with the business in partnership using a pull effect, do not impose yourself on an area. Identify the areas of pain and offer support to help alleviate these. Ask what is keeping the director awake at night.

- Recruit the right people, you need a team who are good communicators, have a positive mindset and have strong stakeholder management skills who work well with others. The technical skills can be taught, the softer skills are more innate.

10. Anything else you'd like to say that might be helpful?

To recognise the pressure that my team were under to pass their Green Belt exam and gain certificated status rapidly, I also opted to complete my own training and gain certificated status at Lean Six Sigma Champion level. This sent out a supportive message to the team and also demonstrated the intent of the programme.

Now Let's Hear About How it Was Done at Sky

1. Why did you start it – what prompted you to get going?

I joined the organisation which had an established Process Improvement team. It became evident to me very quickly that whilst the team had a wealth of experience and had a good track record of delivery, there were huge opportunities to develop the model that was in place. The team was quite hidden and often the work that they did was almost 'cloak and dagger'. Stakeholders were nervous about who the team were and what the team could do. The team was given work to do, rather than working with Operations directly to identify opportunities and install a culture of continuous improvement that tapped into the knowledge of employees and the voice of our customers.

2. Before you started what did you think/what previous experience had you had?

A very different scenario for me as I joined an established process improvement team. However, it became apparent that the team needed training on a process improvement framework to ensure that the team had a toolkit that could be fully utilised and a roadmap for dealing with continuous improvement. There were inconsistent practices and employees were keen to be given the required training that gave them a professional edge. I also felt that the Analyst population was not being fully utilised and allowed to demonstrate their true skills. They were task managed and not able to see a project through from start to finish, often they would be used to complete tasks for project leads and not get to see the full change cycle from start to finish. Training our Analysts at Green Belt level gave them empowerment to lead their own projects and learn and grow.

3. How did you get started?

My approach here was totally different. We had an established Process Improvement team who had varying degrees of experience using Lean Six Sigma. Some of the team were already certificated Green or Black Belts, but there wasn't necessarily a strong structure in place to share knowledge.

Our Senior Analyst population were given the responsibility to lead DMAIC projects, but the Analyst population were just being given tasks and often completed a lot of the 'measure' type activity. They were not being given the opportunity to lead projects and see the full DMAIC cycle through from start to finish. A decision was taken to train all of the team to the same level and everyone is now fully trained to BQF standard at Green Belt as a minimum. This has increased morale and empowerment and given everyone the opportunity to lead, ultimately leading to more completed projects.

Sky is a large company and my main focus has been how we tap into the untouched talent and opportunities for continuous improvement across the organisation. Many areas were approaching the Process Improvement team for support and help, but due to larger priorities and a reduced resource pool, we often turned these types of request away. We decided to explore ways in which we could 'Help the business to help themselves' by introducing our own in-house Yellow Belt programme. We have devised a training course, exam and certification process for delegates to complete. Areas across the business have been encouraged to send their people on the training if they have smaller process improvement projects that they would like to do. The Process Improvement team members have acted as trainers, coaches and mentors to these people and we are now starting to see Yellow Belt projects land across the business and a change in mindset. The skills and knowledge transfer of some of the DMAIC toolkit are helping the business to solve some of their problems in a structured way, placing the customer at the heart of everything that we do.

4. What were you trying to achieve?

We have run with the slogan 'Help the business to help themselves' and again transfer skills and knowledge across the organisation to help them to tackle continuous improvement through a structured framework. Our aim is that on average every Yellow Belt project can save ~£50k per project.

5. How did you go about it?

We tested the Yellow Belt training out as a pilot to practise our training skills and test that the format works and fits within the culture of Sky. We set out our stall that any delegate attending the training must have a project/business need already identified with a sponsor in place and be able to commit towards the full completion of a project.

We joined forces with the Process Improvement teams from other directorates in order to share best practice, resource and knowledge and a standardised approach. Our internal network was formed from representation in Customer Services, HR, Finance as well as the Process Improvement teams in both Sky Germany and Italy.

We have started to see our first Yellow Belt projects land and we are seeing the positive ripple effect where more people, business areas and projects are coming forward.

6. What were the biggest barriers?

- The sheer size of the organisation and trying to ensure that there is no duplication of effort. Often you may feel that you are the only person working on an initiative when you discover that there are many others working on the same project.

- There is always a large sense of urgency within the culture to fix things extremely quickly. The pressure to land a change is large and judgement is given on the speed of delivery rather than the quality of the solution. We spend a lot time managing the unrealistic expectations of our stakeholders.

7. What were the greatest successes?

- We certificated 17 Green Belts landing over £6m in benefit from their first projects delivered.
- We have set up our own internal Yellow Belt training programme which incorporates a two-day training course, an exam and certification panel. To date we have trained over 30 delegates, 4 Yellow Belt projects have been delivered with benefits and we have 16 live projects working through the DMAIC life cycle.

Personal Leadership Perspective Mini Case Study – Barclays

Beau Ormrod, VP Process Improvement & Analytics, Business Transformation.

1. Why did you start it – what prompted you to get going?

I started my Lean Six Sigma life over 12 years ago working as a Governance Manager in Direct Channels. I wouldn't say a prompt but more a forced-hand(!) as the team I looked after was being moved into a Continuous Improvement space and with that came the Lean discipline. Six Sigma came a little later in that transition but the two were introduced within a year of each other and I haven't looked back.

2. Before you started what did you think/what previous experience had you had?

Buzz words! Kaizen, Root Cause, SPC and the more familiar terms – but all fragmented in various discussions and came across as an 'I read this article on the subject, now let me quote tools to you so it sounds interesting' kinda way. No real sense as to, well … why? I initially thought it was going to be another flavour of the month and would soon disappear, along with its predecessors, but it didn't.

3. How did you get started?

Dived in! At that point in my career I was a training/knowledge sponge. I saw the possibilities with what I'd learned from listening to a couple of Lean coaches in the business – so I pursued it. It wasn't long at all before I was using the Ishikawa (which I liked the sound of at first!) in a real-life-business example – and that was it – hooked. I felt the power of a simple tool … I then went through my Green Belt training and became a practitioner. A few projects later and I was looking at a big opportunity.

4. What were you trying to achieve?

I was asked to look at performance across the UK. It flatlined. We were kidding ourselves around better/worse performance and we threw the same resources and thinking at this problem year-on-year. After challenging the problem I decided adopting a Variation Management approach would be the key. Optimising the current capabilities of our colleagues by arming them with new tools – Box Plots (to assess the level of variation/opportunity), Run Charts (to assess the location of this) and Fishbone (to understand why this happens). Not a typical DMAIC/Project approach but the essence of Lean Six Sigma was the backbone. I wanted the business to feel that power I'd felt when using the tools and then to utilise these to move performance in ways never seen before.

5. How did you go about it?

Culture – this had to be culture driven. As all major businesses, across all retail sectors it had a history of sales. Sell, sell, sell. This wasn't about that – it was about optimising performance through Root Cause Insight. What you don't know – you don't know. Get to know it. Repeat the good. Change the not so good. It was a fairly simple message – after all, I wasn't asking for full DMAIC projects – simply to use a few tools in the discipline to help with performance – this carried a heavy challenge.

6. What were the biggest barriers?

Culture! Leaders through to frontline. Unpicking decades of one culture proved insurmountable. That leap of faith in the discipline and that by not driving performance through targets. Use Lean Thinking. Reduce wastes. Create an efficient working environment and therefore productivity.

Have faith! Lean Six Sigma requires a large amount of trust and belief. Instant results and instant gratification drive businesses today and Lean Six Sigma will not provide this in the short term. Medium to long term (for me) – it's the only way. This is true of any installation of Lean and/or Six Sigma methodologies. It takes time – but that time is paid back in abundance when it gets going.

7. What were the greatest successes?

For those with faith, it changed their view of the world/business forever. Top performers became outstanding performers. Those finding it difficult found ways to make it work for them. I could quote numbers on how it stabilised performance and increased productivity – as it did – however, the difference it made to those who had that persistence, it's still paying dividends. I often see colleagues who tell me they will always remember the day they learned how to Fishbone!

8. With hindsight, what would you do differently?

Take time. Too much too soon. Proved it worked and sustained in a smaller scale (rather than the whole of UK plus parts of Europe) and use those closer-to-home examples. It's funny how people want a slice of what looks good.

9. What advice would you give to other leaders?

Whatever you're practising or teaching in Lean Six Sigma, take it to the heart of the business and demonstrate. It has to be relatable, relevant and real. Flatten any hierarchy and you'll be surprised on who and how this is utilised.

10. Anything else you'd like to say that might be helpful?

Belt up. Now a Black Belt it really helps to know the discipline inside out so No.9 is easier. Also – make it fun. I guess a rule I try to apply to as much as I can – but it does go a long way when instilling something potentially technical.

Personal Leadership Perspective Mini Case Study – The UK Government, Central Government Department

Lorraine Daly, Continuous Improvement Manager.

1. Why did you start it – what prompted you to get going?

I had returned from maternity leave and was feeling very lost with my career and where I saw myself in the future. I was working part time and found it a constant challenge to find out what had been happening in the office on the days I didn't work, what progress was being made on things, and I was finding it frustrating that work was often duplicated across other teams in the business – only finding out quite late into a piece of work. The department was starting to set up some small Lean core teams which piqued my interest and after reading some of the Lean principles and doing some research on Google I started to see the potential in what could be achieved

2. Before you started what did you think/what previous experience had you had?

At the time of starting I was a very junior manager, recently promoted with very little people management experience and no improvement experience. I had achieved PRINCE2 qualifications and whilst I enjoyed the structure of the Prince approach my extent of applying it was limited to an administrative role in the project management office.

3. How did you get started?

I applied to be part of a new Lean Core team in the department's Transformation and Products Management Division. I received classroom based training and mentoring/coaching from Lean experts. It was an interesting journey – I was quite surprised that a lot of the learning was around common-sense, practical steps that added some structure to managing work and processes that was quite often missing. Consolidating my training was a challenge.

4. How did you go about it?

- Senior leaders – moving them from supporting to visibly and actively engaging.
- Rolling out awareness sessions to the whole directorate.
- Mini projects – delivering small incremental successes.

5. What were the biggest barriers?
   Where do I start?

- Time
- Middle managers
- Having the confidence
- Bringing people with me

6. What were the greatest successes?

Seeing the change in teams who had previously sat complaining about the way things had been done, and people being creative in their thinking to think differently about the way they worked.

7. With hindsight, what would you do differently?

Wouldn't be prescriptive with tools and techniques to be used and make the learning scenario-led – introducing the tools by 'stealth' as a structured approach rather than a name. Gain more best practice from other organisations – increase my network of support.

8. What advice would you give to other leaders?

- Try to win hearts and minds
- Support middle managers to find the time
- Don't be too prescriptive
- Consolidate, consolidate!

Personal Leadership Perspective Mini Case Study – UK Government, Homes and Communities Agency

Mark Canning, Senior Area Manager, Homes and Communities Agency.

The Homes and Communities Agency (HCA) is the UK government's housing, land and regeneration agency, and the regulator of social housing providers in England. Around 900 people work at the HCA in offices across England. The agency is responsible for:

- increasing the number of new homes that are built in England, including affordable homes and homes for market sale or rent;
- improving existing affordable homes and bringing empty homes back into use as affordable housing;
- increasing the supply of public land and speeding up the rate that it can be built on;

- regulating social housing providers to make sure that they're well managed and financially secure, so maintaining investor confidence in the affordable housing sector and protecting homes for tenants; and
- helping to stimulate local economic growth by using our land and investment, and attracting private sector investment in local areas.

The HCA's Lean Continuous Improvement programme was launched during May 2016 with a programme of awareness-raising delivered during the summer. Eight improvement projects commenced during autumn 2016 to progress a first phase of processes improvement projects, which were largely due to complete around spring 2017.

1. Why did you start your Lean programme – what prompted you to get going?

There were two key prompts which stimulated the HCA's Lean Continuous Improvement Programme:

(i) Delivering Efficiency Savings

The Department for Communities and Local Government (DCLG), like all government departments, had been required by HM Treasury to devise a set of proposals to make efficiency savings across its department and Arms-Length Bodies (the DCLG Group). The efficiency saving required had been agreed between the Secretary of State for Communities and Local Government and Chief Secretary to the Treasury.

The Chancellor's Autumn Statement announcement on the Spending Review on 25 November 2015 also provided details of the government's housing priorities for the next four years. A fundamental objective of future HCA activity was to help deliver these priorities while still making the efficiency savings required and yet maintaining a motivated and skilled work force. The expectations of the HCA were a full commitment to, and engagement with, DCLG in delivering successful continuous improvement by sharing in both the investment costs and the capability development of staff.

(ii) Responding to the HCA Review

In 2011, the Cabinet Office announced that all non-departmental public bodies (NDPBs) should go through a substantive review every three years to assess their capacity for delivering more effectively. The purpose of these reviews is threefold:

- To provide a strong challenge of the continuing need for individual non-departmental public bodies, both their function and their form;
- To review their capacity for delivering more effectively and efficiently, including identifying the potential for efficiency savings and their ability to contribute to economic growth; and
- To review the control and governance arrangements in place to ensure that the public body is complying with recognised principles of good corporate governance. This should also include an assessment of the body's performance.

The HCA Review was completed in early 2016. The introduction of Lean Continuous Improvement principles and practices was embarked upon to help to support the successful delivery of the review.

2. Before you started what did you think/what previous experience had you had?

The Homes and Communities Agency had zero prior experience of Lean Six Sigma, which was a totally new concept for the agency. However, the agency had been made aware of other government departments who had embarked upon such Lean programmes and who had good success with their approach, and this knowledge was shared.

3. How did you get started?

With regards to early governance, the Lean Programme in the HCA was taken forward by a dedicated Programme Board reporting to the Chief Executive and Directors, with a director acting as Senior Responsible Owner (SRO), supported by a PRINCE2 trained Programme Manager. A series of 8 Champions were trained to support the eight pilot projects, and these Champions, along with the SRO and Project Manager formed the Programme Board.

The leading experts in Lean Continuous Improvement, Catalyst, were appointed as the training providers in February 2016.

The agreed training programme included Champion, Green Belt, Yellow Belt and Change Management training courses of between one and six days duration. The wider engagement programme to establish advocates through a series of one-day awareness workshops was made widely available to all staff to introduce core tools and skills.

4. What were you trying to achieve?

The core aim of implementing a Lean Continuous Improvement approach at the HCA was to equip staff with the skills, tools and expertise necessary to make the agency more efficient and effective and support the implementation of new ways of working.

The individual objectives of the HCA Lean Programme are to:

- Support the government's spending review to make resource savings by focusing on what adds value.
- Support the implementation of the HCA Review recommendations to improve core processes, eliminate waste, increase efficiencies, utilise resources more effectively and focus on adding value.
- Make available the tools and materials that will help staff to use Lean Continuous Improvement in their work.
- Identify a network of Lean 'advocates' to share knowledge.
- Provide development opportunities for staff through accredited training.

5. How did you go about it?

- An awareness raising campaign on Lean Continuous Improvement techniques was run through events and communications.
- Capacity Building on Lean Continuous Improvement techniques was developed through direct accredited training. The proposed Lean Continuous Improvement methodology adopted was Lean Six Sigma. Today, Lean Six Sigma is used as an all-encompassing business performance methodology, all over the world, in organisations as diverse as local government departments, the armed forces, banks, and multinational corporations. The methodology will be introduced via a series of one day 'White Belt' workshops.
- Efficiencies were secured through undertaking a series of eight Phase 1 Pilot Projects and implementing the outcomes, e.g. streamlining processes, eliminating waste, reducing bureaucracy.

A separate communication plan has been developed. This is helping to communicate with staff and partners, to achieve their 'buy-in' and involvement in the programme and explain how it will impact on them, i.e. managing the impact of change, improved and streamlined processes, improved service, greater job satisfaction, and career development opportunities. A poster campaign was run throughout all offices to promote visits to the intranet landing page. Three HCA Lean news stories run on HCAnet generated 2,000 views, whilst eight blogs generated 2,500 views.

6. What were the biggest barriers?

There have been very few encountered, as developing a Lean Programme within the agency has been like pushing on an open door. Lean was delivered via a bottom-up approach and the training was seized upon by staff. Some 150 staff were trained over the first two months of the programme and this was so heavily oversubscribed a further 100 training places were quickly added, before the decision was taken by the Chief Executive to train the whole workforce to meet the demand.

Finding the time to train some of the agency's directors did sometimes prove a challenge though – with one senior member of staff memorably quoting that he did not have the time to be trained to become more efficient.

7. What were the greatest successes?

Benefits to date have included:

- A significant contribution towards required efficiency savings through:
  - o Elimination of waste in day-to-day ways of working;
  - o More efficient delivery of government programmes;
  - o Improved satisfaction of partners;
  - o Improved value and reduced costs of delivering HCA activities.
- A staff culture where Lean Continuous Improvement techniques are starting to become business as usual.
- Even more capable and agile staff who are even better able to respond quickly to requests to implement new programmes and products to support government objectives.

8. With hindsight, what would you do differently?

A lesson-learned exercise undertaken after the completion of the phase 1 pilot projects yielded the following advice:

- There is a need to carefully select the improvement projects to be worked upon through a tightly defined problem statement. Scope creep can be a real danger with project teams trying to improve everything.
- Improvement teams should fully understand the process they will work upon at the outset before seeking to improve it.
- Not all Lean benefits are derived from Lean projects – Lean is a mindset that can bring incremental improvements which can bring wider benefits overall.
- The Lean Six Sigma methodology need not be slavishly adhered to – utilising just the parts you need to get the job done can work too. The HCA worked with Catalyst to develop Lean Light (captured on a single side of A3) which has delivered many positive results via rapid improvements that sat outside of the much larger Lean Phase 1 projects.
- It is worth engaging those parties who will help deliver the ultimate improvements at an early stage in the process to ensure their engagement and support when it is required, e.g. IT teams who will upgrade affected systems.

9. What advice would you give to other leaders?

- Need to promote cultural change – train all staff and include Lean in all staff's annual objectives.
- Need to recognise and accommodate for varying levels of Lean improvements:
  o Those taking just a few hours to complete – the 'Just Do It' project;
  o Those taking a few days – Rapid Improvement Projects;
  o Those taking weeks/months – DMAIC Six Sigma Green Belt projects (as per the current eight projects being progressed in the HCA).

- Embark upon a strong PR campaign through your Comms Staff – communicate, communicate, communicate – get your messages of success out there.

10. What next?

The HCA Lean Continuous Improvement Board will continue to reinforce and embed the agency's Lean capability across the performance culture of the agency. Next steps to successfully deliver this will include:

- The programme being supported by a full-time project manager.
- Direct reinforcement and integration of Lean through the agency's performance management process with each employee having a clearly defined annual Lean objective.
- Directors being tasked to identify Lean Advocates to lead and promote Lean within all teams.

Further activity will include:

- The identification and roll out of Phase 2 Projects: The Lean CI Board maintains a schedule of staff suggestions, with 26 being recommended to date, and 5 under active consideration including: the staff performance management process, opportunity cost analysis and the Annual Land Valuations and Validation Exercise.
- Lean Communication and Road Shows on Phase 1 Projects: These will be led by the Green Belts and Champions and were rolled out through the summer of 2017.
- Return On Investment data: Through working with government departments, robust estimates of the return on investment will be assembled and provide clear evidence of the success and value of continuous improvement.

11. Anything else you'd like to say that might be helpful?

The Lean Continuous Improvement Board noted that there are probably three very different types of Lean improvement project:

- Those taking just a few hours to complete – the 'Just Do It' project.
- Those taking a few days – Rapid Improvement Projects.
- Those taking weeks/months – DMAIC Six Sigma Green Belt Projects (as per the current eight projects being progressed in the HCA).

The Lean CI Board accordingly recognised the need to have some form of simple tool kit, which did not readily exist, which enables everyone to apply Lean principles to their role and to be empowered to act to save time and money through 'Rapid Improvement Projects'.

Given the above, a bespoke Lean Rapid Improvement tool has been developed – Lean Light. This is essentially a bringing together of the HCA's current approach on its large Lean projects, distilled down to a technique captured under 3Cs (concern, cause, counter-measure), that has then been captured on a single side of A3. This rapid improvement tool is being rolled out via the current training programme, with a demonstrator example of this approach being illustrated to staff – the HCA finance code generator project, which was a simple two-day Lean business improvement project that will realise savings of £10k per annum. This Lean Light approach has proven very popular with staff.

Personal Leadership Perspective Mini Case Study – Exclusive 5 Star Hotel Group

Business Transformation Project Manager, Exclusive 5 star hotel group.

1. Why did you start it – what prompted you to get going?

The impetus for us came from the top – the regional director had a vision that he wanted to implement a system (and culture) of continuous improvement in the business and, alongside that, a bank of centralised processes.

2. Before you started what did you think/what previous experience had you had?

I had no experience of Six Sigma and had only ever run projects from a pragmatic 'what do we need to do to get this done' perspective.

Actually I was pleasantly surprised at how much sense the Lean Six Sigma methodology seemed to make!

3. How did you get started?

I got in touch with the British Quality Foundation to start with. The EFQM Excellence Model was very helpful for giving an illustration of where our business was at the time, but it didn't help to actually address some of the issues. I had a mentor who recommended that I look into the Lean Six Sigma Green Belt course, so that's how I started

4. What were you trying to achieve?

We wanted to put in place a new 'way of doing business', which was less reactive and more process orientated – so that we could increase efficiency and make life easier!

5. How did you go about it?

We started off by getting the leadership team together and running a big workshop. We showed them the results of the EFQM assessment which got people talking – and also helped them to understand the need for change. Next, we led a 'speed Six Sigma workshop', where each team selected a (real) issue, and then used selected Lean Six Sigma tools to work through the problem.

It was very important to us that we made the methodology 'ours' – in other words, that we stripped as much jargon away from the tools as possible. We never mentioned 'Lean Six Sigma' in any of our communications. Of course, what happened is that we ended up replacing it with jargon of our own ... but the crucial thing was that we 'owned' the system, and the company could recognise it as 'our' way of doing business.

Acceptance and momentum were certainly a gradual process, which snowballed over a five year period. Over time, we were able to cement the gains by linking leadership KPIs to the methodology, and by translating our strategic plan into tactical deployment actions.

6. What were the biggest barriers?

The company had been through two unsuccessful attempts to 'do' continuous improvement before, so there was an element of 'here we go again' amongst some of the senior team. Some people saw the method as a threat. But the biggest barrier we found was 'business as usual': in a 24/7 operation it was very difficult to take people out and form efficient teams. We found that most of the project work ended up being done in our review sessions, rather than in the interim period – this slowed down results and made projects hard to sustain.

7. What were the greatest successes?

We managed to solve a couple of really big operational challenges, like improving the accuracy of our billing, and preparing the bedrooms more efficiently. We were able to demonstrate real monetary benefits in increased efficiencies, such as the way we managed guest requests, processed deliveries, etc. Probably the biggest and most visible success was the implementation of the centralised process library, which is now accessible to all employees across our three sites. In addition, we developed our own training programme for project management and innovation methodology, which was rolled out across our management graduate community.

8. With hindsight, what would you do differently?

We have a very ambitious business culture, but this did mean that – certainly at the beginning – we probably bit off more than we could chew in terms of number of projects running concurrently. This meant that the momentum was sometimes difficult to sustain. It would also have been good to have allowed ourselves more time in developing a more robust strategy deployment template.

9. What advice would you give to other leaders?

(Try to) be patient...! As long as you have the right support, are consistent with your messaging and always keep the end goal in mind – you will see results! It also helps if you try to get key stakeholders on your side sooner rather than later.

10. Anything else you'd like to say that might be helpful ?

The power of as-is process mapping is amazing. Don't cut corners and don't be afraid to show things as they really are; warts and all. Big changes will be easy to make if you understand what currently happens!

Personal Leadership Perspective Mini Case Study: Vanderlande

Alec Gilbert, Strategic Service Development, Vanderlande, describes his lean strategy for delivering sustainable growth in UK logistics automation.

This case study looks at the deployment of a Lean strategy at the UK subsidiary of a global world leader in automation technology. The global organisation has over 4000 staff and a turnover of around £1.5bn, whilst the UK subsidiary is a Small to Medium Enterprise (SME) of around 200 staff, turning over around £50m.

The company designs, builds, operates and maintains automation systems across a number of sectors. It operates business-to-business. It has established world leadership through excellence in product quality and, more recently, through innovation that has moved the company from a supplier of equipment to an integrated control systems partner.

1. Why did you start it – what prompted you to get going?

In 2012 the company suffered some shocks to its UK business – some positive, some negative.

It had just lost some mechanical system service business that it had held for five years, but it had also won some new IT controls service business that was unexpected. We could also see that nearly all the business in the previous ten years had been with one customer, and that this customer was entering a period of reduced investment. It was clear that a fresh appraisal of the business direction was needed.

2. Before you started what did you think/what previous experience had you had?

I could see that just 'fixing our internal processes' as someone suggested I should do, would be akin to 'rearranging the deckchairs' – not on the *Titanic* perhaps, but certainly on a rudderless ship.

My experience in recent years has been deploying Lean Sigma across European organisations. Prior to that I had led business development, sales and marketing activities.

I felt that this challenge was not so much a 'lean process' challenge as a 'business change leadership' opportunity.

3. How did you get started?

I listened. I interviewed the leadership team of the company for their views of the state of the business, its strengths and weaknesses and the market opportunities and threats (voice of the people). We interviewed customers on their experience of the company (voice of the customer). We also mapped some of the key processes to understand some of the issues (voice of the process).

I then sketched out a Kotter change leader roadmap of the eight steps, and planned the approaches and tools that I could apply on that journey. I worked closely with the MD of the company as I developed this journey. His buy-in to this approach and journey was key.

4. What were you trying to achieve?

It was evident that the organisation had become rather inward-looking. So I wanted to move the organisation to a 'customer-centred organisation'.

Three of the four strategies we subsequently developed had the word 'customer' in them.

It was also clear that silo working was interfering in the business (so the fourth strategy was 'teamwork').

5. How did you go about it?

I aimed to apply the principles of Lean to a business change. These included:

- Voice of the customer – listening to customer needs as a driver for strategy.
- Voice of the process – measure what matters.
- Voice of the people – listen to the team and use their strengths.

As we worked through the eight steps of Kotter's change approach, we used a variety of approaches:

1. **Sense of urgency**
   o Interviewed stakeholders to identify their concerns
2. **Guiding coalition**
   o Established who was in the leadership team and their roles
   o Change Readiness Assessment against the Kotter journey: self-audit to highlight our readiness for a change
   o 'Insight' preferred working styles assessment of the leadership team to assess the team style, strengths and weaknesses
3. **Vision development**
   o EFQM self-audit to identify positive and negatives
   o SWOT assessment by the leadership team
   o Innovation workshops
   o Vision and strategy development workshops
   o Developed a 'change programme blueprint':
   o How the strategic actions would develop new capabilities
   o How these capabilities will deliver the desired outcomes
   o What benefits will flow from these outcomes
   o Thus delivering the strategic vision
4. **Communicate the vision**
   o Developed a 'brand' image
   o Created an engaging launch event
   o 'Handouts' that were both useful and communicated the strategies
   o Annual strategy events to communicate progress and direction

5. **Empower people**
   o Created four clear strategies, to give clarity and focus to the whole organisation. Three out of the four included the word 'customer', to move us towards becoming a customer-centric organisation.
   o Deployed Hoshin Kanri policy deployment to cascade the four strategies into ten annual goals. Each functional leader cascaded these to their own functional objectives for the year. This iterative process allowed all staff to see the direct link between their objectives, the annual goals and the strategy.
   o Leadership coaching, for example in Kotter, Covey's '7 Habits', and programme management.
   o We deployed SPIN (Situation, Problem, Implication, Need pay-off) sales training that focuses on listening skills, to develop our focus on the customer's needs.

Measure what you need to manage

As the strategy was a growth strategy, we deployed a new sales process, a new sales and operations planning process and new sales metrics to give more structure and metrics to the sales process. The introduction of new processes and metrics into this area allowed us to proactively manage and measure this process far more objectively than had been the case previously.

The Sales and Operations Plan: by adapting this demand and capacity management tool from manufacturing industry, we collated all the 'demand' data of the pipeline of sales activity into 'one version of the truth', shared across the business. By loading some capacity assumptions, we were able to estimate the 'supply' of sales and delivery resources needed to fulfil the demand. This translated into resource profiles needed across ten key roles in the organisation looking forward a number of months and years, leading to recruitment and development of projected resource shortfalls.

'Decision to Engage (D2E)' and 'Decision to Bid (D2B)' were identified as the two key gateways in the sales process where resources would need to be committed if we proceeded further. We introduced a metric for the strength of our customer engagement at these two gateways. By correlating these scores with the eventual sales outcome we were able to establish scores below which further investment was not justified and scores where sales success was highly likely.

The challenging area was where the scores did not correlate clearly with winning or losing the work: the sales outcome was not certain either way. This 'area of sales opportunity' was where we made decisions either (rarely) to withdraw from the process or (usually) to invest in the relationship to improve the score (and the likelihood of winning) by the next gateway.

1. **Quick wins**
   o Sought quick wins through the improved sales processes
2. **Consolidate the gains**
   o Updated and re-launched the strategy after 3 years to keep it relevant
3. **Institutionalise into the culture**
   o New leaders and staff hired with customer service ethos
   o Customer excellence culture programme started

6. What were the biggest barriers?

Inertia

After we launched the new vision 'Destination 2020' to the whole organisation, with a structured communication engagement, asking people to 'get on board' the journey, things went a bit flat. It was quickly evident that we had not yet 'empowered our people'. People did not know how to get on board or what to do differently.

So we then spent another two to three months redesigning the organisation around the four new strategies. By creating new leadership roles, putting new leaders in post and moving teams below them, this catalysed the change in practice and change started to happen.

The reorganisation and leadership changes tackled the biggest barrier of inertia, because it became evident to everyone that this change was 'real'. Everyone sat up and took notice.

Sustainability

Keeping this strategy alive over four years has been thanks to a couple of main things. First, a consistent MD who supported the approach, encouraged its development, sponsored and visibly supported the changes. Second, the strategy was developed by the whole leadership team of nine. By fully engaging all nine of the leadership team in the strategy development, it took a few months longer to shape the strategy than would have been possible with a small core team. However, as a result, all nine leaders contributed to the strategy, and 'owned' it. This has undoubtedly meant that it has been a non-negotiable basis for the business for the last four years.

We also ensure that we hold a 'Destination 2020' strategy event at least annually to update every employee and keep the strategy visible. At the end of 2015 we consciously refreshed the strategy to ensure that it met our customers' evolving needs. This 'nudge on the tiller' moved the focus towards 'partnership' as a key enabler for sustainable growth.

7. What were the greatest successes?

First: The results of the growth strategy included:

- Increasing our rate of winning bids:
  - From 50% to 75% between 2012 and 2015 on over £300m of work.
- Beating our growth target:
  - We aimed to grow geographically from one customer to ten customers by 2020. We beat this by winning our tenth customer in 2016.
- Diversifying: We aimed to expand into adjacent sectors:
  - We won £40m of business – double our target – in an adjacent sector.
- Doubling the size of our UK office base to accommodate the growth.
- Beating our EBIT target from 2012–2015.

Second: The greatest success was sustaining this journey over several years. This was because the MD of the company 'got' the approach, and sponsored the changes through the leadership team. He made the necessary organisation changes and sponsored the new key processes such as the sales and operational planning meeting and the annual goals setting Hoshin cascade.

Third: The growth in capability of the organisation. The proactive approach to creating a customer-centred organisation has led to us hiring a more customer-centric leadership team and staff. We are empowering customer-facing staff to develop more innovative solutions and to develop a customer service culture.

3. With hindsight, what would you do differently?

Leadership changes were made at a steady pace, and not 'all at once'. It may have been possible to tackle more underperformance issues in a shorter time. However, there was a strong 'family' culture in the organisation, and a more aggressive change approach may have put the culture at risk.

Quick wins were hard to deliver in this 'organic growth' strategy. It took more than a year to start showing tentative sales progress, which meant it took longer to convert 'doubters' to the approach. I would put more focus on delivering some more concrete steps early on.

Final Thoughts and a Warning!

Sustaining Lean Six Sigma – moving from a programme to a culture
As we have seen in this book, Lean Six Sigma contains an extremely powerful set of principles, tools and methodologies which can be deployed to eliminate waste, streamline processes, enhance customer experience and improve safety, quality and productivity. It can also provide both top-line and bottom-line benefits to business performance.

There will also be people benefits in terms of improved capability, increased decision-making authority and greater influence on workplace organisation and standards. When done well, this extends to a genuinely heightened sense of involvement and engagement in shaping the future of the business, where ideas from all sources are encouraged, implemented and recognised in pursuit of a common goal.

However, there is a risk that Lean Six Sigma deployment does not lead to a lasting culture of improvement: after the excitement of the programme 'launch' and the euphoria of early success, projects begin to stall without strong sponsorship or adequate resources, attention of senior leaders is diverted to more pressing matters elsewhere or the next 'shiny new thing', and the focus on culture change diminishes: meanwhile Lean Six Sigma is left in the hands of designated experts, other

277

business priorities impede progress and, over time, the momentum dies and results fade.

So, given the power and the potential of the tools, why do many improvement programmes fail to achieve sustainable success and a long-term culture of operational excellence? Experience and research shows that the following are important factors:

i. Cost reduction focus vs higher long-term purpose. A focus primarily on cost reduction, whilst clearly understandable and useful for creating a sense of urgency, is unlikely to be enough in the long run: ultimately a higher long-term purpose for the organisation will provide a compelling 'why' and fully motivate, engage and align the whole team. Peter Fuda refers to this as moving 'from burning platform to burning ambition'.

ii. Technical perspective vs people perspective. Not everyone is excited by learning and applying tools: those less inclined or confident in using them can feel marginalised or exposed. And if the tools are used in isolation, are imposed or not embedded in the way of working then their use will not be effective. Effective and regular communications, especially good listening, is critical in engaging people in the change.

iii. Abdication vs role models. Too often senior leaders delegate the ownership of the Continuous Improvement or Lean Six Sigma programme to a manager, and after launch consider their work to be done. They then turn their attention to other concerns, and don't reflect personally on their own behaviour and the impact that this has on the culture of the organisation. Personal and social transformation go hand in hand. As Mahatma Gandhi famously said: 'If we could change ourselves, the tendencies in the world would also change'.

iv. Developing experts vs developing all. Whilst the 'Belt' system provides attractive learning and career advancement opportunities for those selected, it can be seen as exclusive rather than inclusive and therefore create division. Long-term success is dependent upon everyone feeling respected and valued, and having fair access to development opportunities. People development – for all – needs to be maintained as a high priority. As Fujio Cho of Toyota said, 'First we build people, then we build cars'.

v. The 'production system' vs total system: If the focus is on improving the performance of operational processes only, then no amount of standard work or control plan deployment will guarantee continued success or further improvements. Nothing sustains itself. However, if consideration is given to the wider business systems, especially management systems, i.e. a combination of visual management, daily accountability and leadership routines (leader standard work), then the improvements can not only be sustained but extended, and indeed the culture of the organisation can be changed. You can't change the culture by directly changing the culture: but changing systems is a good way to change behaviour and mindsets: 'It is often easier to act yourself into a new way of thinking, than to think yourself into a new way of acting' (Jerry Sternin). Furthermore, what a great way for leaders to lead by example, i.e. demonstrating that standard work applies to them as much as it does to associates on the shop floor on in the call centre. It's taking your own medicine.

The End?

At the beginning of this book we asked you to consider what makes a BAD leader, using the negative brainstorm approach. The brainstormed list was then turned around to create a list of positive characteristics. Some ways that Lean Six Sigma can fail to fulfil its promise are outlined above, with 'turnarounds' identified. *Lean Six Sigma for Leaders* brings both of these elements together and highlights the powerful potential of doing so. We wanted to end this book with a call to action. Here's a quote that we use a lot, that we attribute to our dearly missed friend, mentor and colleague John Morgan.

> We've got some big changes to make and you're going to have to make them. If you don't, who will?

Starting the Lean Six Sigma Engine

Before we hit the road with Lean Six Sigma we need to start the engine. To do this, three vital components are required – a spark, fuel and air.

The spark in an engine delivers electric current from an ignition system to the combustion chamber to ignite the compressed fuel and air. The power of the explosion pumps the pistons and keeps the engine going. The fuel powers the engine and the air provides the component required to ignite it.

You could compare these components to the requirements necessary to make a Lean Six Sigma programme work! The spark is provided by leaders in the organisation. Their stimulus ignites the system by bringing the other essential components together. This releases the energy and, ultimately, the 'engine' of Lean Six Sigma is powered and the wheels begin to turn.

The fuel represents the methodology and also the knowledge to apply it. This could come from inside the organisation, from external expertise and input, or from both – external experts used to build the knowledge and capability within the organisation that's required to make it work.

The air represents the people in the organisation, without whose input nothing will work.

If the leadership spark for Lean Six Sigma isn't strong enough, it won't bring the system to life. If, on the other hand, there is too much heat, the 'bang' will be too big and the system could burn out. The spark from leaders needs to be consistent and timely, and it needs to be sustained. In an engine if the spark halts or misses a beat it will stop. In the organisation using Lean Six Sigma there will be the same effect.

Too much fuel can also be problematic, as the system gets 'flooded'. This is true of Lean Six Sigma deployments. Too much theory and technical jargon can get in the way of practical focus and distract us from the real reason we're using it – to deliver our goals, be effective, and be efficient. Futhermore, too many 'external experts' crowding out the system can have the effect of stifling input from the organisation's people. Never let Lean Six Sigma get 'done to you' – always seek a partner who'll work collaboratively with you.

If you have driven a vehicle with a manual choke you might recall having to pull out the choke to let more fuel and air into a cold engine. Putting the choke back in too early (reducing the fuel and air) will stop the engine. Withdrawing resources (your experts and your people) from Lean Six Sigma activities too soon can cause the same effect.

Of the three essential elements, air (people!) is the only one that, if increased, can boost the overall performance. This is called the turbo effect! When the engine is turbo charged it will become more efficient. It doesn't require any more spark than it already has, and draws just as much fuel as it needs.

So now you need to learn to drive. Bon voyage!

Index